ARCO

REAL ESTATE LICENSE EXAMINATIONS

JOSEPH H. MARTIN, MAI, CRE
EVE P. STEINBERG, M.A.

ARCO

THOMSON LEARNING

Australia • Canada • Denmark • Japan • Mexico • New Zealand • Philippines
Puerto Rico • Singapore • South Africa • Spain • United Kingdom • United States

An ARCO Book

ARCO is a registered trademark of Thomson Learning, Inc., and is used herein under license by Peterson's.

About Peterson's

Founded in 1966, Peterson's, a division of Thomson Learning, is the nation's largest and most respected provider of lifelong learning online resources, software, reference guides, and books. The Education Supersite^{SM} at petersons.com—the Web's most heavily traveled education resource—has searchable databases and interactive tools for contacting U.S.-accredited institutions and programs. CollegeQuest^{SM} (CollegeQuest.com) offers a complete solution for every step of the college decision-making process. GradAdvantage^{TM} (GradAdvantage.org), developed with Educational Testing Service, is the only electronic admissions service capable of sending official graduate test score reports with a candidate's online application. Peterson's serves more than 55 million education consumers annually.

Thomson Learning is among the world's leading providers of lifelong learning, serving the needs of individuals, learning institutions, and corporations with products and services for both traditional classrooms and for online learning. For more information about the products and services offered by Thomson Learning, please visit www.thomsonlearning.com. Headquartered in Stamford, Connecticut, with offices worldwide, Thomson Learning is part of The Thomson Corporation (www.thomson.com), a leading e-information and solutions company in the business, professional, and education marketplaces. The Corporation's common shares are listed on the Toronto and London stock exchanges.

For more information, contact Peterson's, 2000 Lenox Drive, Lawrenceville, NJ 08648;
800-338-3282; or find us on the World Wide Web at: www.petersons.com/about

Fourth Edition

Library of Congress Cataloging-in-Publication Data

Martin, Joseph H.
  Real estate license examinations : salesperson and broker / Joseph H. Martin,
Eve P. Steinberg.—4th ed.
    p.   cm.
  ISBN 0-671-84835-6
  1. Real estate business—United States—States—Examinations, questions, etc. 2. Real property—United States—States—Examinations, questions, etc. 3. Real estate agents—Licenses—United States—States. I. Steinberg, Eve P. II. Title. III. Title: Arco real estate license examinations.
HD1381.5.U5M37   1993
333.33'076—dc20   93-4597
                                                          CIP

Printed in the United States of America

10   9   8   7   02   01   00

CONTENTS

Preface

Most people, when they first attempt to enter the real estate field, have little or no understanding of the extent of knowledge necessary for salespeople or brokers. Of particular concern are the examinations conducted by each state for licensure. The purpose and intent of this text is to remove the mysteries that surround license examinations in all fifty states, the District of Columbia, and the Virgin Islands. In all of these areas, state regulatory agencies either conduct their own exams or retain professional test makers to construct and even administer real estate license exams. The authors have studied the license laws of each state and/or district throughout the United States. They have also consulted with authorities in every field concerning the material used herein to insure its accuracy as to test principles and subject matter.

This book, then, is a product of both academic and practical research into all phases of real estate with which you must be concerned for licensure. This material should not be used as a substitute for legal opinion. It is necessary for a student to have a broad understanding of real estate laws, but legal actions are usually narrow interpretations of broad legal principles and, when necessary, a layperson should always consult an attorney.

For you, this book will open the door to a successful career in real estate, but only if you apply its principles and continue your "quest for knowledge" after licensure. Good luck!

Joseph Howard Martin, MAI, CRE
Real Estate Consultant & Lecturer;
State Certified General Real Estate
   Appraiser
Eve P. Steinberg, MA
Real Estate Salesperson & Test
   Analyst

The authors are indebted to the New Jersey Association of Realtors for permission to use its standard forms in this text.

Chapter One

Introduction

If you wish to be a licensed real estate broker or salesperson in the United States, this book is designed for you. Entry into the field of real estate is predicated upon passing a licensing examination. Every state has its own license laws, rules, and regulations governing the licensure and activities of real estate professionals. For licensure, you must demonstrate your understanding of your state's specific laws and rules and of the field of real estate as a whole.

A real estate salesperson is an individual who has passed the required exam and is duly licensed to act as an agent for sellers and lessors under the supervision of a licensed real estate broker. A real estate salesperson operates as an independent contractor but may not conduct business for him- or herself. After satisfactorily acting as a real estate salesperson for a specified period of time (varies by states) and completing a required number of transactions, the salesperson may take an examination for licensure as a broker. (Many states have course requirements as well.) A real estate broker may establish an office and may supervise real estate salespersons. A real estate appraiser estimates and reports on the value of real estate. An informal opinion of value may be prepared by any experienced salesperson or broker. However, appraisals of property which entail federal funding or federal loan guarantees of any kind may be made only by licensed or certified appraisers. Requirements for appraisal licensure or certification include education, experience, and qualifying upon an examination. The final chapter of this book will introduce you to the world of appraisal licensure, explaining its history and special restrictions. The appraisal chapter will prepare you for appraisal licensure and give you a foretaste of an appraisal licensure examination.

This book will provide you with the necessary information to successfully pass a real estate examination for licensure in any state. You may use this book as a text or as a supplement to relate your classroom material to the test-taking experience. The emphasis of this book is upon knowledge expected of all real estate professionals regardless of location and upon applying this knowledge to the test situation. You must complement your study of this book with thorough study of your state's Real Estate License Law.

We have arranged this book so that you may naturally grow in your knowledge of real estate and of test principles. We have placed emphasis on those areas that give new candidates for licensure greatest concern.

There are hundreds of real estate questions and their answers in this text. In addition to supplying correct answers, we have supplied solutions to all mathematical problems for on-the-spot instruction.

The questions at the end of each chapter are typical questions used on real estate examinations throughout the country. The model examinations which follow the text are similar in content and style to the examinations of the three major national real estate test developers—ASI (Assessment Systems, Inc.), PSI (Psychological Services, Inc.), and AMP (Applied Measurement Professionals, Inc.). The full-length model salesperson and broker examinations are not actual examinations, which are secure examinations and not open for public inspection, nor are they official sample examinations, which are copyrighted and may not be reprinted. The model exams are, however, closely patterned on the actual exams to give you excellent practice and to build your confidence in preparation for your test.

The authors have researched various real estate licensing laws and manuals throughout the country to be certain to include all aspects of real estate law which are universally required by the states. All of the material has been pretested by hundreds of students in actual classroom participation. When you have completed this book, you will be very well prepared for the universal aspects of your exam, be it a standardized exam or a state-administered exam.

THE EXAMINATIONS

Each state has its own real estate laws, rules, and regulations, as well as its own method of examination. Some states prepare their own examinations while other states commission one of the standardized test services to develop an examination tailor-made for that state. States that use a standardized exam supplement it with an additional exam based on state laws. This section, too, may be developed by the individual states or by the service that administers the universal portion of the exam.

States are not bound to continue using the same testing method from year to year. Any given state may switch from one national service to another or to its own exam or back again. When you apply to take your real estate exam, you will receive appropriate information. At the time this book was prepared, the examination breakdown was as indicated in the following table.

STATE-UNIQUE EXAMS

The single area of commonality among state-unique exams is that state-specific questions are intermingled among the questions of universal relevance. Thus, state-unique exams are administered as integrated, single-section exams. In all other aspects, there is great diversity from state to state. A state's own exam may be long or short. It may include true-or-false questions, fill-in-the-blank questions, short-answer questions, and multiple-choice questions. A state-unique exam may require you to fill out forms used in real estate and to show your mathematical calculations. Your best preparation for your state's own exam is thorough grounding in all the material covered.

You should be aware that some state-unique exams are not state developed. The Michigan exams, for example, are created by AMP to meet Michigan's specifications. Question styles are similar to the question styles of the AMP standardized exams, but the question content conforms to the requirements set out by the state of Michigan. Similarly, the Wisconsin broker exam is custom-made for Wisconsin by PSI, reflecting Wisconsin's own analysis of the knowledge needed by its brokers.

The state portion of the standardized exams tends to be developed by the same test developers who create the national exams used in that state. However, each state specifies the content and emphases it would like to see on its state portion, and state exams vary along a number of dimensions. The chief variation is, of course, in actual state law as it applies to real estate, but there is also consider-

STATE UNIQUE	AMP	PSI	ASI
California	Alabama	Iowa	Alaska
Florida	Georgia	Nevada	Arizona
Maine	Missouri	New Hampshire	Arkansas
Michigan	Nebraska	Virginia	Colorado
Minnesota	North Dakota	Wisconsin	Connecticut
Mississippi		(Salesperson	Delaware
New York		only)	DC
North Carolina			Hawaii
Ohio			Idaho
Oklahoma			Illinois
Oregon			Indiana
South Carolina			Kansas
Texas			Kentucky
West Virginia			Louisiana
Wisconsin			Maryland
(Broker only)			Massachusetts
			Montana
			New Jersey
			New Mexico
			Pennsylvania
			Rhode Island
			South Dakota
			Tennessee
			Utah
			Vermont
			Virgin Islands
			Washington
			Wyoming

able variation in the number of questions, timing, and proportions of test questions devoted to the topics being tested.

STANDARDIZED EXAMINATIONS

The great majority of the states have contracted with one of three test developers to prepare and administer real estate licensing examinations for the state. Each test developer, in turn, has prepared a national examination which it administers in every state with which it has such a contract and a state examination to accompany it. The national examinations measure knowledge and understanding of the nature of real estate, ownership and land use, contracts, brokerage, financing, etc. National exams also test understanding of federal legislation as it applies to real estate transactions. All exams include many questions designed to ascertain that the candidate has competence to calculate property sizes, taxes, costs, commissions, and financing of purchases. The subject matter of the national portions of the exams prepared by the three testing companies is, of necessity, very similar. The differences lie in question styles and in proportions of questions devoted to the topics being tested.

All standardized real estate examinations are timed. The time allotment is determined by the state contracting for the exam rather than by the testing organization. Thus the exam administered by PSI, for example, may be allotted only 2½ hours for completion in one state while a very similar exam is allotted five hours in another state. The time limits tend to be inclusive of both national and state portions, and the number of questions on state portions is subject to state-by-state variations—anywhere from 30 to 75 questions—but even so, time pressure is determined by the standards of each contracting state.

Another area of variation is in passing scores. Some states require only an overall passing grade, while others require that the candidate achieve a passing grade on each part of the exam. Passing is most commonly set at 75%, but in 12 states the passing grade is 70% and in two states it is 65%.

While the pass-fail cutoff point varies from state to state, the scoring method is the same in all states and on all three standardized examinations. This scoring method is known in the testing trade as "rights only." Under this scoring method each correct answer receives one credit. There is no penalty for wrong answers. The obvious implication is that the test-taker should take risks, answering every question even when uncertain of the correct answer. A wrong answer cannot hurt, but a skipped question most certainly cannot earn a point.

A final area in which all standardized real estate exams are alike is in permissive use of the calculator. Since calculation plays such an important role in real estate practice, proficiency with a calculator is a real plus. All three standardized test-makers specify that the calculators used at the examinations be battery powered and silent and without paper printout capability or alphabetic keypads. For paper-and-pencil administrations any battery power will do; however, light levels are often low for computer or machine administrations, so solar calculators are inadvisable for these. We strongly recommend that you appear for your exam with a spare calculator for backup. Calculator failure is not valid grounds for justifying a failing score.

The following are descriptions of the national portions of the three standardized exams for real estate salesperson or broker. Your state will tell you which of these you must take, or if it provides its own, and will give instructions for applying to take your exam. In some states you will apply for a standardized exam through the state itself; in others you will arrange directly with the testing organization.

ASI (Assessment Systems, Inc.)
Real Estate Assessment for Licensure (REAL) Program
718 Arch Street
Philadelphia, PA 19106
800-274-0999

The national portion of the exam consists of 95 multiple-choice questions of a simple "choose one: A, B, C, D" format. Approximately 20% of the questions require calculation. A few questions on each exam are included for purposes of pretesting for validation. The pretest questions are not counted in the scoring, but are unidentifiable to the test taker so must be answered with the same serious intent as the questions that do count. In some states, the ASI exams are paper-and-pencil exams; in some states all the ASI exams are administered by a machine process called EXPro; and in others the candidate has a choice of method of administration. The EXPro is not a keyboard computer, but a simple touch screen method. Candidates taking the exam by EXPro are offered plenty of time for instruction and familiarization with the machine before testing begins. The machine is programmed to self-score and to turn itself off after the prescribed testing time has elapsed, so test takers are not regimented to begin and end together. This means that the machine-shy candidate may take extra time to feel confident before beginning the exam. Since EXPro provides for instant scoring, the candidate will know whether he or she passed or failed before leaving the test site. In some states, EXPro is programmed to turn itself off when the passing score has been attained, thus saving the candidate time and anxiety.

The content of the ASI salesperson exam national test is roughly:

Real property and laws relating to ownership—20%
- Legal concepts of real property
- Rights of ownership
- Encumbrances
- Government power affecting property

Valuation of real property—14%
- Methods of estimating property value
- Factors influencing value estimates
- Appraisal process

Financing of real estate—20%
- Sources of financing
- Forms of financing
- Methods of repayment
- Terms and conditions
- Lender requirements

Transfer of property ownership—15%
- Titles
- Settlement

Real estate brokerage—31%
- Agency relationships and responsibilities
- Listing of real property
- Negotiating real estate sales contracts
- Federal laws relating to fair practices
- Specialty areas

The content of the ASI broker exam national portion is roughly:

Real property and laws relating to ownership—20%
- Ownership of property
- Transfer of title
- Encumbrances
- Public power over property

Valuation of real property—13%
- Appraisal
- Competitive market analysis
- Influences on value

Federal income tax laws affecting real estate—7%
- Owner-occupied residential
- Investment
- Other tax considerations

Financing of real estate—20%
- Sources of financing
- Characteristics of loans
- Special forms of financing
- Financing instruments
- Clauses in financing instruments
- Foreclosure and redemption
- Terms and conditions

Settlement—12%
    Evidence of title
    Reports
    Settlement procedures

Real estate practice—25%
    Agency relationships and responsibilities
    Listing of real property
    Real estate sales contracts
    Other federal laws
    Specialty areas

PSI (Psychological Services, Inc.)
Real Estate Licensing Examination Services
100 West Broadway, Suite 1100
Glendale, CA 91210
800-733-9267

The national portion of the exam consists of 100 multiple-choice questions of a simple "choose one: A, B, C, D" format. Approximately 10% of the questions require calculation. All of the questions count. In some states the PSI exam is a paper-and-pencil exam; in other states the exam is administered by computer. In those states in which the exam is computer administered, instructions for computer use are repeated on every screen, and a running tally of questions answered, questions skipped, and questions remaining is given to the test-taker. Very few keys are utilized, and learning time is offered before testing begins.

The content of the PSI national exams is roughly:

Property ownership—salesperson 12%; broker 10%
    Classes of property
    Land characteristics
    Encumbrances
    Types of ownership
    Deeds
    Escrow process
    Title insurance

Laws of agency—salesperson 20%; broker 18%
    Representation and disclosure

Contracts—salesperson 16%; broker 14%
    Elements of contracts
    Types of contracts

Federal laws and regulations—salesperson 15%; broker 13%
    Fair housing regulations
    Truth-in-lending (Regulation Z)
    Real Estate Settlement Procedures Act (RESPA)
    Antitrust law and restraint of trade

Real estate mathematics—salesperson 10%; broker 9%

Valuation and real estate economics—salesperson 10%; broker 9%
    Methods of establishing price
    Depreciation
    Capitalization rate
    Difference between comparative market analysis and appraisal

Financing—salesperson 10%; broker 10%

Land use controls and regulations—salesperson 7%; broker 7%

Brokerage Management—broker 10%

AMP (Applied Measurement Professionals, Inc.)
Real Estate Examination Program
8310 Nieman Road
Lenexa, KS 66214
913-541-0400

The national portion of the exam consists of 100 multiple-choice questions. Most of the AMP questions are of the familiar simple "choose one: A, B, C, D" style, but some questions are presented in a two-step format. These questions pose a question followed by a number of statements that may or may not fulfill the requirements of the question. You must answer such a question by choosing which combination of statements meets the demands of the question. Approximately 10% of the questions require arithmetic calculations, and all answers count in your score. AMP offers only pencil-and-paper test administration at this time.

Property ownership, transfer, and use—salesperson 36%; broker 25%
    Nature of real property
    Parties dealing with interests in real property
    Land titles and interests in real property
    Special interests relating to real property
    Special relationships between persons holding interests in land
    Acquisition and transfer of real estate
    Public land use control

Brokerage and laws of agency—salesperson 30%; broker 30%
    Real estate agency
    Federal Fair Housing Laws
    Federal Real Estate Settlement Procedures Act
    Property management

Valuation and economics—salesperson 17%; broker 25%

Finance—salesperson 17%; broker 20%

HOW TO USE THIS BOOK

There are as many ways to study as there are ways to learn. Every student has his or her individual preference. The suggestions we make for using this text have been proven to work for countless students in preparing for their real estate examinations. The text has been designed to flow with clear, basic, concise information about real estate subject matter and to reinforce your knowledge with appropriate questions at each step along the way. Application of our suggestions will insure success in your quest for real estate licensure.

Begin by taking the Diagnostic Examination at the end of this chapter. If you score 70 or better, you are probably adequately prepared to take the licensing exam right now. However, you can increase your chance of success by brushing up on areas of weakness. You need not follow any special procedure for using this book for brushup. You may want to try the questions at the end of each chapter and then read the text as needed. Be sure to take all the sample exams at the end of the book. Regardless of the nature of the exam you will take, the practice in taking real estate exams will prove invaluable to you on exam day.

If your score on the Diagnostic Exam is less than 70, a definite work plan is in order.

WORK PLAN

First: Put aside a definite time period for study. Allow enough time to really "get into" the subject matter. Choose a study area that is as free from distraction as possible.

Second: Handle only one subject area or one chapter at a time. Master a topic before you move on.

Third: Take the test at the end of each chapter immediately after you have studied the subject matter and then grade yourself. If you are satisfied with your score, proceed to the next chapter. If not, reread the chapter and answer the questions again. Be sure you understand the reasoning behind each correct answer.

Fourth: Review each question you miss to determine whether you misunderstood the subject matter or simply misread the question. Learning to read questions is part of learning to take exams.

Fifth: Define each term in the section called "In Your Own Words" at the end of each chapter. Write these terms on small index cards and carry them with you for study as time permits throughout the day.

Sixth: When you have completed the text, attempt one of the model exams. Try to take an entire model exam in one sitting. Score yourself and analyze your errors to see where additional study could help. Return to the chapters that concern your areas of weakness and study some more.

Seventh: Complete the other model exams and direct your study as indicated.

HOW TO TAKE AN EXAM

ATTITUDE

Any student can pass any examination if he or she is prepared for it. You are going to pass your examination because you will have received the best possible preparation for it by using this book. Furthermore, you are going to give the best possible account of yourself by using your common sense to answer examination questions.

First of all, get rid of any negative attitudes you may have toward tests in general. A test is not a device to trip you up; it is an opportunity to show how effectively you have learned.

Working through this book will be no easy task. But when you are done you can be confident that you are well prepared. Self-confidence is one of the greatest assets you can bring into the testing room.

When you take your test, keep calm. There's no reason to panic! If you've done your work, there's no need for it, and, if you haven't, a cool head is your very first requirement. At the very least, this book will dispel the mystery that surrounds examinations. A certain amount of concern is normal and positive, but excessive worry saps your strength and alertness.

PRE-TEST REVIEW

If you know any others who are taking this test, you'll probably find it helpful to review this book and your notes with them. The group should be small, certainly no more than four. Team study at this stage should seek to review the material in a way different from that in which you learned it originally; should strive for an exchange of ideas between you and other members of the group; should be selective in sticking to important ideas; should stress the vague and the unfamiliar rather than that which you all know well; should be businesslike and devoid of any nonsense, and should end as soon as you get tired.

One of the worst strategies in test-taking is to do all your preparation the night before the exam. As a reader of this book, we hope you have scheduled and spaced your study properly so as not to suffer from the fatigue and emotional disturbance that comes from cramming the night before. Cramming is a very good way to guarantee poor test results.

However, you would be wise to prepare yourself factually by reviewing your notes in the 48 hours preceding the exam. You shouldn't have to spend more than two or three hours in this way. Stick to salient points. The others will fall into place quickly.

Don't confuse cramming with a final calm review that helps you focus on the significant areas of this book and further strengthens your confidence in your ability to handle the test questions.

KEEP FIT

Mind and body work together. Poor physical condition will lower your mental efficiency. In preparing for an examination, observe the common sense rules of health. Get enough sleep, eat proper foods, plan recreation, and exercise. In relation to health and your license examinations, two cautions are in order: (1) Don't skip meals prior to an examination in order to get extra time for study; and (2) don't skimp on sleep by sitting up late to cram for an examination. Cramming is an attempt to learn in a very short period of time what should have been learned through regular and consistent study. Not only are these two habits detrimental to health, but seldom do they pay off in terms of effective learning. It is likely that you will be more confused rather than better prepared on the day of the examination if you have broken your daily routine by missing your meals or sleep. On the night before the examination go to bed at your regular time and try to get a good night's sleep.

EXAMINATION DAY

Get started early. Leave time for transit breakdowns or traffic tie-ups. Allow ample time to park. If you have to rush or get flustered along the way, you will not do your best on the exam. Surely you should know the route or plan the connections well ahead of starting out on exam day.

Bring all necessary equipment—two or three sharpened pencils, erasers, a watch, glasses, identification, your admission ticket, required documents, and calculators—as instructed.

Check in and follow directions. Procedures differ greatly at paper-and-pencil sites, EXPro sites, and computer sites. At registration you will have received information for the procedures you must follow. Now you are prepared for the test itself and are on time. Just follow directions, and you'll do fine.

TEST TIME

If your exam is taken with pencil and paper with a test booklet and a separate answer sheet, listen very carefully to the test supervisor. If you don't understand the directions you have heard or read, raise your hand and inform the proctor. Carefully read the directions for each part of the test before beginning to work on that part! If you skip over such directions too hastily, you may miss a main idea and thus lose credit for an entire section.

After reading the directions carefully, look over the entire examination, unless, of course, your exam is divided into separately timed parts in which case you are permitted to look only at the first part. Try to get an overview of the nature, scope, and difficulty of the examination. Note particularly:

- time allowed and number of questions
- scoring method used, if stated
- whether the questions seem to progress from easy to difficult
- which questions, if any, carry extra weight
- what directions apply to each part of the test

On the basis of this overview, you can plan your exam time budget. Unless the exam questions get progressively more difficult, in which case you should have completed more than half at half-time, you should figure that you should answer half the questions in half the time. Do keep track of your time.

Probably the most important single strategy you can follow is to answer the easy questions first, and answer them quickly. Read each question carefully and thoroughly, but do not linger over a question when you know the answer. Likewise, do not spend too much time at the beginning of the exam puzzling over questions that appear to be difficult for you. Read over each difficult question, mark it in the test booklet so that you can find it easily when you return, and *skip its answer space on the answer sheet*. This strategy of answering the easy questions first has at least two advantages for you:

1. You will get credit for all the questions you're sure of. If time runs out, you'll have all the sure shots, losing out only on those that you might have missed anyway. You won't risk getting caught by the time limit just as you reach a question you know really well.
2. By reading and then laying away the tough ones, you give your subconscious a chance to work on them. You may be pleasantly surprised to find the answers to the puzzlers popping up for you as you deal with related questions.

If your exam is administered by a machine, your strategy must be a little different. You cannot circle or make marks next to question numbers on a machine, but you will certainly be issued scrap paper for notes and calculations. Make liberal use of your scrap paper. Write down the numbers of questions you are skipping over for the moment. Keep a running list of the numbers of questions that you answered with a calculated guess or even with a wild guess. Scribble down key words of a question over which you are puzzling. Previewing a machine-administered exam may not be practical, so pace yourself to allow time to go back through the whole exam a second time after a first run-through answering the easiest questions. There will be instructions for getting back to questions you skipped or questions on which you would like to change your answer on the basis of information you synthesized from later questions.

You should know that every question on a properly constructed examination has a purpose. The questions are designed to cover not only all phases of the subject matter but all phases of your reasoning ability. In other words, tests are designed to make you think!

Although it takes a lot of concentration to sit and think for two, three, or four hours, you now know that all tests are nothing more than a series of questions. You will learn to handle them one at a time.

You will see questions that are asked forward or backward, positively or negatively, worst choice or best choice, multiple choice or multi-tiered. Some have common terms, some unusual terms, some seek objective facts, others subjective judgments.

Questions may be based on general knowledge, reasoning ability (interpretive or conceptual), or practical application. This will not bother you. You will read the entire question first, including all choices. Note the key words in the question as you read it. When you understand the question, you will answer it. If you don't understand it or don't know the answer, you will pass it and go on to the next question. One question missed is not going to deter you!

As you proceed through the test, questions that once appeared hard will become easier because of your past study and your growth in confidence during the exam. You can and will analyze each question. Here is the way in which you may analyze the different types of questions previously mentioned.

MULTIPLE CHOICE (GENERAL KNOWLEDGE)

The following question would be labeled a *general knowledge* question. Try the question and see how you do.

Individual ownership in a cooperative apartment is usually held in the form of
- (a) estate in fee simple
- (b) leasehold estate
- (c) stock
- (d) life estate

The answer is (c) *stock*. If you didn't know the answer immediately, then stop and think. Only one answer is possible. Of the four answers given, only one is different from the others (*stock*), and therefore that must be the right answer.

Note what the tester did. The tester tried to give you logical choices, and if you didn't know the difference between a cooperative apartment and a condominium apartment you might have selected (a) *estate in fee simple* as your answer. *General knowledge is important, but test knowledge is also important.*

This same question could be asked backwards or negatively, in a different multiple-choice form. (The style of this next question is not currently in use on any of the standardized real estate exams. However, it is a very common form and is quite likely to appear on a state-developed exam. Furthermore, test-makers change their exams frequently, and you may well encounter this question style by the time you take your exam.) As an example:

Individual ownership in a cooperative apartment is NOT usually held in the form of
- I. estate in fee simple
- II. stock
- (a) I only
- (b) II only
- (c) Both I and II
- (d) Neither I nor II

Read carefully. Note the word *not*. The answer is (a) *I only*. This type of multi-tiered, multiple-choice question stumps many students. It shouldn't. Just remember in answering this type of question that each statement, statement I and statement II, must stand on its own. Read the beginning of the sentence and finish it with one statement at a time. Mark T or F at the end of each statement. You have just reduced a complex multiple-choice question to a simple one.

This question might find its way into still another format.

What do the following people have in common?
I. An owner of a cooperative apartment
II. An owner of a condominium apartment
III. A homeowner in a neighborhood which owns and maintains a swimming pool
    (a) They all hold estates in fee simple.
    (b) They all are stockholders.
    (c) They all have certain interest in common property.
    (d) They all have leasehold estates.

The answer, of course, is (c). In each instance some property is held and enjoyed by the common owners.

SPECIALIZED TERMS

Some questions use specialized terms that real estate salespeople should know but which are generally not used in everyday conversation—in particular, words that end in *or* or *ee* like grant*or*-grant*ee*, lessor-less*ee*, mortgagor-mortga*gee*.

There are two rules for these words that will benefit you. *Rule 1:* Whenever you see a word with the suffix *or*, this person is the giver of something. Whenever you see *ee* at the end of a word, this person is the receiver of something. There are no exceptions to this rule. *Rule 2:* Always change the word to a more familiar word and attempt to answer the question. You'll find it easier. Here is an example of a question in which using these rules can help:

A person who signs a valid listing agreement to sell his property may be known as
    (a) grantee   (c) lienor
    (b) mortgagee   (d) grantor

Because we know the *or* and *ee* rule, we know that the person is not going to be receiving something, so we can cross out (a) and (b) as possible answers. A person who gives a listing contract is also going to be giving title to the property upon its sale and is or can be called the *grantor*. Also note the key word "may" in the question. This word should be circled when you read the question. A person who signs a listing contract is the *principal* in an agency relationship. The student immediately looks for this word in the choices and becomes upset because his word isn't there. But the test-wise student is not flustered because he has noted the key word "may" in the question and knows the principal will be known as the grantor upon the sale and closing of his property. Therefore (d) is the correct answer.

If this question really bothered you, all you have to do is change the words in the answer choices to more familiar words:

• grantee—buyer or receiver of deed
• mortgagee—banker or lender
• lienor—giver of note or bond
• grantor—owner or seller

By doing this, you make the question easier and the answer more obvious.

AMBIGUOUS QUESTIONS

Some testers create questions that at first glance appear ambiguous or incomplete. Every student comes to a test center with a different background and knowledge different from that of every other student, and what appears ambiguous to one is explicit to another. Real estate is so vast and so deep that many questions are not easily marked true or false or a, b, c, or d. If you are confronted with a question that appears ambiguous or incomplete to you, don't fight it! Stop and ask yourself "What does the tester want the general real estate salesperson to know about this subject?" and then answer the question. Put yourself in the place of the tester (particularly if you have a specialized knowledge of a certain facet of real estate) and generalize what the question should be. Here is a simple question that may seem ambiguous to many students.

Which of the following are considered to be contracts?
I. Leases for less than 1 year
II. Oral options
    (a) I only   (c) Both I and II
    (b) II only   (d) Neither I nor II

Most students would place a "true" mark in front of leases and a "false" mark in front of oral options, and answer (a) *I only*. The correct answer is (c) *Both I and II*. The reason is that the question did not ask which are legal contracts, or enforceable contracts, or valid contracts. The question is not ambiguous, but simple! The ambiguity of most questions is created by the student's *reading too much into the question or not reading the question correctly*. A contract, by definition, is nothing more than a mutual agreement between two or more people to do or not to do something. Both a lease for less than 1 year and an oral option, legal or illegal, oral or written, fall within the *common* definition of a contract. There is no question here that, in certain states, these contracts may be unenforceable or invalid. The only question is—are they contracts? By the universal definition, they are. Another example:

When a seller signs a deed, it is said to have been
    (a) ratified   (c) completed
    (b) acknowledged   (d) executed

There are attorneys who would claim all four answers are correct, but in real estate the legal term used is (d) *executed*. This is what the tester wants you to know.

A little thought gives you the best chance of finding the correct answer. The answers are not completely wrong, just partially wrong, and only one answer is complete. Logically, a *ratified* contract or deed implies that more than one party agreed to something. In this instance, only the seller was mentioned in the question. Cross out "ratified." *Acknowledge* is usually an act permitting a legal instrument to be recorded. In the question, the seller signed the deed, not an acknowledgment. Cross out "acknowledged." *Completed* isn't a legal term. Although the lay person may think he has completed everything when he signs a deed, the law just doesn't accept this as a legal term dealing with contracts or deeds. Cross out "completed." *Executed* is the only term left, and is the correct answer and best choice.

BEST CHOICE QUESTIONS

The previous question is also classed as a *best choice question*. Such questions often cause much concern with students. They shouldn't. Most best choice questions have the word "best" in them. As an example:

Money paid to bind an "agreement-to-buy" is best defined as:
(a) surety
(b) legal tender
(c) acknowledgment
(d) consideration

The best answer is (d), even though all the other answers may be correct. *Consideration* is the best word to use when defining any money or thing to bind a contract. The money may be surety, it most certainly is legal tender and it may even be an acknowledgment of the act, but it is always *consideration*.

Remember, the word "best" is a key word and should be circled or underscored when noted in a question. Also, *read and understand* all the answer choices before selecting the best choice answer.

Another way of writing a best choice question is as follows:

Which statement best defines market value?
I. It is present worth for future benefits.
II. It is the price or amount that the property last sold for.
(a) I only
(b) II only
(c) Both I and II
(d) Neither I nor II

The answer is (a) *I only*. Value always denotes worth, and may or may not be the price a property sells for. The best definition is therefore more universal in application and not as restrictive as the second answer, whereas price paid at some unspecified time in the past may or may not denote current market value.

Another best choice question might read:

Which is the best order in which to proceed when establishing a listing price with your principal?
I. Explain the usual commission charged by your office on properties of this type.
II. Present a competitive market analysis.
III. Explain how commissions are split with cooperating brokers.
(a) I, II, III
(b) II, I, III
(c) II, III, I
(d) III, II, I

The *best* order is (b) II, I, III, so the best answer is (b). In establishing a listing price, you and the principal must first agree on a value range for the particular property in the current market. On the basis of the approximate market value of the property, the amount which the principal would like to net, and the commission which will be collected by your office, you and the principal arrive at a listing price. Commission split with a cooperating broker has no bearing at all upon the listing price, but the unsophisticated seller does not know this. The seller may unconsciously try to inflate the listing price so as to protect himself against double commission. It is therefore wise for the salesperson to explain commission splits before the final listing price is established.

KEY OR CLUE WORDS

Be alert for *key* or *clue words* in any question. Obvious key words include "may," "should," "might," "not," "must," "best," "could," "can," "most." Hidden key words include "generally," "normally," "nearly," "required," "prohibit," "usually," or "approximately." An example:

Which of the following is (not intended) to convey legal title?
- (a) warranty deed
- (b) deed-in-trust
- (c) quitclaim deed
- (d) bargain and sale deed

We know by our general knowledge that neither (a) nor (d) is the correct answer. We know this because as we read the question we took notice of the key words in the question, "not intended." Both these deeds are normally used or are intended to convey legal title. That is their purpose. But (b) and (c) are difficult choices. A *deed-in-trust* is a mortgage, and its purpose is to give legal title to a mortgagee if the mortgagor defaults or breaches the mortgage contract. It is not intended to convey title unless an event occurs which forces foreclosure. So by keeping the key words "not intended" in front of you at all times, you now know that the answer is (c). A *quitclaim deed* is used to convey an interest or to correct a flaw in title. Its intention clearly is not to convey legal title.

Key words are important sources of questions to professional test makers. In Chapter 6, "Leases and Management," it is stated that some of the common law requirements of leases are a "date of execution, a date of termination, names of parties, description of the property, and rent to be paid." It is then stated that the "lease *should* state the purpose or use of the premises." A professional tester expects you to know this and may test your knowledge in this fashion:

A valid lease need not include which of the following?
- (a) property description
- (b) terms of lease
- (c) use of premises
- (d) rent

The answer is (c), because by common law the use of the premises is not a requirement. Although most good leases state the use, the question wasn't "what should be in a lease" but "what *must* be in a lease in order for it to be valid." Key in on key words, not only in the test, but throughout this book.

SUMMARY

These are just some of the ways in which you can analyze questions on an examination. It really doesn't take much time, and the results are well worth the effort. As in a basketball game, one point can make the difference between victory and defeat. Each test tip you apply adds points to your score, and the most successful students are the ones who apply these test tips to their advantage.

Remember: An examination is only a series of questions. You can only answer the questions one at a time. So take the time to read, understand, and answer each question and the examination will take care of itself. Be certain that you do answer each question. The scoring method for all three standardized exams is to count only correct answers. No deduction is made for a wrong answer, so even a wild guess cannot hurt you. Most state exams follow this same scoring procedure, but ask to make sure.

The following list consists of important suggestions for taking this exam. Read the suggestions now before you try any of the exams in this book. Read them again the day before you go for your exam. You will find all of them useful.

1. READ every word of every question.
2. READ all of the choices before you mark your answer. It is statistically true that most errors are made when the correct answer is the last choice. Too many people mark the first answer that seems correct without reading through all the choices to find out which answer is *best*.
3. Mark your answers unambiguously, according to instructions.
4. Mark only *one* answer for each question, even if you think that more than one answer is correct. You must choose only one. If you mark more than one answer, the scoring machine will consider you wrong.
5. If you change your mind, change your answer according to instructions. On a paper-and-pencil test, erase completely. Leave no doubt as to which answer you mean.
6. If you do any figuring in the margins of your test booklet or on scrap paper, be sure to mark your answer sheet or the computer screen with your letter choice. Test booklets and scrap paper are not scored.
7. If you are using a separate answer sheet, check often to be sure that the question number matches the answer space, that you have not skipped a space by mistake. If you do slip out of line, you must go back and change your answers. The scoring machine will not read any note of explanation that you write on the answer sheet.
8. If you are unsure of an answer, take your best guess and note the question number on your scrap paper or in the test booklet. Then, if you have time, you can quickly spot those questions to which you would like to give a little extra thought.
9. If you do not know the answer to a question, eliminate the answers that you know are wrong and guess from among those remaining. If you have no idea whatsoever of the answer to a question, guess anyway. Since there is no penalty for a wrong answer, even a wild guess gives you a 25 percent chance to be right. If you leave the space blank, you have no chance at all to be correct.
10. If you notice that time is about to run out and you have not completed all the questions, mark all the remaining questions with the same answer. Some will probably be correct. In doing this, choose an answer other than (A). (A) is generally the correct answer less often than the other choices.
11. Stay alert. Be careful not to mark a wrong answer because you were not concentrating. An example of this type of error might be: The correct answer to a mathematics question is (B) d, and you mark (D) instead of (B).
12. Do not panic. Remember that the real estate license exam is not a competitive exam. You do not have to do better than your neighbor. You do not need to score 100. You want to pass and you want to do well, but a few wrong answers will not hurt you.
13. Check and recheck. If you finish before time is up, do not daydream. Check to be sure that there is an answer—and only one answer—for every question. Return to the difficult questions and rethink them.
14. When you are quite certain that you have done your best, get up and leave even if time has not expired. Too many second thoughts tend to cause changes from right answers to wrong ones.

Good luck!

DIAGNOSTIC EXAMINATION

Directions: Read each question carefully and circle the letter of the best answer. This is a preliminary examination to find out where you stand in your real estate knowledge. Do not be concerned about the time you spend. The correct answers which appear on page 30 are keyed to the chapter which presents each concept. Solutions to the mathematics problems follow the answer key.

1. *Et ux* means
   - (a) and so on and so forth
   - (b) and wife
   - (c) and all others
   - (d) and another

2. A lawsuit is pending against Mr. Jones, and the court rules that his farm should be seized and held as security in case of a negative judgment. This is an act of
   - (a) adverse possession
   - (b) *lis pendens*
   - (c) attachment
   - (d) appurtenance

3. When "time is of the essence" in a contract and a clause is thus included in the agreement of sale specifying that the date of closing will be May 1, 19–, the purchaser
   - (a) has any amount of time after May 1, 19–, in which to fulfill the contract
   - (b) must fulfill the contract on May 1
   - (c) has only until April 30 to fulfill the contract
   - (d) should fulfill the contract on or before May 1

4. Which of the following is (are) true of alterations and addenda to a standard real estate sales contract?
   - I. They should be incorporated into the contract or placed somewhere in the contract where adequate space is available.
   - II. Each alteration or addendum to the agreement should be initialed or signed.
   - (a) I only
   - (b) II only
   - (c) Both I and II
   - (d) Neither I nor II

5. A written agreement in which a purchaser agrees to buy real estate and a seller agrees to sell real estate is called a
   - I. listing agreement
   - II. contract of sale
   - (a) I only
   - (b) II only
   - (c) Both I and II
   - (d) Neither I nor II

6. The term "consideration" as applied to contracts means
   - I. careful thought has been given to the agreement
   - II. that which is given in exchange for something from the other party
   - (a) I only
   - (b) II only
   - (c) Both I and II
   - (d) Neither I nor II

7. If the consideration in a contract is a promise given in exchange for a promise from the second party to the contract, it is
   - I. an installment contract
   - II. a bilateral contract
   - (a) I only
   - (b) II only
   - (c) Both I and II
   - (d) Neither I nor II

8. A contract of sale cannot be valid and enforceable UNLESS
   I. there is an offer and acceptance
   II. the object of the contract is illegal
   (a) I only
   (b) II only
   (c) Both I and II
   (d) Neither I nor II

9. An executory contract is one that is
   I. entered into by the executor of an estate
   II. for the performance of an act in the future
   (a) I only
   (b) II only
   (c) Both I and II
   (d) Neither I nor II

10. The street in front of Mrs. Green's house is paved. Mrs. Green is charged $200 to cover part of the street costs. This charge is known as
    (a) an *ad valorem* tax
    (b) an illegal tax
    (c) an improvement lien
    (d) a special assessment

11. Contracts for the sale of real property must be in writing. The law that established this requirement is known as the
    I. Statute of Frauds
    II. Statute of Limitations
    (a) I only
    (b) II only
    (c) Both I and II
    (d) Neither I nor II

12. Mr. White and Mrs. Black make an oral agreement concerning the sale of Mr. White's apple orchard. Such a contract would be unenforceable in a court of law because of the
    (a) laws of agency
    (b) state licensing laws
    (c) Statute of Frauds
    (d) Statute of Limitations

13. Bill Smith builds a bridge across a stream. Although the entire stream is contained within his property, the anchorings of the bridge extend onto his neighbor's land. This is known as
    (a) adverse possession
    (b) a party wall
    (c) encroachment
    (d) attachment

14. Legality of object in a contract means
    I. an agreement in a contract must be stated in legally correct terms
    II. the contract must be in "plain language" according to the law
    (a) I only
    (b) II only
    (c) Both I and II
    (d) Neither I nor II

15. Which of the following statements regarding the transfer of title by adverse possession is (are) true?
    I. The right of transfer is governed by state laws.
    II. The transfer is voluntary.
    (a) I only
    (b) II only
    (c) Both I and II
    (d) Neither I nor II

16. A contract that is executed for a purpose that is illegal is known as
    (a) a voidable contract
    (b) a lawful contract
    (c) a valid contract
    (d) a void contract

17. Which of the following is NOT considered to be an essential element to a valid contract?
    I. A copy of the previous deed
    II. Signatures of both buyer and seller
    - (a) I only
    - (b) II only
    - (c) Both I and II
    - (d) Neither I nor II

18. A property owner who is selling his own property
    I. is permitted to prepare his own contract of sale
    II. is required to have the contract of sale prepared by a qualified attorney
    - (a) I only
    - (b) II only
    - (c) Both I and II
    - (d) Neither I nor II

19. A lessee's rental is based on 4 percent of his gross sales over $50,000 with a minimum monthly rental of $2,000. This type of lease is generally known as
    - (a) a variable lease
    - (b) a net lease
    - (c) a percentage lease
    - (d) a gross lease

20. When a tenant abandons the leased premises because the landlord has not furnished a vital service, such as hot water, this is known as
    - (a) actual notice
    - (b) constructive notice
    - (c) constructive eviction
    - (d) actual eviction

21. Mary Rogers is going to Europe for the summer. While she is gone, her sister has agreed to occupy Mary's apartment and pay the rent. This is known as
    I. subleasing
    II. abandonment
    - (a) I only
    - (b) II only
    - (c) Both I and II
    - (d) Neither I nor II

22. An option contained in a lease could
    I. grant the lessee the privilege of renewing his lease
    II. grant the lessee the privilege of purchasing the leased premises
    - (a) I only
    - (b) II only
    - (c) Both I and II
    - (d) Neither I nor II

23. A listing agreement may be terminated
    I. by mutual agreement of both parties
    II. by the death of the seller
    - (a) I only
    - (b) II only
    - (c) Both I and II
    - (d) Neither I nor II

24. Each of 12 apartments can be rented thusly:
    (1) at $285 per month with utilities
    (2) at $250 per month without utilities
    If the cost of utilities for each of the 12 apartments averages $25 per month, the net annual income under option (1) is
    - (a) $1,440 more than under option (2)
    - (b) $5,040 more than under option (2)
    - (c) $1,440 less than under option (2)
    - (d) $5,040 less than under option (2)

25. Which of the following sales will yield the seller exactly $208,714?

	Sales Price	Broker's Fee	Other Expenses
(a)	$225,700	6%	$400
(b)	$221,600	5.5%	$698
(c)	$231,000	6%	$301
(d)	$219,900	5%	$272

26. Which of the following is (are) true of exclusive agency listings?
    I. Only one broker is authorized to act as the agent for the buyer.
    II. The seller cannot sell the property himself and avoid paying a commission.
    (a) I only   (c) Both I and II
    (b) II only   (d) Neither I nor II

27. Which of the following is (are) true of VA mortgages?
    I. A purchaser who assumes a VA mortgage must also be a qualified veteran.
    II. A veteran is entitled to only one VA-guaranteed mortgage loan.
    (a) I only   (c) Both I and II
    (b) II only   (d) Neither I nor II

28. Which of the following may not pay discount points charged by the lending institution when obtaining a VA or FHA loan?
    (a) Seller   (c) Vendor
    (b) Broker   (d) Vendee

29. Which of the following is (are) true concerning prepayment privileges?
    I. When a loan insured by the FHA is paid in full before maturity, the mortgagor must pay a prepayment penalty.
    II. In the case of VA loans, prepayment penalties cannot be charged.
    (a) I only   (c) Both I and II
    (b) II only   (d) Neither I nor II

30. The maximum amount of a loan that the FHA will insure on a single-family home is
    (a) 60%   (c) $17,500
    (b) $60,000   (d) None of these

31. The Ace Mortgage Company granted a 20-year, $60,000 mortgage loan to the Olsens at the prevailing interest rate of 12 percent. The monthly payments are $771.66, which includes payments on the principal, interest, and annual taxes. If the taxes are $1,320 per year, what will the balance of the principal be after the first payment? (Round your answer to the nearest dollar.)
    (a) $52,060   (c) $59,938
    (b) $55,100   (d) $59,400

32. In a subordination agreement
    I. the first lender gives first priority to the lien of the second lender
    II. the agreement must be signed by both lenders in order to be valid
    (a) I only   (c) Both I and II
    (b) II only   (d) Neither I nor II

33. What is the rate of interest on a mortgage loan if the principal balance is $80,000 and one month's interest payment is $800?
    (a) 6%   (c) 8%
    (b) 10%   (d) 12%

34. A defeasance clause is most accurately described as
    I. a statement that gives notice to the public that a mortgage debt has been fully paid
    II. a statement that provides that upon full payment of a mortgage loan, the mortgagee will issue a release of mortgage
    - (a) I only
    - (b) II only
    - (c) Both I and II
    - (d) Neither I nor II

35. If a mortgagor defaults on an installment payment, the mortgagee can make the entire debt due immediately by the provisions of the
    I. alienation clause
    II. acceleration clause
    - (a) I only
    - (b) II only
    - (c) Both I and II
    - (d) Neither I nor II

36. What is the remaining principal on a mortgage loan if the monthly interest payment is $325 and the annual interest rate is $8\frac{1}{2}$ percent?
    - (a) $28,528.53
    - (b) $35,697.48
    - (c) $38,235.20
    - (d) $45,882.35

37. Dan Thomas was granted a loan for 80 percent of the purchase price of $165,000. The loan was for a term of 20 years with an annual interest rate of $13\frac{1}{4}$ percent. How much interest will he pay the first month?
    - (a) $1,320.00
    - (b) $1,093.13
    - (c) $1,457.50
    - (d) $1,436.22

38. Using problem 37 as a basis, what will be the remaining principal after the first payment if his total monthly payment is $1,550.00?
    - (a) $131,700.00
    - (b) $131,593.13
    - (c) $131,907.50
    - (d) $131,886.22

39. Which of the following is (are) required to be executed in order to create a mortgage loan that is enforceable?
    I. A document that creates the lien
    II. An agreement to repay the debt
    - (a) I only
    - (b) II only
    - (c) Both I and II
    - (d) Neither I nor II

40. A mortgage that allows a borrower to obtain financing from a second lender while paying off an existing mortgage is known as a(n)
    - (a) wraparound mortgage
    - (b) package mortgage
    - (c) blanket mortgage
    - (d) open end mortgage

41. When a third party purchases a property at a foreclosure sale,
    I. the property is sold free of the first mortgage but not of any junior liens
    II. the property is sold free of the mortgage and all junior liens
    - (a) I only
    - (b) II only
    - (c) Both I and II
    - (d) Neither I nor II

42. What are the quarterly interest payments of a loan of $28,000 if the annual interest rate is $8\frac{1}{2}$ percent?
    - (a) $2,380.00
    - (b) $793.33
    - (c) $595.00
    - (d) $540.00

43. The Millers purchased a property for $130,000. They secured their purchase with a $6,000 earnest money deposit and paid an additional $7,000 at signing of contract of sale. They agreed to assume the seller's mortgage

balance of $50,000 and executed a mortgage and note to the seller to finance the remaining $67,000. This is called

(a) a wraparound mortgage   (c) a balloon note

(b) a junior mortgage   (d) a flexible-payment loan

44. If a VA loan in the amount of $50,000 was in default, for what minimum price must the property be sold at foreclosure in order for the lender to recover the full value of the loan?

(a) $20,000   (c) $32,500

(b) $22,500   (d) $50,000

45. If a VA loan was made for $20,000, how much would the seller be charged at closing if the mortgage was discounted 5 points?

(a) $500   (c) $850

(b) $700   (d) $1,000

46. An interest rate that is charged on a loan is higher than the legal limit. This violates which of the following?

(a) Statute of Frauds   (c) Regulation "Z"

(b) Usury laws   (d) Fair housing law

47. Which of the following would provide the greatest protection to the buyer of real property?

(a) Bargain and sale deed   (c) Quitclaim deed

(b) General warranty deed   (d) Special warranty deed

48. The accumulation of soil on an owner's property caused by the movement of water is known as

(a) accretion   (c) assemblage

(b) erosion   (d) annexation

49. Possession of *equitable title* to a property gives a buyer the right to

(a) move in

(b) lease the premises to another

(c) sell his interest

(d) make capital improvements, but not move in

50. Which of the following is correct in reference to a valid and complete transfer of title to real property?

I. The grantee may be a fictitious person.

II. The grantor's spouse is never required to sign the deed.

(a) I only   (c) Both I and II

(b) II only   (d) Neither I nor II

51. Title is said to pass at which of the following times?

I. Acknowledgement of an executed deed

II. Delivery of an executed deed

(a) I only   (c) Both I and II

(b) II only   (d) Neither I nor II

52. When a person uses another's land for a certain period of time without the owner's approval, he may acquire

(a) easement by necessity   (c) easement by prescription

(b) easement in gross   (d) easement appurtenant

53. An encumbrance
    I. prevents the transfer of title of a property
    II. may be a lien, easement, or restriction
    - (a) I only
    - (b) II only
    - (c) Both I and II
    - (d) Neither I nor II

54. Which of the following statements is (are) correct in reference to life estates?
    I. A life estate ends with the death of the person to whom it was granted.
    II. A life estate is passed on to the owner's heirs.
    - (a) I only
    - (b) II only
    - (c) Both I and II
    - (d) Neither I nor II

55. Which of the following is not a leasehold estate?
    - (a) Estate at will
    - (b) Life estate
    - (c) Estate at sufferance
    - (d) Estate for years

56. Police powers are most accurately described as
    I. the right to acquire private property for a public use
    II. the right to place a charge on real estate to raise revenue
    - (a) I only
    - (b) II only
    - (c) Both I and II
    - (d) Neither I nor II

57. When a deed specifically states that a parcel of real property is granted as long as it is used for church purposes, the estate is
    - (a) a fee simple
    - (b) a determinable fee
    - (c) ecumenical
    - (d) an estate at will

58. Which of the following statements is (are) true regarding condominium ownership?
    I. One tax bill is received by the condominium project's managing agent, divided equally between all unit owners, and included in a monthly assessment charge.
    II. Default in the tax payments by one unit owner affects the title of the remaining owners.
    - (a) I only
    - (b) II only
    - (c) Both I and II
    - (d) Neither I nor II

59. Residents of a cooperative apartment are subject to
    I. regulations of the co-op board
    II. laws of the municipality
    III. prohibitions of the landlord
    - (a) I only
    - (b) II only
    - (c) I and II only
    - (d) I and III only

60. The condominium owner-occupant holds his title as a
    - (a) partial estate
    - (b) determinable fee estate
    - (c) fee simple estate
    - (d) leasehold estate

61. Which of the following is (are) NOT covered under the Federal Fair Housing Act?
    I. Industrial loft buildings
    II. Vacant land acquired for the construction of commercial buildings
    - (a) I only
    - (b) II only
    - (c) Both I and II
    - (d) Neither I nor II

62. The term "blockbusting" is most accurately described as
    I. the purchase of a home in a homogeneous neighborhood by a member of a minority group
    II. directing homeseekers to particular areas to maintain the homogeneity of a particular neighborhood
    (a) I only
    (b) II only
    (c) Both I and II
    (d) Neither I nor II

63. The guidelines contained in the Federal Fair Housing Law apply to
    I. a real estate broker or salesperson
    II. an owner using the services of a real estate broker
    (a) I only
    (b) II only
    (c) Both I and II
    (d) Neither I nor II

64. Discrimination on which basis is NOT prohibited by Federal Fair Housing legislation?
    (a) Race
    (b) Age
    (c) Sex
    (d) Religion

65. A savings and loan association holding a first mortgage has allowed a lender of a second mortgage to take priority over its loan. This is called
    I. redemption
    II. subordination
    (a) I only
    (b) II only
    (c) Both I and II
    (d) Neither I nor II

66. A property management agreement should include
    I. the duties of the property manager
    II. description of the property
    (a) I only
    (b) II only
    (c) Both I and II
    (d) Neither I nor II

67. Which of the following would be considered to be a fixed expense in a property management budget?
    I. Employees' salaries
    II. Repairs
    (a) I only
    (b) II only
    (c) Both I and II
    (d) Neither I nor II

68. A broker's contract for selling a property stipulated that he was entitled to 5 percent of the first $15,000 and $3\frac{1}{2}$ percent of all over that amount. The broker received $1,100 for selling a property. What was the sales price?
    (a) $10,000
    (b) $15,000
    (c) $20,000
    (d) $25,000

69. You have the opportunity to buy a piece of property for $45,000, which is 10 percent less than the original listed price. What percent profit can you make if you resell it immediately for 20 percent more than the originally listed price?
    (a) 20%
    (b) 17%
    (c) $33\frac{1}{3}$%
    (d) 25%

70. Which of the following is NOT a responsibility of a broker towards his principal?
    (a) Account for all monies entrusted to the broker by the principal.
    (b) Disclosure to a buyer that the seller will accept a price lower than the listing price.
    (c) Act according to a principal's instructions and authority.
    (d) Inform the seller of a low offer.

71. A broker may represent and collect a commission from both the buyer and seller as long as
    I. he has the prior knowledge and agreement of the seller, who is his principal responsibility
    II. he has the prior knowledge and agreement of the buyer in such a transaction
    - (a) I only
    - (b) II only
    - (c) Both I and II
    - (d) Neither I nor II

72. The owner of a block of 14 building lots, each with a frontage of 75 feet, desires to realize $161,400 from the sale of said lots, withholding 2 lots for himself. What must the sales price be per front foot on the lots sold?
    - (a) $179.33
    - (b) $153.71
    - (c) $215.20
    - (d) $161.40

73. A house sold for $86,480, which was 8 percent under the original list price. The broker's commission fee was 5 percent. What was the original list price?
    - (a) $94,000
    - (b) $83,398
    - (c) $87,561
    - (d) $91,032

74. When a contract for sale has been signed, the buyer receives
    - (a) equitable title to the property
    - (b) legal title to the real estate
    - (c) the right of possession of the property
    - (d) none of the above

75. The synopsis of all recorded instruments in reference to the title of a piece of real property is known as
    - (a) subrogation of title
    - (b) metes and bounds of title
    - (c) an abstract
    - (d) a certificate of title

76. On June 16, a property was sold. The annual taxes of $775.00 and the water bill of $86.00 for the current calendar year had been paid in full on January 1. If these payments are prorated, what amount will be returned to the seller? (Please round answer.)
    - (a) $357.00
    - (b) $466.00
    - (c) $430.00
    - (d) $394.00

77. Title insurance on a property was $232.70. In addition, the following costs were incurred: title search fee—$65.00; cost of preparing the papers—$20.00; appraisal fee—$40.00; and miscellaneous fees—$8.30. If the seller paid 70 percent of the total charges and the buyer paid the rest, how much more did the seller pay than the buyer?
    - (a) $109.80
    - (b) $366.00
    - (c) $146.40
    - (d) $256.20

78. When J. Sutherland sold his house, the buyer assumed the unpaid balance of the mortgage. The monthly mortgage payment had been paid on August 10. The unpaid balance of Mr. Sutherland's 8 percent interest mortgage was $11,500. What was the amount of accrued interest if the closing was held on September 2?
    - (a) $168.67
    - (b) $58.88
    - (c) $51.11
    - (d) $20.44

79. Which of the following is NOT usually charged to the buyer as a settlement charge?
    - (a) Recording of the deed
    - (b) Termite inspection
    - (c) Recording a new mortgage
    - (d) Broker's commission

80. An office building is listed at $175,000. One offer received from a prospective buyer was the assumption of the $85,000 mortgage and $80,000 in cash. If the seller accepts this deal and authorizes the broker to deduct the transfer tax of $577, $650 for title insurance, and a 10 percent commission fee, how much will the seller receive from a 20 percent earnest money deposit?
    (a) $16,273
    (b) $14,273
    (c) $17,273
    (d) $15,273

81. Louis Townsend agreed to assume a $15,000 mortgage on a property he was purchasing at the price of $35,000. He also deposited 15 percent earnest money with the seller's broker. If the seller authorized the broker to deduct his 7 percent commission, title insurance expenses of $195, and the transfer tax fee of $70, how much will the broker owe the seller at closing?
    (a) $3,300
    (b) $3,450
    (c) $3,247
    (d) $2,535

82. The Real Estate Settlement Procedures Act
    I. requires that all finance charges be disclosed only to the buyer
    II. requires that the buyer and seller be informed of all settlement costs
    (a) I only
    (b) II only
    (c) Both I and II
    (d) Neither I nor II

83. The recording system was enacted in order to
    I. give notice to anyone interested in the title to a parcel of property of the interests of all parties
    II. insure title against all claims by third parties
    (a) I only
    (b) II only
    (c) Both I and II
    (d) Neither I nor II

84. "Market value" is best defined as
    I. the price that a property sells for
    II. the highest price that a property will bring in the open market
    (a) I only
    (b) II only
    (c) Both I and II
    (d) Neither I nor II

85. Which of the following methods of appraising would best be utilized in finding the value estimate of a church?
    (a) Cost approach
    (b) Rental approach
    (c) Market approach
    (d) Income approach

86. Which of the following does not apply to depreciation?
    (a) Physical deterioration
    (b) Locational obsolescence
    (c) Functional obsolescence
    (d) Original cost

87. An appraiser has estimated the current replacement cost of a one-year-old building to be $557,000. The building is situated on a plot of land valued at $90,000. If the depreciation has been calculated to be $35,000 annually, what is the estimated value of this property?
    (a) $682,000
    (b) $612,000
    (c) $502,000
    (d) $432,000

88. A 15-year-old building has a useful life of 25 years and a current replacement cost of $42,000. By what percentage has the building depreciated in 15 years?
    (a) 100%
    (b) 37½%
    (c) 60%
    (d) 40%

89. Using problem 88 as a basis, what is the estimated value of this real estate if the land is valued at $13,000?
    - (a) $25,200
    - (b) $16,800
    - (c) $29,000
    - (d) $29,800

90. Which of the following is true in reference to the metes and bounds method of describing property?
    - (a) Always ends at the point where it started
    - (b) Always uses north as a base line
    - (c) Is based on principal meridians and base lines
    - (d) Section number 16 is always set aside for school purposes

91. Zoning laws are
    - I. made by federal agencies and laws
    - II. used to regulate and control the use of land
    - (a) I only
    - (b) II only
    - (c) Both I and II
    - (d) Neither I nor II

92. Building codes are used to
    - I. set the requirements for sanitary equipment
    - II. set the requirements for the type of materials that may be used in the alteration of a commercial building
    - (a) I only
    - (b) II only
    - (c) Both I and II
    - (d) Neither I nor II

93. A house is assessed at $47,200. The tax rate was formerly $6.50 per $100. Due to a recent revaluation, the tax rate is decreased by $3.40 per $100. What is the new monthly property tax payment?
    - (a) $255.66
    - (b) $121.93
    - (c) $133.73
    - (d) $146.32

94. In the municipality of Kenope, the local tax rate has been increased from $0.024 per dollar to $0.032 per dollar. What is the increase in local tax that must be paid on a house that has an assessed value of $20,000?
    - (a) $1,120
    - (b) $16
    - (c) $640
    - (d) $160

95. The Piersons went to Europe for the summer and forgot to pay their annual real estate taxes of $1,200 due on June 1. When they returned, they paid the amount in full on October 1. What was their total payment if there was a penalty fee of 1 percent per month on all overdue taxes?
    - (a) $1,212
    - (b) $1,260
    - (c) $1,248
    - (d) $1,152

Questions 96–100 refer to the map on page 29.

96. How many lots on the plat are encumbered by easements?
    - (a) One
    - (b) Two
    - (c) Three
    - (d) Four

97. Which of the following statements is (are) true?
    - I. The lots on the easterly side of School Lane would be found on Sheet No. 8.
    - II. Lot 17 in Block 34 has 100 feet of frontage on School Lane.
    - (a) I only
    - (b) II only
    - (c) Both I and II
    - (d) Neither I nor II

98. If the owner of Lot 17 in Block 34 decided to subdivide the lot into 13 lots, each containing a frontage of 50 feet, how much would he have to charge per front foot in order to realize $198,354?
    - (a) $360.64
    - (b) $233.35
    - (c) $305.16
    - (d) $264.47

99. Which of the following statements is (are) correct?
    - I. Lot 14 in Block 34 is in the shape of a square.
    - II. Lot 7 in Block 36 is in the shape of a triangle.
    - (a) I only
    - (b) II only
    - (c) Both I and II
    - (d) Neither I nor II

100. Which of the following has the greatest frontage on Berry Drive?
    - (a) Lot 6 in Block 36
    - (b) Lot 15 in Block 35
    - (c) Lot 18 in Block 35
    - (d) Lot 4 in Block 36

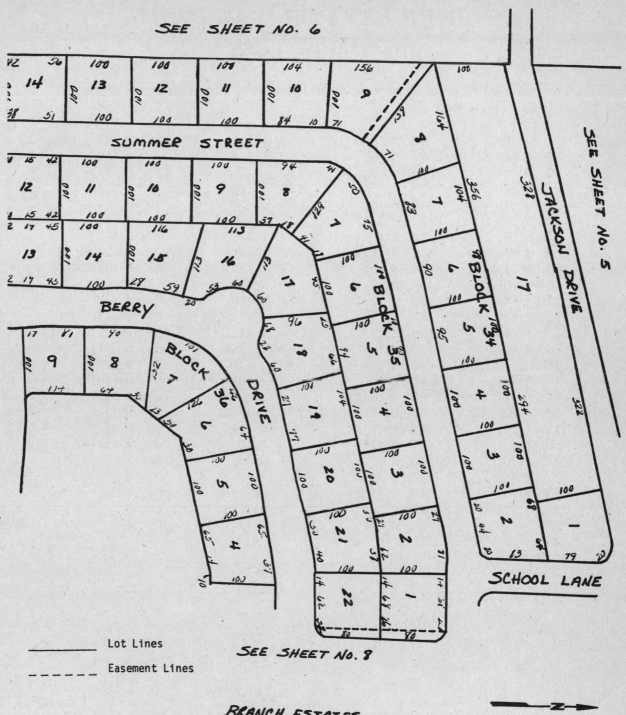

BRANCH ESTATES
SHEET No. 7

ANSWER KEY FOR DIAGNOSTIC EXAMINATION

The number following the correct answer letter refers to the chapter in which the concept is presented.

1. b (13)	26. d (3)	51. b (4)	*76. b (11)
2. c (13)	27. d (5)	52. c (2)	*77. c (11)
3. d (4)	28. d (5)	53. b (2)	*78. b (11)
4. c (4)	29. b (5)	54. a (2)	79. d (12)
5. b (4)	30. d (5)	55. b (2)	*80. d (11)
6. b (4)	*31. c (11)	56. d (2)	*81. d (11)
7. b (4)	32. c (5)	57. b (2)	82. b (12)
8. a (4)	*33. d (11)	58. d (2)	83. a (2 and 5)
9. b (13)	34. b (5)	59. c (2)	84. b (8)
10. d (5)	35. b (5)	60. c (2)	85. a (8)
11. a (4)	*36. d (11)	61. c (10)	86. d (8)
12. c (4)	*37. c (11)	62. d (10)	*87. b (11)
13. c (2)	*38. c (11)	63. c (10)	*88. c (11)
14. d (4)	39. c (5)	64. b (10)	*89. d (11)
15. a (4)	40. a (5)	65. b (5)	90. a (7)
16. d (4)	41. b (5)	66. c (6)	91. b (10)
17. a (4)	*42. c (11)	67. d (6)	92. c (10)
18. a (3)	43. b (5)	*68. d (11)	*93. b (11)
19. c (6)	*44. b (11)	*69. c (11)	*94. d (11)
20. c (6)	*45. d (11)	70. b (3)	*95. c (11)
21. a (6)	46. b (13)	71. c (3)	96. c
22. c (6)	47. b (4)	*72. a (11)	97. a
23. c (3)	48. a (13)	*73. a (11)	*98. c
*24. a (11)	49. c (4)	74. a (4)	99. d
*25. b (11)	50. d (4)	75. c (2)	100. c

*Solutions provided

SOLUTIONS TO MATH PROBLEMS

24. (1) $285 per month × 12 apts = $3,420 − ($25 per month × 12 = $300) = $3,120 net income per month × 12 = $37,440 net per year
    (2) $250 per month × 12 apts = $3,000 net per month × 12 = $36,000 net per year
    $37,440 − $36,000 = $1,440 more than under option (2)

25. (a) $225,700 × 6% = $13,542
    $225,700 − $13,542 = $212,158 − $400 = $211,758
    (b) $221,600 × 5.5% = $12,188
    $221,600 − $12,188 = $209,412 − $698 = $208,714
    (c) $231,000 × 6% = $13,860
    $231,000 − $13,860 = $217,140 − $301 = $216,839
    (d) $219,900 × 5% = $10,995
    $219,900 − $10,995 = $208,905 − $272 = $208,633

31. $60,000 × 12% = $7,200 ÷ 12 months = $600 interest per month
    $1,320 ÷ 12 months = $110 taxes per month
    $600 + $110 = $710 non-principal payment per month
    $771.66 − $710 = $61.66 principal payment first month
    $60,000 − $61.66 = $59,938.34 balance of principal rounded to $59,938

33. $800 per month interest × 12 months = $9,600 interest per year
    $9,600 ÷ $80,000 = .12 = 12% interest

36. $325 × 12 months = $3,900 interest ÷ .085 = $45,882.35

37. $165,000 × 80% = $132,000 mortgage × 13¼% = $17,490 annual interest
    $17,490 ÷ 12 = $1,457.50 interest first month

38. $1,550.00 − $1,457.50 = $92.50 principal
    $132,000 − $92.50 = $131,907.50 remaining principal

42. $28,000 × .085 = $2,380 ÷ 4 = $595 per quarter

44. The VA will guarantee 60% of the loan or $27,500 whichever is less.
    $50,000 × .60 = $30,000. Therefore VA will guarantee $27,500.
    $50,000 - $27,500 = $22,500

45. $20,000 × .05 = $1,000

68. $15,000 × .05 = $750
    $1,100 − $750 = $350 ÷ .035 = $10,000
    $15,000 + $10,000 = $25,000 sales price

69. $45,000 ÷ .90 = $50,000 original listed price
    $50,000 × 1.20 = $60,000 − $45,000 = $15,000
    $15,000 ÷ $45,000 = .333 or 33⅓%

72. 12 lots for sale × 75 front feet = 900 front feet
    $161,400 ÷ 900 = $179.33 per front foot

73. $86,480 ÷ .92 = $94,000

76. 5½ months between date paid and closing
    Taxes $775 per year, $64.58 per month
              $64.58 × 5.5 = $355.19 used by seller
              $775 − $355.19 = $419.81 returned to seller

Water $86.00 per year, $7.17 per month
$7.17 × 5.5 = $39.44 used by seller
$86.00 − $39.44 = $46.56 returned to seller
$419.81 + $46.56 = $466.37 rounded to $466.00 returned to seller

77. $232.70 + $65.00 + $20.00 + $40.00 + $8.30 = $366.00
$366.00 × .70 = $256.20 paid by seller
$366.00 − $256.20 = $109.80 paid by buyer
$256.20 − $109.80 = $146.40 more paid by seller

78. $11,500 × .08 = $920 ÷ 12 months = $76.67 per month ÷ 30 days = $2.56 per day
August 10 to September 2 = 23 days
$2.56 × 23 days = $58.88

80. $85,000 + $80,000 = $165,000 × .20 = $33,000 deposit
$165,000 × .10 = $16,500 commission fee
$577 + $650 + $16,500 = $17,727
$33,000 deposit − $17,727 charges = $15,273 remaining

81. $35,000 × .15 = $5,250 deposit
$35,000 × .07 = $2,450 commission
$2,450 + $195 + $70 = $2,715 charges
$5,250 − $2,715 = $2,535 owed to seller

87. $557,000 replacement value − $35,000 depreciation = $522,000 + $90,000 land value = $612,000 estimated value

88. 100% ÷ 25 years
1.00 ÷ 25 = .04 or 4% yearly depreciation
15 years × 4% = .60 or 60% total depreciation

89. 100% − 60% = 40%
$42,000 × 40% = $16,800 cost of building
$13,000 cost of land
$29,800 total estimated cost

93. $6.50 − $3.40 = $3.10 per $100 new tax rate
$47,200 ÷ 100 = $472 × $3.10 = $1,463.20 ÷ 12 = $121.93 per month

94. $20,000 ÷ 1.00 = $20,000 × .024 = $480
$20,000 ÷ 1.00 = $20,000 × .032 = $640
$640 − $480 = $160 increase

95. June 1 to October 1 = 4 months × .01 = .04
$1,200 × .04 = $48.00 penalty + $1,200 = $1,248

98. 13 lots @ 50 front feet = 650 front feet
$198,354 ÷ 650 = $305.16 per front foot

Chapter Two

Interests in Real Estate

All real estate in the United States is either *privately* or *publicly* owned. In this chapter, we will discuss the nature of the different kinds of interests that people may own in property. The interest that a person owns in real estate is called an *estate*.

REAL VS. PERSONAL PROPERTY

Generally, property can be divided into two classes—real and personal. *Real property* is normally defined as "land, and all that is permanently attached, affixed, or growing thereon." This is broken down as follows:

1. *Land:* The crust of the earth and all rights above and below the surface that would insure its full use, including mineral rights, air rights, and water rights.
2. *Attached:* Implies a permanent relationship with land such as footings, foundations, superstructures, buildings, sidewalks, curbs, driveways, fencing, etc.
3. *Affixed:* Those things that are the essential elements of the structure, such as heating plants, lights, and built-in features, such as plumbing fixtures, that are wedded to the structure in such a way that to remove them would cause harm to the structure.
4. *Growing thereon:* Anything that has roots of a permanent nature; not annual crops that have to be planted each year, but bushes, trees, shrubs, and lawns that mature and grow *each* year.

Personal property is normally defined as "anything that isn't real property." In a practical sense, most real estate practitioners consider anything movable as personal property and anything immovable as real property. When real estate agents are in doubt, they incorporate the specific article into a contract to avoid misunderstanding.

It is interesting to note that real property is always voluntarily conveyed by a deed and personal property by a bill of sale, but a contract for sale in real estate may incorporate both real and personal property items.

FIXTURES

To know whether something is so affixed to real property as to become real property itself, a test is made of that article known as "the test of a fixture." A *fixture* is defined as something that was once personal property, but is now real property if it passes this test affirmatively:

1. What is the method of annexation? Is the article affixed to the real property in such a way that its removal would destroy all or part of the real property?
2. What is the intention of the parties? In placing the article in the property, did the parties intend it to become real property?
3. What is the relationship of the parties? An owner's improvement of real property is normally assumed by the courts to be permanent, whereas a tenant's improvement of a property he is renting is assumed to be temporary. In the first instance (owner) the article would be classed as real property, and in the second instance (tenant) it would be classed as personal property.

OWNERSHIP RIGHTS

Ownership of property in the United States is under an *allodial system* of title; that is, absolute possession and control are vested in the holder, and the interest a citizen has is considered free of servitude to or ownership rights of the government.

This does not mean that the government has no rights, or that the citizen has no responsibility to the government but that a person can own property freely, subject only to the obligations of our social order. These ownership rights and/or interests can be classified into various categories that express the degree of ownership a person has. As an example, the highest and most complete form of ownership a person can have in real property in this country is known as *fee simple.* This form of ownership is normally acquired by deed in the standard sales transaction of buying and selling a parcel of real property. It implies that the person who acquires title has the right to do with it as he pleases, subject only to certain public and/or private restrictions. The rights that one acquires in ownership of property are known as the *bundle of rights* and include the rights to possess, use, or dispose of the property as one sees fit. Obviously, if you acquire a right of possession through a lease or with a limitation on your ownership, such as a "life estate," you do not have the complete bundle of rights and, therefore, do not have a fee simple ownership. Regardless of the extent of ownership a person may have in real property, there are limitations to his estate that are imposed by government. They are:

1. *Police power:* Since we are a part of a social order, laws have been made controlling the health, welfare, and safety of each of us. These controls include building codes, zoning ordinances, traffic and health regulations, environmental rules, laws against discrimination, agency laws, and laws governing contracts.
2. *Eminent domain:* This is the power to take private property for the public good. It is commonly referred to as *condemnation* and is applied in the building of roads, parks, and schools.

3. *Taxation:* Taxes are necessary to preserve our way of life and support our public institutions. Taxes limit the return and, therefore, the value of real property.
4. *Escheat:* In order to insure that all property is under some form of ownership, the power of escheat enables government to take private property that has an unknown ownership. Some people die without a will and without heirs, leaving private property without ownership and responsibility. Government thereby takes title and resells it at an escheat sale.

The definitions of these four limitations on the ownership of property have only been generalized. They are becoming quite extensive (especially police power) and are increasing each year. Any law, statute, court decision, or regulation by any federal, state, or local government unit that limits the use or disposition of property would fall within these public restrictions.

PRIVATE RESTRICTIONS

There are *private restrictions* that also affect the ownership of real property, and they are known as *deed restrictions.* An owner can transfer ownership of real property with a private restriction as to land use, building size, or occupancy as long as that restriction is not in conflict with the laws of the land. If there were a conflict, the private restriction would be meaningless. For example: The owner of a large tract of land made a deed restriction that permitted the tract to be subdivided into lots of 5,000 square feet each, but the zoning of the property requires 10,000 square feet; zoning would prevail and the deed restriction would be declared ineffective. However, in most instances deed restrictions are used to impose greater, not lesser, restrictions on property than those permitted by government.

ESTATES

When an ownership right is conveyed by a deed, contract, or will, an *estate* is created. If it is for an indeterminate period of time, such as in a normal purchase, it is known as a *freehold estate.* If it is for a determinable period of time, such as a lease, then it is known as *estate of less than freehold* or *leasehold estate.* Leasehold estates are discussed fully in Chapter 6, "Leases and Management."

Freehold estates are further broken down into two classifications, those *of inheritance* and those *not of inheritance.* These types of estates mean exactly what they say; that is, if a person dies having an estate for inheritance, he or she can devise (transfer) it by a will or it will go to the proper person(s) listed under that state's *laws of distribution.* If the estate is not of inheritance, such as a life estate, then upon death the estate vanishes and the property reverts to the original owner or remains with (or goes forward to) another person.

A breakdown of the Classification of Estates follows, as a memory aid. Definitions of these estates are contained in Chapter 13, "Real Estate Terminology." Generally, an interest a person has in real property can be defined by knowing the quality, quantity, time, and miscellaneous characteristics of that ownership.

As an example, if a husband and wife purchased a home as a married couple, they would have a fee simple, joint, present ownership of that property. As two or more persons, they could take title as tenants by the entireties, joint tenants, or tenants in common, depending on their own wishes. They could also acquire miscellaneous interests, such as easements, encroachments, licenses, or emblements with their title, subject only to others' rights. By knowing this outline, a real estate salesperson is equipped to know that there are different ways in which ownership rights can be broken down and is therefore able to protect the interests of all concerned when negotiating a sale. The real estate salesperson should always refrain from giving legal advice or opinions regarding title and/or these rights.

Classification of Estates

A. As to Quality (Degree)

    I. Freehold Estates

        a. Those of Inheritance
           1. Fee Simple (absolute)
           2. Fee Tail, Fee Determinable, and Fee Conditional
        b. Not of Inheritance
           1. Life Estates (for the life of the tenant)
           2. Estates *Pur Autre Vie* (for life of another)

    II. Less than Freehold Estates (Leasehold Estates)

        a. Estate for Years
        b. Year to Year (Month to Month)
        c. Estate at Will
        d. Estate at Sufferance

B. As to Quantity (Number of Owners)

    I. Estate in Severalty (single person or corporation)
    II. Joint Estates (two or more)
        a. Tenancy by Entireties (by marriage)
        b. Joint Tenants (more than one with right of survivorship)
        c. Tenants in Common (more than one)
        d. Estates in Partnership (rare)

C. As to Time of Enjoyment

    I. Present (current ownership)
    II. Future (reverters or remainders)

D. As to Miscellaneous Interests

    I. Encroachment (an overlapping)
    II. Emblement (a right in future crops)
    III. Easements (a non-possessory right in property)
    IV. License (a permit to use certain real estate for a special purpose, as to place a billboard)

An interest, or estate, a person has in real estate is usually indicated in two ways—by possession and by title. Possession is normally considered *actual notice* of a right a person has in real estate. Title, by deed properly recorded, is considered *constructive notice* of a person's right.

All states have laws or regulations governing the recording of instruments affecting the right, title, or interest a person has in real property. Normally the recording acts give legal *priority* to those interests which are recorded first.

When purchasing real property, the lender or purchaser will demand proof of ownership and marketable title from the seller. Marketable title is one that is free of liens, encumbrances, and defects. Proof of ownership is acquired by reviewing the public records for evidence of title. Title evidence may be acquired by (1) certificate of title, (2) abstract of title, (3) title insurance policy, (4) Torrens certificate. It must be remembered that a *deed* only conveys the interest a person has in property, but does not state the true condition of that interest. Only a proper search or examination of the records will indicate the complete ownership rights a person has and whether there are any recorded liens, encumbrances, or claims upon that deed.

An examination of the public record would produce a *chain of title.* This examination is known as a title search. The chain of title may go back from the present owner to the original owner, depending upon the state statutes. Upon ascertaining the complete chain of title, the attorney or searcher would produce an *abstract of title,* which is a condensed history of all recorded instruments that affect title. Based upon the abstract of title, the attorney or abstractor would write an opinion of title, which would also be called a *certificate of title.* In some states, a certificate of title need not be based upon a written abstract, but only upon an examination of the public record.

If a title company prepared the abstract of title or made an examination of the record, it could give a report of title or a commitment to issue a title insurance policy. A title insurance policy is a contract whereby the owner or mortgagee is indemnified against a loss as a result of a future claim on title, subject to the terms of the policy.

Some states have adopted a state title registration system known as Torrens. It is not compulsory. Upon proof of ownership, the registrar of titles produces a certificate of title to the owner. Any claims upon the future title to this property, under this system, must be passed through the registrar of titles. It is the registration, not a deed, that transfers title or interests to a new grantee. At any time, the original Torrens certificate will reveal the true owner of lands and all claims thereto.

SPECIAL TYPES OF OWNERSHIP

Two special types of ownership of property which have become prevalent in the past few years involve a combination of private and common ownership. These two special instances are *cooperatives* and *condominiums.*

Cooperative ownership exists when a group of individuals owns a large piece of property in common. Each owner owns a certain number of shares in the whole. The shares entitle the owner to exclusive use of a designated unit and shared use of common areas. The property as a whole pays taxes assessed on the entire property. Each owner pays a portion of the taxes (deductible from Federal Income Tax) and a portion of the maintenance of the entire property proportional to his share holdings. A management committee or board elected from among the shareholders makes rules governing policies of the property. An individual may finance purchase of a co-op with a co-op loan rather than with a mortgage. Since ownership is technically of shares rather than of property, some states require the real estate salesperson to obtain a securities license as well as a real estate license.

Ownership of a *condominium* consists of outright ownership of a specific unit along with common ownership of corridors, elevators, grounds, and special amenities. Condominium owners pay taxes individually. A monthly maintenance charge covers the cost of care of common areas. Since there is greater individual ownership, the rules of the condominium board tend to be less restrictive than those of a co-op board, though this need not be the case. Purchase of a condominium unit is financed with a mortgage. Some states require the salesperson to hold a securities license in order to sell condominiums.

IN YOUR OWN WORDS

These are terms you should be familiar with. Check your definition by referring to the text or to the glossary beginning on page 140.

allodial system	laws of distribution
bundle of rights	leasehold estate
condemnation	life estate
condominium	personal property
cooperative	police power
eminent domain	private restrictions
escheat	public restrictions
fee simple	real property
fixture	taxation
freehold estate	trade fixture

TEST YOURSELF

1. Which of the following statements is (are) true?
   I. Real property is always voluntarily conveyed by a bill of sale.
   II. Both real and personal property can be incorporated in a contract of sale.
   (a) I only
   (b) II only
   (c) Both I and II
   (d) Neither I nor II

2. A life estate
   I. is a fee simple estate
   II. is included in the bundle of rights
   (a) I only
   (b) II only
   (c) Both I and II
   (d) Neither I nor II

3. Which of the following is (are) included as part of the police power?
   I. Building codes
   II. Taxation
   (a) I only
   (b) II only
   (c) Both I and II
   (d) Neither I nor II

4. Property with an unknown ownership is usually taken by the government by the power of
   I. eminent domain
   II. escheat
   (a) I only
   (b) II only
   (c) Both I and II
   (d) Neither I nor II

5. Private property which is taken for the public good is achieved by
    (a) taxation
    (b) escheat
    (c) eminent domain
    (d) police power

6. Which of the following is (are) true?
    I. A deed restriction can be imposed on private property.
    II. A deed restriction is usually used to impose greater restrictions than that of the government.
    (a) I only
    (b) II only
    (c) Both I and II
    (d) Neither I nor II

7. Two or more persons can take title to property as all except which of the following?
    (a) Joint tenants
    (b) Tenants in common
    (c) Partnership
    (d) Severalty

8. Which of the following is defined as a leasehold estate?
    I. Estate at will
    II. Estate at sufferance
    (a) I only
    (b) II only
    (c) Both I and II
    (d) Neither I nor II

9. When selling a cooperative apartment, the owner must surrender the keys to the unit and
    (a) a bill of sale
    (b) stock shares
    (c) warranty deed
    (d) certificate of title

10. The owner of a condominium apartment owns
    (a) a leasehold estate
    (b) a life estate
    (c) a freehold estate
    (d) an estate at will

ANSWERS: 1. b 2. d 3. a 4. b 5. c 6. c 7. d 8. c 9. b 10. c

Chapter Three
Law of Agency

In our individualistic society a person always has the right to do things for himself. Thus, though it may not always be in the individual's best interest, he may draw his own will, advertise and sell his own property, and even prepare and record his own deed. If, however, the individual elects another to act in his behalf, the person so chosen, the agent, must conform to certain standards of behavior and, for many functions, must meet certain licensing requirements.

An *agency relationship* exists whenever one person contracts to another the right (or rights) to do something in his stead. An example of this is a general power of attorney, whereby a person (known as a principal) gives to another person (known as a general agent) the complete power to execute all legal acts in that person's (the principal's) name. In this case, anyone of legal age with complete contractual capacity has the right to act as principal or agent. However, it should be noted that most powers of attorney are given by a layperson to an attorney-at-law to close or sign some legal papers in the layperson's absence.

Over the years there has been created, both in custom and law, a general understanding of the obligations of a person who has accepted an agency relationship. These include: (1) absolute loyalty; (2) care; and (3) accountability. These principles are true regardless of the type of agency created.

COMMON PURPOSES FOR CREATING AN AGENCY RELATIONSHIP

In real estate, an agency relationship is created when a broker is retained to perform an act for another. Again, the broker is known as an agent, and the other party is known as the principal. A principal may be anyone with a need in real estate, but most often is:

- A property owner who lists his house with the broker to sell.
- A person seeking funds (mortgage) for a property he owns or intends to buy.
- A landlord seeking tenants for a property he wishes to lease.
- A builder or developer attempting to assemble land for construction purposes.
- An investor seeking others for syndication of a parcel or parcels of investment real estate.
- A person or corporation desiring to purchase a property or properties.

As noted, the preceding list is not complete, but represents the common specific purposes for which a real estate salesperson or broker may accept an agency relationship. Every state has its own real estate license laws, rules, and regulations. These laws expressly list all the acts a licensed real estate broker or salesperson may legally perform in that state to earn a commission. It is essential for every student to obtain a copy of his or her state's licensing laws and to study it. Chapter 9, "License Laws" contains a complete list of all state real estate commissions. Write to your state commission and ask for the real estate laws for your state.

GENERAL VS. SPECIAL AGENCIES

Because of the specific nature of the assignments received by brokers and salespersons in real estate transactions, their agencies are known as *special agencies*, as distinguished from *general agencies*; real estate brokers are usually retained to do one special thing for a principal and not to act in his or her complete legal stead. Furthermore, all agencies are limited by the implications in their contracts or as expressed by the nature of the agency. As an example, if a broker receives a listing contract to sell a specific parcel of real property for an owner, at a given price and within a certain time period, it is *implied* that he will use every legal marketing tool within his knowledge to do so, including advertising the property, although the listing (agency) contract may be silent in this regard. Also, all the obligations of a general agent are imposed on a special agent; i.e., absolute loyalty, care, and accountability. Included in this would be the broker-agent's responsibility to submit all offers fairly and without bias. As with most contracts, a principal may insert into an agency contract any legal instructions that are consistent with the purpose of the agency. If accepted, the agent must adhere to these instructions, but no obligation may be imposed that would require the broker to make an unfair representation to the buyer.

ORAL CONTRACTS

Oral contracts, including agency relationships, involving real estate are governed by state laws. In most states, a broker must have a written contract to act as an agent and to collect a commission. It is essential that real estate salespersons and brokers understand the nature of their obligations and responsibilities as agents, created by contract or law, to faithfully fulfill their fiduciary responsibilities and to truthfully earn their fee or commission. Consumer protection laws have entered the field of real estate, and the old adage, *caveat emptor* (let the buyer beware), is becoming extinct.

LISTING CONTRACTS

In most cases, the agency relationship in real estate is created by a *listing contract.* This is a contract between the principal and the real estate broker. It authorizes the broker to attempt to sell, buy, lease, exchange, or negotiate any bona fide interest or partial interest in real estate for a certain price, always within a certain time period and for a specific fee or commission.

TYPES OF LISTING CONTRACTS

There are three types of listing contracts. These are: (1) a "sole and exclusive listing" contract; (2) an "agency listing" contract; and (3) an "open listing" contract.

Each listing contract has its root in the protection afforded to the broker for the collection of his commission. In the sole and exclusive listing, the broker will collect his commission regardless of who sells the property during his listing period. It gives to the broker the maximum protection of his commission and also gives to the principal the knowledge that the broker (agent) will expend his greatest effort. In the agency listing, the broker collects a commission only if the broker or another agent performs the real estate act. The principal may sell the property (or reserve the right to sell) and thereby avoid paying a real estate commission or fee. In an open listing, the broker has the least assurance of collecting a commission. The listing is open to anyone and is in fact nothing more than an offer to sell, on the part of a principal, which may be accepted by anyone but may be rescinded by the principal at any time without prior notice.

As an example, an owner of a parcel of real estate wishing to sell same may go to a licensed real estate broker and give him a listing to do so. If the owner reserves the right to sell the property himself, he has given the broker an agency listing. If he gives the listing to many brokers, all with the same rights, and reserves the right to sell or withdraw the listing, he has given to the broker an open listing. If he gives to the broker the complete right to act in his stead to sell the property at a given price within a certain period of time and guarantees a commission to that broker, then the owner (principal) has given a sole and exclusive listing. Most listing contracts are of the latter form although they need not be. There are other forms or variations of these three basic listing contracts, but generally they are derivatives of these three. In many cases, custom dictates the type of listing contracts used in certain geographical areas. Again, state license laws may prohibit a broker from accepting certain types of variations in a listing contract.

NET LISTING

A *net listing* is usually a variation of a sole and exclusive listing contract, and it may be illegal in certain states. It is a listing whereby the owner only wishes to realize a certain *net* amount on his real estate transaction, and anything over that net sum of money may be retained by the agent (broker) as his commission.

MULTIPLE LISTING

A *multiple listing* is not so much a listing contract as an agreement between certain licensed real estate brokers to mutually share a lead. They normally form an organization, and whenever one broker within the group receives a listing, he sends it to a central clearing house which then sends it to all other brokers within the system. It assures a principal that his property or request will receive maximum exposure among many brokers.

As brokers share a listing, they also then share in the commission. The owner (principal) is only obligated to pay a single commission rate which is shared by the two or more brokers. If there are two brokers in a single transaction, one is known as the *listing broker* and the other as the *selling broker*. The commission split is usually 50–50 but may be any agreed-upon division.

SAMPLE EXCLUSIVE LISTING CONTRACT

EXCLUSIVE RIGHT TO SELL AGREEMENT

THIS AGREEMENT is effective ___March 10___ 19_--_, and confirms that ___John C. Green and___

___Barbara T. Green___ XXX(have) appointed ___Good Earth Realty Co.___ to act as Agent for the

sale of property known as ___1620 Osborne Road, Bramlee___, New York.

In return for the Agent's agreement to use Agent's best efforts to sell the above property, the Owner(s) agree(s) to grant the Agent the exclusive right to sell this property under the following terms and conditions:

PERIOD OF AGREEMENT

1. This agreement shall be effective from the above date and shall expire at midnight on ___July 9___, 19_--_

PRICE AT WHICH PROPERTY WILL BE OFFERED

2. The property will be offered for sale at a list price of $ ___186,000___ and shall be sold, subject to negotiation, at such price and upon such terms to which Owner(s) may agree.

COMMISSION TO BE PAID TO AGENT

3. The Agent shall be entitled to one commission of ___6___% of the selling price. Both the Owner(s) and the Agent acknowledge that the above commission rate was not suggested nor influenced by anyone other than the parties to this Agreement. Any commission due for a sale brought about by a Sub-agent (another broker who is authorized by the Agent to assist in the sale of your property) shall be paid by the Agent from the commission received by the Agent.

OWNER(S) OBLIGATIONS AFTER THE EXPIRATION OF THIS AGREEMENT

4. Owner(s) undertands and agrees to pay the commission referred to in paragraph 3, if this property is sold or transferred or is the subject of a contract of sale within ___3___ months after the expiration date of this agreement involving a person with whom the agency, any sub-agent or the Owner(s) negotiated or to whom the property is offered, quoted or shown during the period of this listing agreement. Owner(s) will not, however, be obligated to pay such commission if Owner(s) enters into a valid Exclusive Listing Agreement with another New York State licensed real estate broker after the expiration of this agreement.

WHO MAY NEGOTIATE FOR OWNER(S)

5. Owner(s) agree(s) to direct all inquiries to the Agent. Owner(s) elect(s) to have all negotiations submitted through Agent☒ or Sub-agent☐.

SUBMISSION OF LISTING TO MULTIPLE LISTING SERVICE

6. Both Owner(s) and Agent agree that the Agent immediately is to submit this listing agreement to the Westchester Multiple Listing Service, Inc., for dissemination to its Participants. No provision of this agreement is intended to nor shall be understood to establish or imply any contractual relationship between the Owner(s) and the Westchester Multiple Listing Service, Inc., nor has the Westchester Multiple Listing Service, Inc. in any way participated in any of the terms of this agreement, including the rate of commission.

AUTHORIZATION FOR "FOR SALE" SIGN

7. Agent ☐ is (☒ is not) authorized to place a "For Sale" sign on the property.

REQUIREMENTS FOR PUBLICATION IN WMLS COMPILATION

8. This listing agreement is not acceptable for publication by the Westchester Multiple Listing Service, Inc. unless and until the owner(s) has duly signed both the face of this agreement and the reverse side or an attachment to the listing agreement reflecting receipt of the definitions of "Exclusive Right to Sell" and "Exclusive Agency" required by New York State Department of Law - Division of Licensing Services.

9. Additional Points of Agreement, if any: ___Includes refrigerator, washer & dryer;___

___excludes freezer and dining room chandelier___

ALL MODIFICATIONS TO BE MADE IN WRITING

10. Owner(s) and Agent agree that no change, amendment, modification or termination of this Agreement shall be binding on any party unless the same shall be in writing and signed by the parties.

___John C. Green___ ___3/9/--___
(OWNER) (DATE)

___Barbara T. Green___ ___3/9/--___
(OWNER) (DATE)

Owner's Mailing Address: ___1620 Osborne Road___
___Bramlee, NY 09900___

Owner's Telephone: ___123-4567___

___Good Earth Realty Co.___
(AGENT)

By: ___Joanne Chu___ ___3/9/--___
(Authorized Representative) (DATE)

Agent's Address: ___230 Main Street___
___Bramlee, NY 099-00___

Agent's Telephone: ___123-7654___

DEFINITIONS

In accordance with the requirements of the New York State Department of State the undersigned owner(s) does (do) hereby acknowledge receipt of the following:
1. Explanation of "Exclusive Right to Sell" listing;
2. Explanation of "Exclusive Agency" listing;
3. A list of Participants of Westchester Multiple Listing Service, Inc.

EXPLANATION OF EXCLUSIVE RIGHT TO SELL: (as worded verbatim by the Department of State)
"An Exclusive Right to Sell listing means that if you, the owner of the property, find a buyer for your house, or if another broker finds a buyer, you must pay the agreed commission to the present broker."

EXPLANATION OF EXCLUSIVE AGENCY: (as worded verbatim by the Department of State)
"An Exclusive Agency listing means that if you, the owner of the property, find a buyer, you will not have to pay commission to the broker. However, if another broker finds a buyer, you will owe a commission to both the selling broker and your present broker."

"THE FAIR HOUSING ACT"

"The Civil Rights Act of 1968 known as the Federal Fair Housing Law makes illegal any discrimination based on race, color, religion, sex or national origin in connection with the sale or rental of housing."

Article X of the REALTOR Code of Ethics states:

"The REALTOR shall not deny any equal professional services to any person for reasons of race, creed, sex, or country of national origin. The REALTOR shall not be a party to any plan or agreement to discriminate against a person or persons on the basis of race, creed, sex or country of national origin."

John C. Green
——————————————
Owner

Barbara T. Green
——————————————
Owner

SAMPLE MULTIPLE LISTING CONTRACT

SUBMIT ORIGINAL AND ONE COPY TO MLS OFFICE
WESTCHESTER MULTIPLE LISTING SERVICE, INC.
RESIDENTIAL FORM
CLASS 1:
CHECK ONE BOX ONLY:
ZONE (PROPERTY LOCATION)

☐ 01   ☐ 05
☐ 02   ☐ 06
☐ 03   ☐ 07
☐ 04   ☐ 08

RLTR CODE GERC

Exp.Date 7/9/-- Co/Ex Code -- 4 Price $ 186,000
Style colonial Bedrooms 4 Baths 2½

RESIDENTIAL

O/H:3/15/-- TIME: 10:30 - 12:00	
# 1620 P.O.ADD: Osborne Road	$: 186,000
ZONE 6 TWNSHP: Bramlee	PROP.SZ: 75 x 110
CONST: frame/alum. YR.BLT.: 1968 RMS: 8 BR: 4 BTH: 2½	
STLE: colonial COLR: white SQ.FT: 2600 GAR: 1 EE	
ZONING: R-5 BSMT: full, unfinished, laundry	
SFL: --	
1FL: CH, LR/fpl, DR, den, MEIK, PR -- deck	
2FL: MBR/bath, 3BR, bath	
3FL: bessler	
E.S Douglas J.H. Bramlee H.S. Central	
ASMT:41,000 TX.LT.: 10-28-42 TAX $: 3412	
SEW/SEPTIC WTR.SUPP. city PLUMB: copper ELEC: 220	
FUEL: oil HEAT:steam COST: 2000 A/C: 3 units	
WALLS: SR INSUL: fibregla ROOF: asph POSS: 7/1/--	
REMARKS: Dead-end street; beautiful landscaping. Inclusions: refrigerator, washer, dryer; Exclusions: freezer, dining room chandelier	
MAP: 24 GRID: 8-Q	
RLTR CODE: GERC L/A: Good Earth--Chu PH: 123-7654	
CO/EX CODE: -- CO/EX: -- PH: --	
OWNR: Green DATLSTD: 3/10/-- S/B 3% 3%	
All information believed accurate but not warranted. Neg. Thru L/A ☒ or S/B ☐	

Joanne Chu -- 123-2468
Extra Photos

FOLLOWING, PLEASE GIVE DIRECTIONS FOR PHOTOGRAPHER TO HELP HIM LOCATE THE PROPERTY. (A picture will not be taken if the listing does not contain an adequate address to locate the property).

Signed (Person that types the form) _____

BROKER COOPERATION

Regardless of whether or not a broker belongs to a multiple listing system, broker cooperation is required in all license laws throughout the country, unless specifically waived by the principal. Remember, it is the broker-agent's responsibility when accepting a listing to make every effort to perform the services required, and our laws have insured this by mandating broker cooperation.

LEGAL REQUIREMENTS FOR A LISTING CONTRACT

Every state has its own special legal requirements pursuant to the laws of that state dealing with listing contracts. A definition that has all the basic national requirements would be: "A written contract that has a proper legal description, a specific sales price, a definite termination date, a commission basis, and is signed by the owners of the property and duly acknowledged by the broker-agent."

Other inclusions in a listing contract could be:

- a possession date
- items of personal property
- financing offered
- requirements on non-discrimination
- method or methods of promotion

DISCRIMINATION

It is also true that over the years the laws governing a real estate agent's responsibilities have increased. One area of increased responsibility includes the laws concerning discrimination. Most states have adopted their own civil rights laws, and most real estate license laws require the real estate agent to abide by either the state or federal law.

Generally, through federal law in fair housing, court interpretations, and laws enacted on state levels, real estate licensees may not discriminate and should not accept restrictive listings or publish any notice or advertisement with respect to the sale or rental of a property which suggests discrimination because of race, sex, religion, color, handicap, familial status, or national origin, and, in many areas, age or marital status as well.

INTERSTATE LAND SALES

The Federal Interstate Land Sales Full Disclosure Act regulates, to protect the consumer, the filing and registration of lots that are for sale interstate. Real estate agents who participate in the sale or promotion of interstate land sales must also abide by these regulations. An important aspect of the federal law is that a contract or agreement for the purchase or lease of a lot in a subdivision or condominium is voidable at the option of the purchaser if he has purchased the property without inspecting same. This rescission right can be exercised up to

48 hours after receipt of the property report. A *property report* is the official statement of the developer filed with the Federal Office of Interstate Land Sales Registration. The contract must provide notice to the purchaser for his option to rescind.

The federal act includes civil and penal sanctions. Violations of any of the provisions of the law are punishable by a fine of not more than $5,000 or by imprisonment of not more than five years, or both.

IN YOUR OWN WORDS

These are terms you should be familiar with. Check your definitions by referring to the text or to the glossary beginning on page 140.

agency listing	listing contract
agency relationship	multiple listing
agent	net listing
broker	obligation
caveat emptor	open listing
commission	oral contracts
consumer protection laws	power of attorney
contractual capacity	principal
fiduciary	sole and exclusive listing
general agency	special agency

TEST YOURSELF

1. A person who authorizes a broker to sell his home and signs a listing contract for that purpose is known as a(n)
   - (a) grantor
   - (b) principal
   - (c) agent
   - (d) attorney

2. Which of the following is not an agent's responsibility in a listing agreement?
   - (a) Submission of all offers
   - (b) Fair representation to the buyer
   - (c) Advertising the property for sale
   - (d) Revealing the seller's financial status to the buyer

3. An agency listing is most accurately described as
   - I. a listing contract in which the owner reserves the right to sell the property and thereby avoid paying a commission
   - II. a listing contract in which the broker receives a commission only if the broker or another agent is the procuring cause of the sale
   - (a) I only
   - (b) II only
   - (c) Both I and II
   - (d) Neither I nor II

4. A net listing is
   I. the most widely used type of listing contract
   II. used when the buyer wishes to net a certain amount from the sale of his home and the broker retains anything over that amount as his commission
      (a) I only
      (b) II only
      (c) Both I and II
      (d) Neither I nor II

5. Under a multiple listing service, if two brokers are involved in the sale of a property
   I. the owner must pay a total individual commission to each broker
   II. the owner pays a single commission which must be split 50–50 between the listing broker and the selling broker
      (a) I only
      (b) II only
      (c) Both I and II
      (d) Neither I nor II

6. Which of the following is not required to be included in a listing contract?
   (a) Definite termination date
   (b) Specific sales price
   (c) Items of personal property
   (d) The commission rate

7. John Jones receives a listing from Mary Johnson in which he is guaranteed a commission and Ms. Johnson gives up her right to sell the property herself. This type of listing is known as a(n)
   (a) open listing
   (b) sole and exclusive listing
   (c) net listing
   (d) agency listing

8. Broker cooperation is
   I. required only of brokers belonging to a multiple listing service
   II. required of all brokers in all states
      (a) I only
      (b) II only
      (c) Both I and II
      (d) Neither I nor II

9. Which of the following would most likely be a purpose for creating an agency relationship?
   I. A person seeking a mortgage for a property he owns
   II. A landlord seeking tenants for a property that he wishes to rent
      (a) I only
      (b) II only
      (c) Both I and II
      (d) Neither I nor II

10. Dave Smith, a developer, retains a licensed real estate broker in order to assemble land to be used for a new residential development. This relationship creates a(n)
    (a) general agency
    (b) open listing
    (c) special agency
    (d) power of attorney

ANSWERS: 1. b 2. d 3. c 4. b 5. d 6. c 7. b 8. b 9. c 10. c

Chapter Four

Contracts and Deeds

CONTRACTS

A contract is always thought of as a mutual consent between two or more parties to do or not to do some lawful thing. Many test questions evolve around this general area of contractual law. All real estate transactions have as their nucleus a contractual relationship, and it is the licensee, as middleman, who brings the parties together in order to earn a fee or commission. A well-made contract, therefore, ensures his earnings and enhances his reputation.

All contracts have certain *essential requisites* in order for them to be considered complete. These essentials are necessary, regardless of the type of contract with which you are dealing. As we proceed with certain types of real estate contracts, we will add to these basic essential requirements those additional elements that are necessary to make each type of real estate contract complete.

ESSENTIAL REQUISITES TO A VALID CONTRACT

The essential requisites all contracts have in common are as follows:

Competent Parties. Since a contract is a promise between two or more parties, all of those parties must have competency to contract; i.e., they must be of legal age, not insane, or under intoxication or undue force or pressure.

It is incumbent upon a licensee to know the legal age of competency in his state (it varies from 18 to 21) and to verify the competency of all parties in a transaction. For example, since many married people own property jointly, *both* parties must sign any contract affecting the title to real property in order for it to be a binding contract, and both must be legally competent to do so. Corporations must have the legal power to contract, either created by their charter or by law, expressed or implied by the nature of their business.

Consideration. The law universally acknowledges that parties in a contract must have an *award* of some sort. The compensation is usually in the form of money, but could be anything that could be transformed into dollars, such as expert services, other types of employment, or personal articles of value. It could be nominal, such as one dollar, or it could be excessive. Normally, courts will not review the adequacy of consideration unless fraud or deceit has been alleged in the making of the contract. However, without any consideration a contract is without substance and is therefore void.

Meeting of the Minds. This is also known as *offer and acceptance*, and some textbooks place these as separate requisites of a contract. Modern practitioners, however, regard these as one and the same, and until the offer is fully and completely accepted bilaterally the contract cannot exist. This issue applies to the mutual consent of both parties as to all the terms and conditions set forth in the agreement. As an example, if a property owner wished to sell his property for $60,000 and a potential buyer offered $50,000, no meeting of the minds ensued, and hence no contract. But if the seller reoffers the same property to the buyer for $55,000, and the buyer accepts, then there has been a meeting of the minds and a contract is made. (Please note that in most states this type of offer and counter offer would have to be in writing to be enforced and would normally have more conditions and/or contingencies than those expressed herein to be a complete real estate contract.)

Legal Purpose. It should be obvious that you cannot contract to injure someone or to do something against the public purpose. In real estate contracts, care should always be exercised in the wording of conditions in a transaction that changes the purpose of the transfer. As an example, if the consideration is excessively stated with the intent to deceive a financial institution, then the entire contract may be declared illegal. This practice is against the public purpose since banks and savings institutions are trust agents for the public's funds.

Proper Form. Most contracts should be in writing, but some oral contracts are accepted in the courts. Every state has its own set of laws (known as the *Statute of Frauds*) which require certain contracts to be in writing if they are to be enforced in the courts. It is important to note here that an oral real estate contract that should be in writing according to the state's Statute of Frauds is not necessarily an illegal contract; it is, however, an unenforceable contract. Furthermore, most real estate contracts require a proper legal description, which may be a street address, a survey, a tax-map description, deed book and page, or a block and lot. (Legal descriptions are further discussed in Chapter 7.) The property to be affected by the contract must be specifically defined, and the contract cannot be ambiguous and uncertain in purpose.

Each type of real estate contract has its own special requisites and/or form. In this chapter we will discuss binders, options, installment sales contracts, and agreements of sale. Other chapters covering leases, mortgages, and listings have their requisites fully discussed.

CONDITIONS AND CONTINGENCIES IN A CONTRACT

As stated earlier, each type of contract has its own form or requirements. In addition to these requirements, there may be *conditions* or *contingencies* to the benefit or detriment of one of the parties. A *contingency* is a clause in a contract that normally limits the validity of the contract until the contingency is fulfilled. An example would be the signing of a contract of sale "subject to the procurement of a mortgage acceptable to the buyer." Until a mortgage acceptable to the buyer is secured, the contract is not completely *valid* and is *voidable* at the buyer's option. Contingencies could include clauses on procuring financing, building permits, variances, health inspections, or engineer's reports. A contingency can be anything that the parties to the contract agree to that delays the validity of the contract.

A *condition* in a contract relates to the acceptance or acknowledgment of things unique to the property, such as easements, restrictive covenants, type of deed, closing date, rights of tenants, or possession. It is said that the *agreement of sale* is the single most important contract in real estate because from it flow all the rights of both parties. It is therefore important that all parties read and understand a contract before they sign it. If, however, a party fails to read a contract and still signs it, that party will be bound by its contents. Failure to read a contract does not affect its legality or render it void.

CHANGES IN A CONTRACT

In some instances, changes are made in a contract after it has been signed and accepted by both parties. This is done either by inserting a new clause in a contract or by annexing a *rider* to the contract. If a contract is changed by a rider, both parties must sign the rider in order for it to be legal. The basic contract should also note that a rider is attached by inserting new words to the contract, and both parties should also initial and date the new insertion. The same requirement applies if they later change any wording in the contract. What two people agree to do, they can mutually agree not to do—as long as they both agree.

EQUITABLE TITLE

When a contract is fully executed (signed and accepted by all parties) the buyer (vendee) receives an interest in the ownership of the property known as *equitable title.* That is, the buyer will receive the benefits of any increase in the value of the property from the date of signing the contract until the date of closing on title. Under common law the vendee likewise suffers whatever loss occurs to the property prior to closing. That is why, in most real estate contracts, one of the obligations of the seller (vendor) is to maintain insurance adequate to cover loss until title passes at closing.

LEGAL EFFECT

A *valid* contract is fully enforceable. A *voidable* contract may be terminated by one of the parties. A *void* contract is one that cannot be enforced. Most contracts are fully *enforceable.* Some states have "blue laws" which make contracts signed on Sunday unenforceable. Other examples of unenforceable contracts would be contracts between minors and incompetents, fraudulent or blank contracts, double contracts, or some incomplete contracts. Legal counsel should always be recommended when a person is in doubt about the wording or legality of a contract. The principal reason for this is that real estate has always been treated as unique by the courts, and a breach of a real estate contract can bring a suit of "specific performance"; that is, one of the parties (either seller or buyer) can require the other party to sell and/or buy.

Time is of the essence is a feature in some real estate contracts. It implies that time is important and closing of title must take place "on or before some date." If a sales contract reads "closing shall take place on or about January 1, 19 – –," the courts might interpret that closing can take place almost any reasonable time thereafter. But if "time is of the essence" is inserted or demanded by contractual right, then all damages, benefits, rights, and obligations are computed from the date expressed therein.

It is a mistaken opinion by many that the nonperformance on their part in a contract of sale in real estate will result only in the loss of their deposit as a damage claim. When a real estate contract has been breached, the injured party may sue for *specific performance* or *damages*. He cannot sue for both, but the injured party has the right to sue for either. Since a contract is a mutual agreement, the injured party can also forgive the breach. But it must be remembered that it is his choice to sue or not to sue and for what.

STATUTE OF LIMITATIONS

States have enacted *Statutes of Limitations* which create legal periods of time that parties in various types of contracts have in case they decide to sue for breach of contract. Courts have been very liberal in the interpretation of these statutes in order to protect the rights of all parties in a contract. Real estate salespersons should always consult an attorney when they have a question on contractual law.

TYPES OF REAL ESTATE CONTRACTS

Four of the basic real estate contracts that deal with buying and selling real estate are:

1. Agreement of Sale
2. Binder
3. Installment Land Contract
4. Option

They are defined as follows:

Agreement of Sale. An *Agreement of Sale*, also known as a *Contract of Sale*, is the promise of an owner (vendor, seller) to transfer title to a buyer (vendee) of a specifically defined parcel of real property on a certain date for a stated consideration (price). It is the most common and the most important of all real estate contracts.

Binder. An informal agreement to hold off the market a parcel of real property, at a stated price and for a short period of time, until the parties can enter into a more formal contract of sale. It is sometimes referred to as an *agreement to agree* and has little force in law.

Installment Land Contract. An installment purchase of real estate, whereby the owner sells his property to a purchaser over a period of time. The purchaser pays money over the time (like rent) to the owner and receives title to the property only upon the complete payment of all monies due the seller. It is called a *land contract*, but also is used on improved real estate, especially urban areas where normal financing may be difficult. It is also known as an *installment contract* or *contract for deed*.

Option. A contract that gives the buyer the right to purchase a parcel of real property within a specific time period for proper consideration. It is usually used in large land acquisitions where the buyer can only develop or purchase a portion of the seller's property at one time, but wishes to reserve the right (option) to purchase the balance of the land at a later time.

Know then that all contracts, not just real estate contracts, have to have *five essential requisites* in order to be declared fully legal and binding agreements. The absence of one of these requisites will destroy the validity of a contract. As stated earlier, these requisites are:

1. competent parties
2. consideration
3. meeting of the minds
4. legal purpose
5. proper form

DEEDS

The transfer of ownership in real property can be accomplished by a voluntary or involuntary act. Conveyances through a *deed* (gift or sale) or a *will* (devise) are considered the voluntary acts of an owner, whereas the transfer of title by a court order is considered an involuntary conveyance. Involuntary conveyances may come about through:

- *Non-payment of liens.* A court may order, through foreclosure, title conveyance to a lienholder.
- *Condemnation.* A court may order title to be conveyed to a governmental agency for a public improvement against the owner's wishes. The court would also give to the owner just compensation for the property taken.
- *Escheat.* If a person dies intestate (without a will) and with no apparent heirs, the court would give title to the state agency to resell.
- *Adverse Possession.* If a person uses another's property for a continuous period of time and against that person's wishes, then the courts, upon petition, could grant title to the user. Known in some states as squatter's rights, it is difficult to prove and/or to acquire title through this method. Each state has its own adverse possession period.

In most instances, a deed is used to indicate that a transfer of title has been completed, although a will or court order is sufficient evidence of a conveyance in those cases where they are used. Since a deed is the most common method used to reflect a transfer of ownership, the student should know that there are basically three general types of deeds used.

1. **Warranty Deed.** The basic warranty deed is known as a *General Warranty Deed.* Warranty, of course, implies a promise (covenant), and within this deed the owner (grantor) conveying title assures the purchaser (grantee) all of the following: that grantor is the legal owner, that he or she has the right to convey title, that no one will disturb ownership, that there are no liens or encumbrances that affect clear title to the property, and that grantor will defend the title always. All of these promises are also known as covenants and run permanently with the land.

Sometimes there are limitations placed by the owner on one or more of these covenants (promises). The deed is then known as a *Special Warranty Deed.*

2. **Bargain and Sale Deed.** This deed usually has limited covenants against the grantor, whereby the owner (grantor) states only that he or she has done nothing to adversely affect the title of the property and will always defend it against his or her own acts.

   There is also a Bargain and Sale Deed that contains no promises whatsoever and is used by executors when transferring property after a decedent's death or by a sheriff after a foreclosure sale. It is sometimes called an *Executor's Deed, Sheriff's Deed,* or *Tax Deed.*

3. **Quitclaim Deed.** This is a deed used to correct an error in a previous deed, such as a misspelled name or improper legal description. It contains no covenants whatsoever. Sometimes this deed is used to release an interest a person may have in property, such as in the case of a questionable heir. The intention is not to convey valid title to property, but, if the person executing the deed has a valid interest, the property would be legally transferred by virtue of the quitclaim deed.

REQUIREMENTS

Deeds, like contracts, have certain minimum essentials in all states in order to be valid. By definition, a deed is a written legal instrument whereby the interest of a person or persons in and to real property is conveyed to another person or persons. The following elements are generally required:

1. The deed must be in writing.
2. Parties (grantor and grantee) must be competent.
3. Consideration must be recited.
4. It must have a *granting clause* which states the type of deed and the presence or absence of covenants.
5. It must have an adequate (legal) description of the property conveyed.
6. It must be signed by the grantor and properly witnessed.
7. It must be delivered to the grantee (purchaser).

A deed should have a *habendum clause* which is used to limit the type of estate granted. It should be acknowledged by a notary so that it may be recorded. An unrecorded deed is a valid deed, but between two deeds conveying title to the same property the deed first recorded takes priority over subsequent recordings.

In the absence of any one of the foregoing elements or requirements, the ownership rights (title) may be defective at the least and invalid in most cases. As an example, an undelivered deed conveys nothing. Delivery is as essential as the deed itself. Unless both possession and control of the deed pass out of the hands of the grantor (seller), title does not pass.

WILLS

Title to real property may also be conveyed by a *will.* A person who dies and leaves a will is known to have died testate. One who dies without a will is said to have died intestate. The will, in the former instance, is itself a legal conveyance. No deed is required. If a person dies intestate, then the administrator appointed by the courts will dispose of the property under the laws of descent and distribution of that state.

Progress of a Typical Transaction

Owner gives exclusive right to sell listing to broker

Broker gives listing information to multiple listing services
places advertising
holds Open House for other brokers; points out features
shows property
assists other brokers in showing property

Buyer gives offer to buy to broker who showed property

Buyer's Broker transmits offer to seller's broker
negotiations proceed through brokers
meeting of the minds: buyer and seller agree to price, financing, occupancy, inclusions/exclusions

Buyer with help of broker, if desired, secures inspections by engineer and termite inspector

Seller's Attorney contacts buyer's attorney
contract of sale is drawn and signed by buyer and seller
buyer makes specified downpayment which seller's attorney deposits in escrow account

Buyer applies for mortgage loan

Lender does credit check, appraises property, approves loan

Buyer's Attorney orders title policy

Buyer secures fire insurance

At Closing

Seller satisfies own mortgage
pays taxes and fuel in arrears
pays certain recording costs
pays brokers' commissions
signs deed
hands deed and keys to buyer

Buyer pays cash balance as agreed
pays prorated share of taxes and fuel
pays for title policy
pays certain recording costs
pays into tax escrow account as requested by lender
signs mortgage note

Seller's Attorney releases downpayment from escrow account to seller
takes satisfaction of mortgage for recording

Lender pays loan amount to seller

Buyer's Attorney takes deed for recording
takes mortgage for recording

IN YOUR OWN WORDS

These are terms you should be familiar with. Check your definition by referring to the text or to the glossary beginning on page 140.

adverse possession	meeting of the minds
agreement of sale	offer and acceptance
bargain and sale deed	option
bilateral contract	quitclaim deed
binder	specific performance
competency	Statute of Frauds
condemnation	Statute of Limitations
consideration	testate
contract	time is of the essence
deed	valid
enforceable	vendee
equitable title	vendor
escheat	void
essential requisites	voidable
executed contract	warranty deed
installment land contract	will
intestate	

TEST YOURSELF

1. A contract which has as its purpose an illegal gain would be
   - (a) voidable
   - (b) unenforceable
   - (c) void
   - (d) invalid

2. A contract entered into with a minor can be disavowed by which of the following?
   - I. The minor
   - II. The competent party
   - (a) I only
   - (b) II only
   - (c) Both I and II
   - (d) Neither I nor II

3. Which of the following sets forth that contracts must be in writing to be enforced?
   - (a) Statute of Limitations
   - (b) Blue laws
   - (c) Statute of Frauds
   - (d) Uniform Contract Act

4. Which of the following is not considered to be an essential requisite of a real estate contract?
   - (a) Offer and acceptance
   - (b) Competent parties
   - (c) Legal purpose
   - (d) Contingency

5. Which of the following would be cause for a voidable contract?
   - I. A contract signed on Sunday and ratified subsequently by both parties
   - II. The failure of one of the parties to read the contract before signing
   - (a) I only
   - (b) II only
   - (c) Both I and II
   - (d) Neither I nor II

6. Which of the following alternatives can be taken by the injured party when a contract has been breached?
   I. Claim the earnest money deposit for damages
   II. File a suit for specific performance
      (a) I only   (c) Both I and II
      (b) II only   (d) Neither I nor II

7. The term *time is of the essence* is best defined by which of the following?
   I. The amount of time over which a person has to sue when a contract has been breached
   II. The amount of time the parties have to perform all promises and obligations in a contract
      (a) I only   (c) Both I and II
      (b) II only   (d) Neither I nor II

8. A purchaser in an installment land contract
   I. receives legal title to the property upon signing the contract
   II. possesses equitable title to the property upon signing the contract
      (a) I only   (c) Both I and II
      (b) II only   (d) Neither I nor II

9. If a residence under a sales contract was damaged by a fire prior to closing, who would bear the loss if the contract was silent on this point?
      (a) Seller   (c) Buyer
      (b) Broker   (d) Vendor

10. Which of the following statements is (are) true?
    I. A binding contract must be signed by both spouses when a property is owned jointly.
    II. A contingency in a contract would cover any easements affecting the property.
       (a) I only   (c) Both I and II
       (b) II only   (d) Neither I nor II

ANSWERS: 1. c   2. a   3. c   4. d   5. d   6. c   7. b   8. b   9. c   10. a

NOTE: Problem 6 is a good illustration of the need to remember that "both" can mean "either." As you know, both remedies are available to the injured party when a contract has been breached, but the party must choose which remedy to seek. Both alternatives *cannot* be taken, though the correct answer to the exam question is (c).

Chapter Five

Mortgages and Liens

MORTGAGES

A *mortgage* is a written contract that creates a specific lien *on the title* to real property. It may also be known as a *deed of trust*.

REQUISITES OF A MORTGAGE CONTRACT

Some of the requisites of a mortgage contract are:

1. It must be in writing.
2. It must describe the property encumbered.
3. It must have a defeasance clause which gives the method the borrower can use to redeem his property free and clear.
4. It must have a granting clause to state the interest mortgaged.
5. It must be signed by mortgagor (borrower).
6. It must be acknowledged.

Mortgages, similar to deeds, are usually recorded and delivered. There are other clauses in a mortgage, depending upon the lender's (mortgagee's) requirement. As an example, most mortgages have an *acceleration clause* which permits the mortgagee to demand the entire debt due if the borrower defaults. Other clauses that are typical in today's financial world include requirements that the borrower keep the property in good repair, maintain adequate fire insurance, and pay property taxes promptly. Charges for prepayment and/or late payment are also usually included.

The mortgage is usually created by intention of the parties and is most common in aiding in the purchase or refinancing of real property. The parties to the mortgage are known as the mortgagor (borrower) and mortgagee (lender). The mortgage can be written for any period of time, can lien more than one parcel of real estate, or can be repaid in various ways. Most residential mortgages and/or deeds of trust are accompanied by a *personal note* or *bond*.

TYPES OF MORTGAGES

Various types of mortgages and their definitions are as follows:

FHA Mortgage. This is a mortgage that is *insured* by the Federal Housing Administration (FHA). The FHA creates rules on the types of mortgages it will insure through its approved lenders. The FHA does not lend money to individual purchasers, it only insures loans. By FHA insurance rules and regulations, lenders are encouraged to accept lower interest, smaller down payments, and longer terms than they would conventionally. To finance this operation, the borrower pays a mortgage insurance premium (MIP) of one-half of 1 percent throughout the life of the loan. The interest rate on an FHA mortgage is established by the Secretary of Housing and Urban Development (HUD). The FHA-approved appraiser values the property at its *fair market value* and issues a *conditional commitment* to the lender on this value. This commitment is conditional to the FHA's approval of the borrower. By its underwriting standards, the FHA will issue a *firm commitment* when it approves both the property's value and the borrower's credit ability. The lender, by the firm commitment, may close on the mortgage. The mortgage must be a first mortgage. The lender has the right to charge a 1 percent processing charge to the borrower. Any points charged for the mortgage must be paid by someone else, usually the seller. A *point* is a discount charge to increase the yield on the mortgage. As an example, if the FHA interest rate is established at 9 percent and the market rate is $9\frac{1}{4}$ percent, the lender would request that the seller pay 2 points (2 percent of the mortgage) at closing. It is said that 2 points equal a yield increase of one-quarter of 1 percent on an average residential mortgage. This type of discounting encourages lenders to lend on FHA mortgages when the FHA interest rate is less than the market rate.

VA Mortgage. This is a mortgage that favors eligible veterans. The Veterans Administration *guarantees* to a qualified lender, against the loss of mortgage, loans to veterans under certain conditions. The mortgage given to the veteran may be 100 percent of the purchase price, including closing costs, and for a term of up to 30 years. The interest rate is normally, though not necessarily, the same as for FHA mortgages and is set by the Secretary of Housing and Urban Development (HUD). Property qualifications are established by the VA and appraised by VA-approved appraisers. After establishing the property's value, the VA issues a *Certificate of Reasonable Value* (CRV). Eligibility of the veteran is also determined by the VA, which upon approval issues a *Certificate of Eligibility*. A lender will process and close on the mortgage upon presentation of these two certificates. Processing fees, points, and interest rates are usually the same for VA mortgages as they are for FHA mortgages.

Conventional Mortgage. Any mortgage not guaranteed or insured by the government is considered a conventional mortgage. This basically means that the lender accepts all the risks of the mortgage and, subject to federal or state laws, creates all its own loan requirements.

TYPES OF CONVENTIONAL MORTGAGES

All *non-residential* mortgages are automatically considered conventional mortgages. Although the FHA and VA are important residential mortgage sources, the bulk of residential lending is done by conventional standards. Some of the types of conventional mortgages are as follows:

- *Construction mortgage.* A mortgage designed to advance funds to a builder during various construction stages.
- *Blanket mortgage.* A mortgage that covers more than one parcel of real property as security for the indebtedness.
- *Package mortgage.* A mortgage that includes a lien on both real and personal property.
- *Open-end mortgage.* A mortgage that can be increased during its term at the option of the borrower.
- *Wraparound mortgage.* A mortgage that absorbs an existing mortgage due to the favorable terms of the earlier mortgage.
- *Variable-rate mortgage.* A mortgage with an interest rate which changes with market conditions. This mortgage is also called an ARM or adjustable rate mortgage.
- *Flexible-payment mortgage.* A mortgage which permits a varied payment during the life of the mortgage, depending upon the borrower's present and future financial expectations.
- *Straight-term mortgage.* A mortgage in which the principal is repaid in one lump sum at the time of maturity. Only interest is paid during the term of the mortgage.
- *Amortized mortgage.* Most mortgages fall within this classification as far as payments are concerned. Each payment includes the proper amount of interest and a partial repayment of the principal.

As previously noted, mortgages are highly flexible and can have variations of each classification as noted. As an example, a savings and loan association could give a variable-rate mortgage that amortizes (pays out) the indebtedness over the term of the mortgage. The mortgage could include both real and personal property (package mortgage).

INTEREST

Interest charged during the life of the mortgage, as well as penalties for late payments or prepayments, is normally governed by state laws. It should be noted that mortgages insured or guaranteed by the federal government are exempt from state usury laws. *Usury* is an interest rate in excess of the legal rate permitted by state laws.

RECORDING MORTGAGES

Most mortgages are recorded to give *constructive notice* to the world that there is a valid lien on the property. Most states have laws that require any lien affecting real property to be recorded. The lender who records the lien first in time has first priority of payback in a foreclosure proceeding. There can be as many mortgages on a property as there are lenders foolish enough to lend same.

SUBORDINATION

Each mortgage after a first mortgage is known as a *junior lien* or *second mortgage* and takes a lesser position in repayment at foreclosure than the prior lien. Since a mortgage is a contract between two or more parties, the contract may be extended, modified, forgiven and/or rescinded by mutual assent anytime during its term. It can even be *subordinated* to a later lien; i.e., a lender who has a first mortgage can subordinate his position to a later recorded mortgage, making the latter mortgage a first mortgage and his first mortgage a second mortgage. This is done frequently in the construction field where a holder of a land mortgage subordinates his land mortgage to the construction of a building or site improvements.

Mortgagee position, i.e., first, second, third, etc., is very important in case the mortgagor (borrower) *defaults* in the payment and the lender has to file a *foreclosure action* to protect his financial interest. At the foreclosure sale the most successful bidder will acquire title to the property, subject only to the borrower's (owner's) *redemption* right in that state. State, county, or local taxes that are unpaid usually take precedence over all private liens (mortgages, mechanic's liens, judgments) regardless of their priority. Borrower's redemption rights vary in some states from ten days to two years after a foreclosure sale. If the period of time is ten days or less, that state has a strict foreclosure law and the mortgagor (borrower) is forever barred from redeeming or reacquiring his property. The period of time is normally known as *equity of redemption*, and the student should know this period of time in his state.

If the monies received at the foreclosure sale are sufficient to satisfy the debt (or debts), then the bond (note) the borrower signed with the mortgage becomes unimportant. If it is insufficient, then the lender (mortgagee) can sue on the bond and/or note. The *bond* is the personal guarantee of the borrower that he will pay the monies advanced by the lender. If the property does not repay the lender completely (principal, interest, reasonable costs, etc.) upon its sale, then the lender has the right, by virtue of the personal bond, to go after other income and assets of the borrower.

PENAL SUM

Sometimes bonds or notes which accompany a mortgage are written in a sum in excess of the mortgagor's indebtedness. This is known as a *penal sum* and is necessary in some states to protect the lender's interest and costs during litigation to reacquire the property.

ASSIGNMENT OR ASSUMPTION

The mortgage contract may be *assigned* to another lender or *assumed* by another borrower unless specifically prohibited by the contract itself. If assumed by another borrower, as in those cases where a person sells his property subject to a mortgage, the original borrower remains liable on the mortgage and bond unless released by the mortgagee. It should be understood that the contract between the lender (mortgagee) and borrower (mortgagor) is dependent not only on the property offered as security for the loan, but upon the credit worthiness of the borrower as well. Therefore, if there is to be a change in the borrower so named in the original contract, the mortgagee usually retains the right to accept or reject the assumption.

The mortgagee always reserves the right to assign the contract to another lender. The mortgage, to a lender, is viewed as an investment or an asset— something that can be converted to money if the need arises. Mortgage brokers or bankers specialize in the sale of mortgages from one lending institution to another.

GOVERNMENT AGENCIES

Two major government agencies, The Government National Mortgage Association, also known as "Ginnie Mae," and the Federal National Mortgage Association, also known as "Fannie Mae," aid in this process of selling or buying mortgages. It is done principally to improve the flow of funds from one area to another. There are basically two types of mortgage markets—primary and secondary. The primary mortgage market consists of those lenders who lend money directly on real estate, such as savings and loan associations. The secondary mortgage market consists of those lenders who buy and sell mortgages already in existence. In most cases, real estate salespeople work with the primary mortgage lenders.

MORTGAGE SOURCES

Most lenders in the primary mortgage market specialize in financing certain types of real estate. It is required, in order to be successful in the real estate profession, to know the sources for mortgages of all kinds. Some of these sources are:

• Savings and loan associations
• Savings banks
• Commercial banks
• Private lenders
• Insurance companies
• Mortgage bankers

LIENS

There are both *liens on title* and *liens as to physical condition*. A mortgage is a specific lien or encumbrance on the title of the real property. Other specific or general liens as to title are:

1. *Mechanic's Liens.* An encumbrance placed on the property due to construction or improvements by someone other than the owner.
2. *Taxes.* General or special assessments placed on a property by a governmental agency are a valid lien against the free and clear title of the owner.
3. *Judgment.* A court decision affecting the assets of an owner.

It is important to note that every state has a procedure to protect property owners from unlawful liens. As an example, in most states before a builder can place a mechanic's lien on a property he has improved, he must file a *lis pendens* in the court. A *lis pendens* is a notice of pending action and gives constructive notice to the world that a lien may be placed on the property in the future. In most states this notice must be filed before work begins. If the builder completes the work and is then unpaid, he may file a mechanic's lien. The lien protects his labor and materials in case the property is sold. The builder can also institute foreclosure proceedings on his lien in the same manner as a mortgagee.

IN YOUR OWN WORDS

These are terms you should be familiar with. Check your definitions by referring to the text or to the glossary beginning on page 140.

acceleration clause	blanket mortgage
amortization	bond
assumption of mortgage	construction mortgage
conventional mortgage	mortgage
deed in trust	mortgagee
defeasance clause	mortgagor
discount points	open-end mortgage
equity of redemption	package mortgage
FHA mortgage	penal sum
flexible-payment mortgage	straight-term mortgage
foreclosure	subordination
judgment	usury
junior mortgage	VA mortgage
lis pendens	variable-rate mortgage
mechanic's lien	wraparound mortgage

TEST YOURSELF

1. Which of the following is (are) true of an acceleration clause found in a mortgage?
   I. It gives to the borrower the method of redemption when the mortgage loan has been satisfied.
   II. It gives the mortgagee the right to declare the entire unpaid sum due immediately if the borrower defaults.
      (a) I only
      (b) II only
      (c) Both I and II
      (d) Neither I nor II

2. A purchaser is seeking a mortgage loan for a restaurant he wishes to buy. If the loan needed is to include the trade fixtures as well as the building itself, which type of mortgage should the purchaser seek?
      (a) Package mortgage
      (b) Blanket mortgage
      (c) Wraparound mortgage
      (d) Open-end mortgage

3. A young couple is purchasing a starter home. A savings and loan gives them a mortgage which will allow them to make smaller payments in the earlier years of the loan with payments to increase as their income increases. This type of loan is known as a(n)

    (a) variable rate mortgage   (c) flexible payment mortgage
    (b) VA mortgage   (d) amortized mortgage

4. A savings and loan association holding a first mortgage has allowed a lender of a second mortgage to take priority over its loan. This is called

  I. redemption
  II. subordination

    (a) I only   (c) Both I and II
    (b) II only   (d) Neither I nor II

5. A mortgage may be

  I. assigned to another lender
  II. assumed by another borrower

    (a) I only   (c) Both I and II
    (b) II only   (d) Neither I nor II

6. A *lis pendens* is normally filed

    (a) before work begins
    (b) within 30 days after work begins
    (c) at anytime during the construction phase
    (d) after work is completed

7. In the event of a foreclosure, the lender who holds the first mortgage has priority over

  I. tax liens
  II. second mortgage

    (a) I only   (c) Both I and II
    (b) II only   (d) Neither I nor II

8. Which of the following is (are) true concerning Veterans Administration mortgage loans?

  I. The funds are lent directly by the Veterans Administration.
  II. An eligible veteran can receive a mortgage loan only up to 85% of the purchase price.

    (a) I only   (c) Both I and II
    (b) II only   (d) Neither I nor II

9. The variation of a variable rate mortgage is based upon

    (a) a predetermined rate table
    (b) the current rate of fixed term mortgages
    (c) a combined index of money market indicators
    (d) government regulations

10. A conventional mortgage is most commonly sought because

  I. it is guaranteed by the government
  II. it is insured by the government

    (a) I only   (c) Both I and II
    (b) II only   (d) Neither I nor II

ANSWERS: 1. b   2. a   3. c   4. b   5. c   6. a   7. b   8. d   9. c   10. d

Chapter Six

Leases and Management

LEASES

A *lease* is an agreement between two parties known as a *landlord* (lessor) and *tenant* (lessee) whereby the lessor gives up possession of real property (or a portion thereof) to the lessee for consideration known as rent. The lease may be in many forms and in some states is required to be in writing before it can be enforced under that state's Statute of Frauds. In fact, each state, by various statutes, rules, regulations, or laws, has established responsibilities between landlord and tenant that take precedence over common law. Students are advised to know their state's laws governing leases.

LEASE DEFINED

Generally, a lease is a contract for a specific period of time, from one day to 99 years or beyond. It may be oral in some states if the period of time is less than three years. A lease may be recorded when it is in writing and properly acknowledged.

ESSENTIAL ELEMENTS OF A LEASE

In common law, the lease must have a date of execution and a date of termination; it must name the parties to the lease, describe the property, and state the consideration (rent) to be paid. Rent may be anything of value including services to be rendered. The lease should state the purpose or use of the premises, the right to assign or sublet, the liability or responsibility of both parties, and improvements or alterations permitted. In common law the tenant (lessee) must return the premises in the same condition as originally leased, normal wear and tear excluded.

TYPES OF LEASES

Most leases acquire their name from the manner in which rent is paid to the landlord. The most common types of leases are as follows:

Gross Lease. A lease where the landlord receives a gross (total) sum of money out of which he pays all the expenses associated with the property. Residential apartment leases are typical of gross leases.

Net Lease. A lease where the landlord receives a net sum of money and the tenant pays for expenses associated with the property, such as maintenance and upkeep. There are net leases; net, net leases; and net, net, net, leases. Each net represents an expense item that the tenant assumes. As an example, a single net indicates that the tenant pays for utilities and electricity; a double net indicates that the tenant pays for utilities and upkeep; and a triple net indicates that the tenant pays for utilities, maintenance, taxes, and insurance. The main thing to remember is that these leases are usually associated with commercial, office, or industrial leases and are usually in various combinations of the tenant paying expenses plus a base rental to a landlord.

Percentage Lease. A lease that is based upon a percentage of the business that the tenant performs on the property in lieu of a regular base payment. As an example, if the tenant has a pharmacy, the landlord may wish a percentage of the gross business as rent. This type of lease is very common in shopping centers, either as a straight percentage or as a percentage on top of a base rent.

Graduated Lease. A lease that increases over the term for whatever reason is known as a graduated lease. It could be based upon a consumer index or some other standard, or could just be increased arbitrarily throughout its term. It is just a lease that has a rental base that changes, usually upward.

Revaluation Lease. A lease that is changed throughout its term by a revaluation of the property and/or its economic rent. A procedure is usually established in the lease for the revaluation that is then binding upon both parties.

Ground Lease. A lease upon vacant land which normally requires the tenant to improve the property with a structure within a certain time period. The improvements usually revert to the landlord at the end of the leased term.

EFFECT ON OWNERSHIP RIGHTS

Each one of these above leases affects the ownership rights in real property. In fact, any lease given by an owner of real property reduces that person's ownership rights. Each fee simple owner of real property has a bundle of rights which include use, enjoyment, possession, and disposition. When the owner of a fee simple estate gives possession to someone else (a tenant), the owner has reduced the bundle of rights by this act. The owner now holds a *leased-fee estate* and the tenant has a *leasehold estate*. These estates exist as long as the contract (lease) exists or as long as the laws governing leasehold estates permit them to exist.

TYPES OF ESTATES

The estates capable of being created by various types of leases (or by law) are four in number. They are:

1. *Estate for years.* Any leasehold estate that exists by contract for one year or more.
2. *Estate from year-to-year.* Any lease for less than a year; usually a renewable monthly lease.
3. *Estate at will.* Any possession of property at the expiration of the lease with the consent of the landlord.
4. *Estate at sufferance.* Any possession of property at the expiration of the lease but without the consent of the landlord.

EVICTION

In the case of estate at sufferance, the owner (lessor) is being deprived possession of his property at the expiration of a lease because the tenant (lessee) refuses to move out. The tenant is known as a *holdover tenant.* The owner cannot just bodily move in and evict the tenant. The lessor must file an *actual eviction* notice with the courts and seek dispossession in a lawful manner. *Eviction* means depriving the tenant of enjoyment of the leased premises. It can be done at any time during the lease if the tenant breaches any of the provisions of the lease or after the lease if he fails to move out. Usually a statutory notice is given to the lessee (tenant) which informs him of a proposed court order of eviction and gives him time to appear in court to show why he should not be evicted. If he fails to appear or show good cause, a judgment is entered against him and a warrant to dispossess is issued. All of the above fall under the heading of *lawful or actual eviction.*

There is also *constructive eviction,* which is unlawful. This occurs when the lessor (landlord) interferes with the tenant's use, control, or possession of the real property. In these cases the tenant would be justified in many states in abandoning the premises and quitting the lease. An example of constructive eviction is where a landlord cuts off a major utility (water, gas, electricity) that serves the property. Without these essential services it would be impossible for the tenant to enjoy the property.

SECURITY DEPOSITS

Most leases have a requirement that a *security deposit* be made at the time the lease is executed. Some states require (1) that a residential security deposit cannot exceed a certain number of months' rent, (2) that the security deposit earn interest which accrues to the lessee, and (3) that it be returned to the tenant at the expiration of the lease if the tenant returns the property in the same condition he received it (normal wear and tear excepted). Regardless of the law, most security deposits are governed by the lease provisions and are used to protect the landlord from a lessee's quitting the property before the expiration of the lease and leaving the landlord with a vacant property.

TERMINATION OF LEASE

A lease can be terminated by contract, surrender, abandonment, or forfeiture. In the first two there is consent by both parties and all obligations are terminated. In the last two, abandonment or forfeiture, damages may be sought by the lessor (landlord) in a lawsuit although the lease may already be terminated.

FEDERAL CRIME INSURANCE

It is a federal requirement on all residential rental properties of ten or more units that the landlord notify the tenant of the availability of burglary insurance coverage. Usually federal crime insurance applications may be obtained by any state-licensed property insurance agent. Residential insurance coverage may be purchased in amounts up to $10,000. Rates for this insurance, even in high crime areas, are controlled.

TRUTH-IN-RENTING

Some states have passed legislation requiring landlords to inform all residential tenants of their rights under state laws. The student should know whether his state has a "truth-in-renting" statute and, if so, he should become familiar with its terms.

MANAGEMENT

Since a lease is applicable to all types of real property (single-family, multi-family, commercial, industrial, agricultural, and special purpose), real estate salespeople in all states have the capacity by state laws to earn a commission by either renting or managing other people's property.

In renting real property, a listing is accepted by the broker-agent in the same manner as he or she would accept a listing for sale. If the agent finds a tenant willing to lease the property under terms acceptable to the landlord, then a commission is considered to have been earned. Again the rate and method of compensation are at the discretion of the landlord and agent. The same laws of agency are applicable in this type of listing as they are in listing a property for sale.

Many owners of rentable real property do not wish to manage it. Instead, they retain professional managers for this task, and many real estate agents have developed successful management offices to do this. The management contract can take the form of complete power of attorney or merely collector of rents, depending only upon the wishes of the owner. Normally the real estate manager receives a percentage of collected rents, and the percentage received is based upon the obligations assumed.

Some of the management duties include:

1. Acquiring and qualifying tenants
2. Collecting rents
3. Advertising
4. Hiring maintenance personnel
5. Settling disputes with tenants
6. Disbursement of funds

IN YOUR OWN WORDS

These are terms you should be familiar with. Check your definitions by referring to the text or to the glossary beginning on p. 140.

abandonment	ground lease
actual eviction	lease
constructive eviction	leased-fee estate
essential elements of a lease	leasehold estate
estate at sufferance	lessee
estate at will	lessor
estate for years	net lease
estate from year-to-year	percentage lease
forfeiture	revaluation lease
graduated lease	security deposit
gross lease	surrender

TEST YOURSELF

1. A tenant in the Millstone Mall is required to pay as rent 3% of his gross business with a minimum monthly rent of $900. This type of lease is known as a
   - (a) gross lease
   - (b) percentage lease
   - (c) net lease
   - (d) variable lease

2. The type of ownership which the landlord of the leased premises holds is a
   I. fee simple estate
   II. leasehold estate
   - (a) I only
   - (b) II only
   - (c) Both I and II
   - (d) Neither I nor II

3. A lease that provides for an increase in rent should the property be valued later at a higher price is called a
   I. revaluation lease
   II. graduated lease
   - (a) I only
   - (b) II only
   - (c) Both I and II
   - (d) Neither I nor II

4. A landlord permits his tenant to remain in possession of the leased premises after the lease has expired until the tenant can move into his new home. This type of possession is known as
   I. estate at sufferance
   II. estate at will
   - (a) I only
   - (b) II only
   - (c) Both I and II
   - (d) Neither I nor II

5. By which of the following means may a lease be terminated without the possibility of a lawsuit being brought against the lessee by the lessor?
   I. Surrender
   II. Contract
   (a) I only
   (b) II only
   (c) Both I and II
   (d) Neither I nor II

6. Which of the following is not required to be included in a lease?
   (a) Consideration
   (b) Termination date
   (c) Amount of taxes
   (d) Description of property

7. A net lease is most commonly associated with which of the following types of properties?
   (a) Residential properties
   (b) Apartment complexes
   (c) Vacant land
   (d) Industrial properties

8. An "actual eviction" notice may be served
   I. any time during the term of the lease if the lessee breaches any provision of the lease
   II. after the lease has expired and the tenant fails to remove himself from the property
   (a) I only
   (b) II only
   (c) Both I and II
   (d) Neither I nor II

9. The purpose of a security deposit is
   I. to protect the landlord in case of damages to the property
   II. to provide funds for the general upkeep of the property
   (a) I only
   (b) II only
   (c) Both I and II
   (d) Neither I nor II

10. Which of the following types of leases is typical of those used in residential apartment complexes?
    I. Ground lease
    II. Gross lease
    (a) I only
    (b) II only
    (c) Both I and II
    (d) Neither I nor II

ANSWERS: 1. b 2. d 3. a 4. b 5. c 6. c 7. d 8. c 9. a 10. b

Chapter Seven

Property Descriptions

All contracts and deeds must clearly describe the property to be transferred in such a way that the contract or deed can be enforced, if necessary. There are three ways in which a description of real property would be declared by a court as certain in "subject matter" and therefore legal. They are (1) metes and bounds, (2) recorded plat (block and lot number), and (3) rectangular survey system. In some states all three of these descriptions can be used, and in others only the first two are used. Basically, the original thirteen states do not use the rectangular survey system.

METES AND BOUNDS

A *metes and bounds description* is also known as a *surveyor's description*. It begins at a definite point (known as the point of beginning), proceeds around the boundaries of a tract by reference to linear measurement and direction, and always ends at the point where it began. This is also referred to as a description by *monuments and boundaries.* Monuments are any natural or man-made markers (such as the intersection of two named streets) that a surveyor would use to establish a point. Once having established the *point of beginning* (POB), the surveyor recites the course of the property lines by use of a transit and tape.

Certain real estate licensing examinations require the student to understand this method in order to find a tract of land in a hypothetical subdivision.

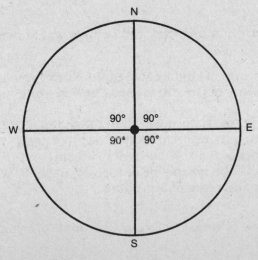

If you can visualize a circle (a compass) which has a circumference of 360 degrees and which is broken down into four quarters of 90 degrees each, respectively labeled north, south, east, or west, you have a good idea of the methodology employed.

Now, if you were proceeding in a northeasterly direction, 45° 100 feet along a property's line, all you would have to do is put the center of the circle (compass) over the point of beginning and proceed with the tape 100 feet to your next point. Directions around a parcel are always taken clockwise.

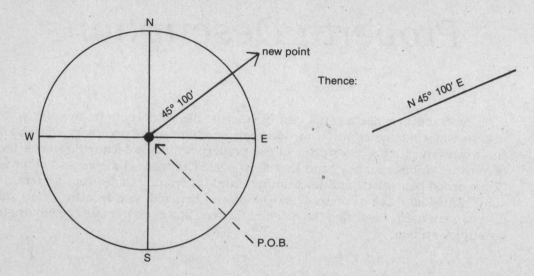

It should be noted that degrees are also broken down further into minutes and seconds. These are not time indicators, but refined physical measurements on the circle (compass) that enable you to more adequately describe a parcel of real property and are similar to measurements on a ruler.

A typical legal description by metes and bounds would read like this:

All that tract or parcel of land located in the Sunnyview Estates, in the City of Greatness, County of Greatness, State of New York, and being described as follows:

BEGINNING at a point on the north side of Rich Road, 200 feet east of Happy Street, and running thence N 45° E 300 feet to a point; thence S 45° E 150 feet to a point; thence S 45° W 300 feet to a point on the north side of Rich Road, thence along the north side of Rich Road N 45° W 150 feet, more or less, to the point and place of beginning.

See if you can draw or visualize this lot. A sample drawing is at the end of this chapter on page 75.

RECORDED PLAT

Most states require all new subdivisions of land to be properly recorded on a filed subdivision map. A subdivision is the division of a larger tract of land into smaller parcels. These smaller parcels are given block and lot numbers. By referral to the filed map, any parcel thereon can be cited by its block and lot number. The map could be either a private subdivision plat or a municipal tax map. No two parcels on any map have the same block and lot numbers. The map may contain actual or proposed roads, alleys, easements, or other information of a physical or topographical nature.

In some real estate exams, students are given a recorded plat where they must locate various easements or compute and compare lots or street frontages. A simulation of this problem is contained in one of the final exams. The student should not be overly concerned with this problem. It is nothing more than a reading comprehension problem.

RECTANGULAR SURVEY SYSTEM

Used in all states except the original thirteen, this is sometimes called the *government survey system.* It is formed around sets of two intersecting lines— principal meridians and base lines. The *principal meridians* are north and south lines and the *base lines* are east and west lines. Theoretical *townships* are formed when the lines are parallel with the base line 6 miles apart. Each township then contains 36 square miles (6 × 6). Each square mile in a township is called a *section.*

There are 640 acres in a section. A legal description from this survey is then taken similar to locating a property in a subdivision, but instead of calling the property by block and lot it is known by township and section number.

SURVEYS

Legal descriptions should not be changed or altered without adequate information and competent authority such as a licensed surveyor or qualified title attorney. Legal descriptions should always include the municipality, county, and state where the land is located. Surveys may be used in conjunction with all three aforementioned descriptions and are required in many real estate transactions such as: (1) conveying a portion of a given tract of land, (2) conveying real estate as security for a mortgage loan, (3) locating roads and highways, and (4) showing the location of improvements on the parcel.

Legal descriptions may show *air rights* and/or *water rights.* An owner may subdivide the air space above his land into lots such as a high-rise condominium. *Datum* is a point above the earth's surface from which elevations are measured or indicated, generally taken at levels above the mean sea level at the New York harbor.

The owner of land which borders on a non-navigable stream is considered to own land to the center of the stream. However, navigable waters are considered to be public highways in which the public has an interest or right to travel. *Water rights* (also known as *riparian rights*) can be acquired or leased from the appropriate state agency on navigable streams by the upland owner who wishes to use the waterway for access, for docking, or for pleasure.

LAND UNITS AND MEASUREMENTS

For some real estate exams the student needs to know the following measurements. Please copy them down on an index card and memorize them.

1 Circle = 360 degrees
1 Acre = 43,560 square feet
1 Mile = 5,280 linear feet
1 Section = 1 Square Mile or 640 acres

IN YOUR OWN WORDS

These are terms you should be familiar with. Check your definitions by referring to the text or to the glossary beginning on p. 140.

air rights   principal meridian
base line   recorded plat
block & lot number   rectangular survey system
datum   riparian rights
metes & bounds   section
monuments   subdivision
point of beginning   township

TEST YOURSELF

1. Which of the following statements is (are) true?
   I. The metes and bounds method of describing property always utilizes township and section numbers.
   II. A monument can be used as a reference point for a surveyor when using the metes and bounds description.
   (a) I only   (c) Both I and II
   (b) II only   (d) Neither I nor II

2. Which of the following is not a term found in a metes and bounds description?
   (a) Minutes   (c) Section
   (b) Degrees   (d) Point of beginning

3. For which of the following reasons may a survey be required?
   I. When using real property as security for a mortgage loan
   II. To show the location of improvements on a parcel of real estate
   (a) I only   (c) Both I and II
   (b) II only   (d) Neither I nor II

4. Which of the following is (are) true?
   I. An owner can subdivide air space above his land.
   II. Non-navigable waterways are considered to be public highways.
   (a) I only   (c) Both I and II
   (b) II only   (d) Neither I nor II

5. An owner of land which borders on a navigable waterway can acquire
   I. riparian rights
   II. monument rights
   (a) I only
   (b) II only
   (c) Both I and II
   (d) Neither I nor II

ANSWERS: 1. b 2. c 3. c 4. a 5. a

SAMPLE DRAWING OF LEGAL DESCRIPTION ON PAGE 72.

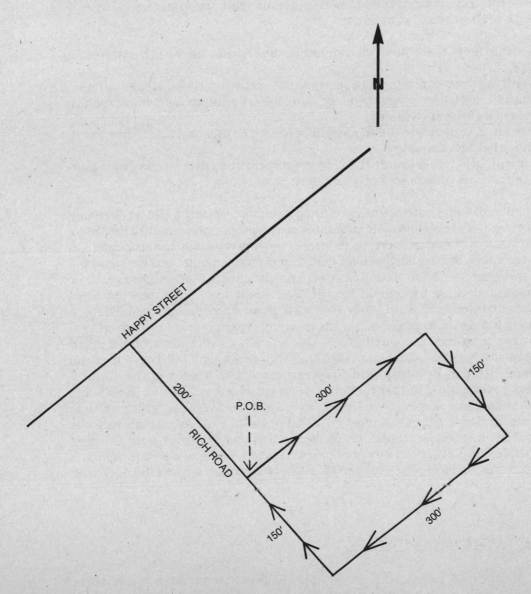

Chapter Eight

Appraising

An *appraisal* is always defined as an *opinion of value*. It may be a written or an oral opinion of value, but it is always documented. *Documentation* means *support* and implies that the person making the appraisal can logically defend it. Real estate brokers are often called upon to give an opinion of value for many reasons. Some of these reasons include:

1. The transfer of real estate, so that either the seller or buyer can establish a price.
2. Financing prior to placing a property up as security for a mortgage or loan.
3. Taxation, either for property, income, or inheritance, to determine the fair basis of a government's lien.
4. Insurance, to estimate the replacement cost in case of loss due to fire, flood, wind, or other casualties.
5. Condemnation, to estimate the proper compensation due an owner for public takeover of private property (eminent domain).

Any opinion of value not documented is a *guesstimate*. Many builders, lenders, and real estate salespersons offer estimates or ranges of price and/or cost that a particular parcel of real property is worth. *Estimates* normally are documented opinions of value but are subjective, based upon a particular builder's cost, a lender's mortgage policy, or a broker's own knowledge of sales the broker's office has consummated. An *appraisal* is objective, made by a disinterested third party. This disinterested third party is known as an *appraiser*. In real estate, a broker may act as an appraiser in a transaction separate and apart from personal broker or agency responsibilities. One usually cannot act as both agent and appraiser in the same transaction. The provisions of the Financial Institutions Reform, Recovery and Enforcement Act of 1988 require that all appraisers participating in transactions which entail federal money in any way be licensed by their states. Since there is federal involvement with banking, guarantees, and mortgages in almost all instances, all formal appraisals must be conducted by licensed or certified appraisers. This chapter deals with the general principles and practices of appraisal. Chapter 15 addresses requirements and procedures for licensing and certification of appraisers in conformity with FIRREA.

APPROACHES TO VALUE

The support or documentation in an appraisal usually involves one of three approaches to value. It should be noted that all three approaches to value listed below may be used to value a single parcel of real property, but it would be unusual to use all three in an appraisal report. These approaches are:

1. *The Cost Approach.* This process involves the cost or outlay of money to replace or reproduce the real estate being valued, including land.
2. *The Market Data Approach.* A method by which the property under appraisement is compared to other properties that have been sold.
3. *The Income Approach.* A system of using the rentals achieved or capable of being achieved and converting them to a present worth.

An outline of each of these approaches to value is as follows. The steps listed here represent a simplified format for easy reader comprehension. It is more than adequate for salesperson examinations throughout the country. Broker candidates may wish to further expand their knowledge of these steps by referring to their own textbooks. Licensed appraiser candidates should direct their attention to Chapter 15. Each approach to value listed herein has particular use for the various types of real property being appraised. A description of the class or age of property best suited for the particular approach to appraisal accompanies the detailing of each approach.

COST APPROACH

This approach is used on newer or "special purpose" real estate where there are few sales of entire properties, such as large industrial plants, churches, schools, etc. It is also used to value new or like-new real estate. It is rarely applicable to obsolete or old real estate holdings.

Step 1: Estimate the current value of the land. Normally, sales of unimproved, similar lands are used to value the improved land as of the valuation date.

Step 2: Estimate the current cost of duplicating the improvement. Usually, known building costs of similar new structures are used and compared to the property under appraisement.

Step 3: Estimate the amount of depreciation the building has experienced. There are three types of depreciation the valuator must consider: physical, functional, and economic. Depreciation is more fully discussed later in this section.

Step 4: Deduct the amount of estimated depreciation from the cost of the new improvement in Step 2.

Step 5: Value all "on-site" improvements either as is or by the same criteria as Step 2 and Step 3. On-site improvements include lawn, driveways, curbs, sidewalks, swimming pools, sheds, etc.

Step 6: Add the value of the land to both the depreciated value of the improvement and the on-site improvements.

MARKET DATA APPROACH

This approach is used on "general purpose" real estate such as residences, vacant land, farms, small commercial or industrial properties. It is also the only approach used to value vacant land.

Step 1: Carefully inspect the property under appraisement, noting all features and amenities that are typical to that class of real property. As an example, in a single family residence the ceiling height, number of bedrooms or baths, layout, yard improvements, kitchen, etc. are important to purchasers of this type of property.

Step 2: Research the community to discover recent sales similar in benefits to the property under valuation. Sales must be bona fide transactions that have occurred between a willing seller and a willing buyer. Sales must be similar in order that the valuator can compare "apples with apples" and not "apples with oranges."

Step 3: Compare the sales that have occurred to the property under appraisement, making appropriate adjustments for time, location, and physical differences.

Step 4: Select a value for the property after considering all the adjusted sales based upon a logical analysis of the facts as indicated by the comparisons rendered.

INCOME APPROACH

This approach is used on "income-producing" real estate such as apartment buildings, office buildings, nursing homes, shopping centers, industrial loft buildings, warehouses, etc. It is used whenever income is thought of as the main purpose of the structure.

Step 1: Analyze the property to be appraised as to its maximum current income potential. This is known as *gross income* and can be determined by comparable properties which are similarly rented.

Step 2: Determine the typical expenses in order to obtain the gross income, including vacancy allowances, operating expenses, and fixed charges.

Step 3: Deduct the total expenses from the gross income (Step 1 minus Step 2) to achieve the *net income* potential from the property.

Step 4: Estimate the return rate required to entice an investor to purchase this class of property. Return rates vary with different types of investment properties based upon the quality, quantity, and durability of the net income stream. Return rates are also known as *capitalization rates, overall rates, dividend rates,* and *equity rates.*

Step 5: Convert the net income stream into a capital value by dividing the rate into the net income. This process is known as capitalization. As an example, if a property produced a net income of $10,000 and a typical investor wanted a 10 percent return on his money, then $10,000 divided by 10 percent equals $100,000. The $100,000 represents the value the investor believes the property is worth to guarantee him a $10,000 annual net income on his investment.

VALUES

The purpose of each approach to value is usually to estimate the market value of the property as of a certain date. However, as there are different purposes for which an appraisal can be made on the same parcel of real estate, there are different values that can also result. Some of these are:

- Market value
- Tax value
- Insurance value
- Mortgage value
- Condemnation value
- Use value
- Salvage value

One author lists over 52 different values that a given property can have as of a certain date. It suffices to say that value commonly means worth, and any word in front of value limits the type of value being defined.

VALUE CHARACTERISTICS

It is obvious that in order for anything to have value or worth it must possess certain characteristics. Among these are *scarcity, utility, transferability,* and *desirability.* The greater the degree to which these characteristics are present in an economic good (such as shelter), the greater the value it would have. As an example, air is a commodity that has a great degree of usefulness and desirability, but it is not scarce and therefore has little economic value. Basic shelter, housing for individuals, commerce, and industry are limited and therefore scarce. Something has value because it is desirable, useful, scarce, and capable of transfer. The more desirable or useful or scarce it is, the greater its value. The function of an appraiser is to measure those characteristics. He does this by knowing that value is: (1) determined by the interaction of buyers and sellers in the market (Market Data Approach); (2) measured by the cost to duplicate a substitute property (Cost Approach); (3) estimated by the future returns or benefits the property can produce over its economic life (Income Approach).

HIGHEST AND BEST USE

Most properties have one thing in common in relationship to their value—as of a given date they have a use which would produce highest value or greatest net return. This use is called the property's *highest and best use.* The highest and best use of a property is always estimated upon that use which is legal, feasible, and possible. Not every vacant tract of land along a highway can be used as a service station or bank site. It must be zoned for that use (legal), there must be a demand for that use (feasible), and the site must have the physical attributes to be used for that purpose (possible). Normally, if the answer to those limitations is affirmative, then that use would be the highest and best use.

DEPRECIATION

One of the special concepts a student has to know is that depreciation means *a loss in value.* It can be caused by many factors, but is generally classed into three categories—physical, functional, and economic.

Physical depreciation is any loss in value a property suffers due to age, general wear and tear, or the elemental actions of sun, wind, rain, and cold. This loss in value begins the day the property is newly completed and extends throughout the property's life. It may be offset by upkeep and maintenance but is generally at a constant rate. Measurement of this class of depreciation is usually through an age-life table such as accountants use to write off an asset for the Internal Revenue Service; however, in real estate valuations the age-life expectancy is determined by the market and not by IRS charts. As an example, if the appraiser discovers in the market that 40-year-old single family homes are selling at 20 percent less than their cost new, he could say that depreciation is at the rate of one-half of 1 percent per year (40 times .05 = 20%). Although depreciation rarely occurs in real life on a straight-line basis, the measurement indicates an overall value loss that could be used to analyze a comparable property. There are other mathematical ways to compute depreciation which are discussed in the math section of this book.

Functional depreciation is a value loss that has to do with style, layout, utility, or features that are no longer acceptable by modern tastes. It is said that "more buildings are torn down than fall down," and this is a reflection of their lack of usefulness. As an example, years ago homes were built with outside toilets. Today inside plumbing is not only desirable but mandated by many health authorities. Homes that have bath facilities away from the sleeping quarters of a house lose appeal and value in the market. This loss of value is called *functional obsolescence* and is usually measured by either the cost to correct same or by the value loss if incurable. Any value loss a property suffers within its boundary lines that is not a physical loss in value can be classed as functional obsolescence. Examples of this would be inadequate service equipment (electrical, heating, plumbing); improper or unusual style (gingerbread or outlandish room layout, materials, high ceilings, shape); oversized or undersized rooms; mix and match architectural types, or inappropriate relationship of land to building.

Economic depreciation is a loss that occurs outside the boundary lines of a property. It has to do with the principle of conformity which confirms that the maximum value of any physical object occurs when that object is in balance with its surroundings. An overimprovement or underimprovement is an example of a property that is larger than or smaller than properties within the neighborhood and causes a loss in buyer appeal. Few people would buy a $100,000 residence in a $50,000 neighborhood. Also, if fronting streets become heavily trafficked or if heavy industrial plants are constructed on adjacent or nearly adjacent properties, residential properties would suffer in value. The measurement of value loss would be the loss of income or the price the property could obtain if located in a proper area.

IN YOUR OWN WORDS

These are terms that you should be familiar with. Check your definitions by referring to the text or to the glossary beginning on p. 140.

appraiser	highest and best use
capitalization	income approach
cost approach	market data approach
depreciation	market value
documentation	net income
economic obsolescence	on-site improvement
functional obsolescence	opinion of value
gross income	physical deterioration
guesstimate	return rate

TEST YOURSELF

1. A residential appraisal which uses comparable sales located in the same neighborhood to support the appraised value would be described as a(n)
   I. opinion of value
   II. guesstimate
   (a) I only
   (b) II only
   (c) Both I and II
   (d) Neither I nor II

2. The method which would give the best indication of the value of a high-rise apartment building would be the
   (a) cost approach
   (b) market approach
   (c) economic approach
   (d) income approach

3. The market approach to value would best be used to estimate the value of
   (a) a church
   (b) a new residence
   (c) vacant commercial land
   (d) an industrial plant

4. Gross income is achieved by
   I. analyzing the property to find the maximum current income potential
   II. deducting the operating expenses from the net income
   (a) I only
   (b) II only
   (c) Both I and II
   (d) Neither I nor II

5. An appraiser who estimates the cost of duplicating a property minus any depreciation which has occurred utilizes the
   (a) income approach
   (b) market approach
   (c) cost approach
   (d) depreciation approach

6. A property contains an undersized kitchen with little cabinet space. Due to this loss in utility, the depreciation would be classed as
   (a) physical
   (b) functional
   (c) straight-line
   (d) economic

7. A residential property which is affected by noxious fumes from a nearby factory would suffer
   (a) economic obsolescence
   (b) functional obsolescence
   (c) curable obsolescence
   (d) physical depreciation

8. Which of the following characteristics is (are) important in estimating the value of a property?
   I. Scarcity
   II. Transferability
   (a) I only
   (b) II only
   (c) Both I and II
   (d) Neither I nor II

9. Which of the following statements is (are) correct?
   I. The purpose of an appraisal is always to estimate the market value.
   II. The value of a property is determined by the purpose for which the appraisal is being made.
   (a) I only
   (b) II only
   (c) Both I and II
   (d) Neither I nor II

10. Highest and best use is best described as
    (a) the use for which the property is zoned
    (b) the use which causes the least amount of depreciation
    (c) the use which would attract the greatest number of buyers
    (d) the use which would produce the highest net return at a given time

ANSWERS: 1. a 2. d 3. c 4. a 5. c 6. b 7. a 8. c 9. b 10. d

Chapter Nine

License Laws

Real estate, real property, and realty are all synonymous terms and are universally used interchangeably to denote a physical asset. That asset is sold, purchased, traded, exchanged, mortgaged, leased, and contracted for in many ways with the aid of real estate professionals who are licensed as real estate brokers and real estate broker-agents (or salespeople licensed to work under the supervision of a broker). Every state has its own licensing laws that govern the actions of these agents and establish the education and experience requirements for licensure.

Each student should write to the appropriate Real Estate Commission and acquire a copy of the rules, regulations, and licensing laws of his state for home study purposes. At the end of this chapter is a list of addresses of all the Real Estate Commissions. It is impossible to place all of their requirements in one text; however, we have reviewed the rules and have outlined the essentials. Once you receive your copy of your state's licensing laws, follow the outline presented herein and fill in your state's requirements. Most states have a two-part examination, one part of which is on the licensing laws, rules, and regulations of that state. This outline singles out those points that would be part of your state's examination.

Summary of License Law Provisions

I. General Provisions

    A. Define real estate broker

    B. Define real estate salesperson

    C. Exemptions from license requirements

D. Broker office requirements

E. Experience requirements—broker

F. Experience requirements—salesperson

G. Educational requirements—broker

H. Educational requirements—salesperson

II. Real Estate Commission

A. Number of members

B. Qualifications and appointment

C. Powers of enforcement

D. Penalties for violation

E. Consent agreements and fees

III. General Licensing Requirements

    A. Necessity for license

    B. Qualifications for license

       1. salesperson

       2. broker

       3. corporation

       4. partnership

    C. Application procedures and fees

    D. Displaying of licenses

    E. Expiration and renewal of licenses

    F. Effect of revocation of broker license on licenses of salespersons in his employ

    G. Transfer of license

    H. Branch offices

    I. Discharge or termination of employment of salesperson

J. Change of location requirements

K. Death of broker

L. Effect of contracts negotiated by licensed persons; unlicensed persons

M. Provisions for trust accounts

N. Bonding

O. Convictions

P. Sponsorship

Q. Fee splitting with unlicensed persons

R. Commingling

S. Fingerprinting

T. Other rules or regulations

1. rental housing

2. appraisals

3. advance fees

4. guaranty fund

5. trust accounts

6. steering/blockbusting

7. reciprocity

8. interstate land sales

9. business opportunity sales

U. Grounds for suspension or revocation of license

If you are studying for your real estate salesperson's or broker's exam in a state which uses one of the standardized national real estate license exams—the ASI Real Estate Assessment for Licensure, the AMP Real Estate Examination Program, or the PSI Real Estate Licensing Examination Services—you will find yourself taking two exams at the same sitting. The first of these is the standardized national exam which tests your knowledge of real estate in general, of universal principles of real estate law and of real estate mathematics. The second, shorter exam asks questions that pertain specifically to your state's licensing laws, rules, and regulations. If your state does not subscribe to a national testing service but administers its own exam, then questions pertaining specifically to the state will be mingled with the more general questions.

The questions that follow are typical state-law related questions. The answers will differ depending upon each state's laws; therefore we cannot present an answer key. You must do your own research to confirm the correct responses for your state.

TEST YOURSELF

1. Your license as a real estate salesperson could be suspended or revoked for which of the following activities?
   I. Listing a property for more than 6% commission
   II. Offering a property for sale at a price other than that stipulated by the owner
      (a) I only   (c) Both I and II
      (b) II only   (d) Neither I nor II

2. A broker candidate, in addition to other requirements for licensure, normally must
    I. be of legal age
    II. have served a prescribed period as a salesperson
    (a) I only
    (b) II only
    (c) Both I and II
    (d) Neither I nor II

3. Under the licensing law, which of the following is legal?
    I. A broker keeping personal funds in his trust account
    II. A broker depositing a buyer's "good faith" deposit in his personal account
    (a) I only
    (b) II only
    (c) Both I and II
    (d) Neither I nor II

4. Which of the following is required by the Real Estate Commission regarding out-of-state real estate offerings?
    I. Photographs of the property
    II. A description of the property
    (a) I only
    (b) II only
    (c) Both I and II
    (d) Neither I nor II

5. The license law
    I. regulates the commission a broker may charge in selling real estate
    II. permits a salesperson to sue his broker for commissions due him upon termination of his employment
    (a) I only
    (b) II only
    (c) Both I and II
    (d) Neither I nor II

6. If a firm's broker dies and there are no other brokers in the office
    I. a temporary license may be issued to an individual who qualifies as a broker as long as he applies for said license within 30 days of broker's death
    II. a temporary license will be valid for 30 days
    (a) I only
    (b) II only
    (c) Both I and II
    (d) Neither I nor II

7. If you were found guilty of discrimination, the penalty would be
    I. an order to cease and desist
    II. a fine of not more than $500
    (a) I only
    (b) II only
    (c) Both I and II
    (d) Neither I nor II

8. The Real Estate Commission has the power to
    I. suspend or revoke licenses
    II. impose fines
    (a) I only
    (b) II only
    (c) Both I and II
    (d) Neither I nor II

9. Which of the following is governed by the license laws in the sale of real estate?
    I. Guardians
    II. Trustees
    (a) I only
    (b) II only
    (c) Both I and II
    (d) Neither I nor II

10. Which of the following activities most accurately describes "blockbusting?"
    I. Soliciting leases in a neighborhood by claiming that minorities moving into the area will decrease the values
    II. Soliciting sales in a neighborhood by claiming that minorities moving into the area will decrease the values
    (a) I only   (c) Both I and II
    (b) II only   (d) Neither I nor II

11. As a licensed salesperson, you may receive a commission for selling a neighbor's property
    I. directly through the neighbor
    II. only through your employing broker
    (a) I only   (c) Both I and II
    (b) II only   (d) Neither I nor II

12. Which of the following constitutes commingling of funds?
    (a) Mixing a salesperson's funds with a broker's personal funds
    (b) Mixing a client's funds with a broker's personal funds
    (c) Mixing a broker's savings account with funds in his checking account
    (d) Maintaining a minimum fee in a trust account to keep the account active

13. In which of the following may a broker maintain his office?
    I. In the living quarters of his residence
    II. In the residence of one of his salespersons
    (a) I only   (c) Both I and II
    (b) II only   (d) Neither I nor II

14. Which of the following may the Real Estate Commission take action against?
    I. A salesperson violating the license act
    II. A person acting as a salesperson without a license
    (a) I only   (c) Both I and II
    (b) II only   (d) Neither I nor II

15. Which of the following is (are) exempt from the provisions of the licensing act?
    I. A licensed attorney acting in accordance with his legal practice
    II. The owner of a property handling his own real estate
    (a) I only   (c) Both I and II
    (b) II only   (d) Neither I nor II

16. A real estate salesperson's license must be
    I. maintained in the office of the employing broker
    II. carried on the salesperson whenever he is engaged in a real estate transaction
    (a) I only   (c) Both I and II
    (b) II only   (d) Neither I nor II

17. Which of the following activities requires a real estate broker's license?
    I. Transferring the title to a warehouse, including all equipment, from father to son
    II. Transacting the sale of commercial property for a commission
    (a) I only   (c) Both I and II
    (b) II only   (d) Neither I nor II

18. Which of the following statements is (are) true?
    I. A licensee may collect part of his commission from the buyer and part from the seller without each other's knowledge.
    II. A licensee may collect part of his commission from the buyer and part from the seller as long as both parties know in advance.
    (a) I only
    (b) II only
    (c) Both I and II
    (d) Neither I nor II

19. Which of the following is (are) exempt from the educational requirements for licensure as a real estate salesperson or broker?
    I. Certain disabled veterans
    II. Attorneys-at-law
    (a) I only
    (b) II only
    (c) Both I and II
    (d) Neither I nor II

20. Which of the following may an unlicensed employee of a broker do?
    I. Provide listing information to a prospective purchaser
    II. Take a listing
    (a) I only
    (b) II only
    (c) Both I and II
    (d) Neither I nor II

STATE REAL ESTATE LICENSING BOARDS AND COMMISSIONS

ALABAMA
Real Estate Commission
4121 Carmichael Road, Suite 401
Montgomery, AL 36106
(205) 242-5544

ALASKA
Real Estate Commission
3601 C Street, Suite 722
Anchorage, AK 99503-5934
(907) 563-2169

ARIZONA
Department of Real Estate
202 East Earll Drive, Suite 400
Phoenix, AZ 85012-2633
(602) 255-4345

ARKANSAS
Real Estate Commission
1 Riverfront Place, Suite 660
North Little Rock, AR 72114-5646
(501) 682-2732

CALIFORNIA
Department of Real Estate
P.O. Box 187000
Sacramento, CA 95818-7000
(916) 739-3600

COLORADO
Real Estate Commission
1776 Logan Street, 4th floor
Denver, CO 80203-1248
(303) 894-2166

CONNECTICUT
Real Estate Commission
165 Capitol Avenue
Hartford, CT 06106-1630
(203) 566-5131

DELAWARE
Real Estate Commission
Federal Street, O'Neil Building
Box 1401
Dover, DE 19903
(302) 739-4522

DISTRICT OF COLUMBIA
Real Estate Licensing Division
614 H Street NW
Washington, DC 20005
(202) 727-7480

FLORIDA
Division of Real Estate
400 West Robinson Street
Orlando, FL 32801-1736
(407) 423-6053

GEORGIA
Real Estate Commission
148 International Boulevard, NE, Suite 500
Atlanta, GA 30303-1734
(404) 656-3916

HAWAII
Real Estate Commission
P.O. Box 3469
Honolulu, HI 96801-3469
(808) 548-7464

IDAHO
Real Estate Commission
633 North 4th Street
Boise, ID 83702-4500
(208) 334-3285

ILLINOIS
Real Estate Commission
320 West Washington Street
Springfield, IL 62786-0001
(217) 785-0800

INDIANA
Real Estate Commission
100 North Senate Avenue, Room 1021
Indianapolis, IN 46204
(317) 232-2980

IOWA
Real Estate Commission
1918 SE Hulsizer Avenue
Ankeny, IA 50021
(515) 281-3183

KANSAS
Real Estate Commission
900 SW Jackson Street, Room 501
Topeka, KS 66612-1226
(913) 296-3411

KENTUCKY
Real Estate Commission
10200 Linn Station Road, Suite 201
Louisville, KY 40221
(502) 425-4273

LOUISIANA
Real Estate Commission
9071 Interline Avenue
Baton Rouge, LA 70809-1904
(504) 925-4800

MAINE
Real Estate Commission
State House Station 18
Augusta, ME 04333-0001
(207) 582-8727

MARYLAND
Real Estate Commission
501 St. Paul Place
Baltimore, MD 21202-2269
(410) 333-6230

MASSACHUSETTS
Board of Registration of Real Estate Brokers
and Salespersons
100 Cambridge Street, Room 1518
Boston, MA 02202-0001
(617) 727-7376

MICHIGAN
Department of Licensing and Regulation
611 West Ottawa Street
Lansing, MI 48909
(517) 373-1870

MINNESOTA
Department of Commerce, Licensing Division
133 East 7th Street
St. Paul, MN 55101
(612) 296-6319

MISSISSIPPI
Real Estate Commission
1920 Dunbarton Drive
Jackson, MS 39216-5087
(601) 987-3969

MISSOURI
Real Estate Commission
3523 North Ten Mile Drive
Jefferson City, MO 65101
(314) 751-2628

MONTANA
Board of Realty Regulation
1429 9th Avenue
Helena, MT 59620
(406) 444-2961

NEBRASKA
Real Estate Commission
301 Centennial Mall South
Lincoln, NE 68508-2529
(402) 471-2004

NEVADA
Real Estate Division
1665 Hot Springs Road
Carson City, NV 89710-0001
(702) 885-4280

NEW HAMPSHIRE
Real Estate Commission
107 Pleasant Street
Concord, NH 03301-3818
(603) 271-2701

NEW JERSEY
Real Estate Commission
20 West State Street
Trenton, NJ 08625-0001
(609) 292-7053

NEW MEXICO
Real Estate Commission
4125 Carlisle NE
Albuquerque, NM 87107-4806
(505) 841-6524

NEW YORK
Department of State, Division of Licensing
Services
84 Holland Avenue
Albany, NY 12208-3490
(518) 474-4750

NORTH CAROLINA
Real Estate Commission
1313 Navaho Drive
Raleigh, NC 27609-7461
(919) 733-9580

NORTH DAKOTA
Real Estate Commission
P.O. Box 727
Bismarck, ND 58502-0727
(701) 224-2749

OHIO
Division of Real Estate
77 South High Street, 20th floor
Columbus, OH 43215
(614) 466-4100

OKLAHOMA
Real Estate Commission
4040 North Lincoln Boulevard, Suite 100
Oklahoma City, OK 73105-5283
(405) 521-3387

OREGON
Real Estate Agency
158 12th Street Northeast
Salem, OR 97310-0001
(503) 378-4170

PENNSYLVANIA
Bureau of Real Estate
North Office Building, Room 505
Harrisburg, PA 17125-0001
(717) 787-4394

RHODE ISLAND
Real Estate Division
233 Richmond Street, Suite 2320
Providence, RI 02903
(401) 277-2255

SOUTH CAROLINA
Real Estate Commission
1201 Main Street, Suite 1500
Columbia, SC 29201-3228
(803) 737-0700

SOUTH DAKOTA
Real Estate Commission
212 East Capitol Avenue
Pierre, SD 57501-2518
(605) 773-3600

TENNESSEE
Real Estate Commission
500 James Robertson Parkway,
Suite 180
Nashville, TN 37243
(615) 741-2273

TEXAS
Real Estate Commission
P.O. Box 12188
Austin, TX 78711-2188
(512) 459-6544

UTAH
Real Estate Division
P.O. Box 45802
Salt Lake City, UT 84145-0802
(801) 530-6747

VERMONT
Real Estate Commission
26 Terrace Street
Montpelier, VT 05602-2154
(802) 828-3228

VIRGINIA
Real Estate Board
3600 West Broad Street
Richmond, VA 23230-4915
(804) 367-8526

WASHINGTON
Real Estate Licensing
P.O. Box 9012
Olympia, WA 98504-0001
(206) 753-6874

WEST VIRGINIA
Real Estate Commission
1033 Quarrier Street, Suite 400
Charleston, WV 25305-0001
(304) 558-3555

WISCONSIN
Bureau of Direct Licensing and Real Estate
P.O. Box 8935
Madison, WI 53708-8935
(608) 266-5511

WYOMING
Real Estate Commission
Barrett Building, 3rd floor
Cheyenne, WY 82002-0001
(307) 777-7141

Chapter Ten

Zoning and Public Regulations

Zoning, health regulations, building codes, master plans, environmental rules, traffic controls, and even historic preservation laws are all part of the many public regulations that affect land use in every state. For the most part these public regulations are local in character; i.e., they are either municipal, county, or state enforced.

ZONING

Zoning means exactly what the term implies. Land within a particular zone is restricted in its use. A certain governmental area, be it county, borough, city, township, or ward, is divided into various zones permitting and/or limiting certain development. The zones begin by having certain general classifications. These general classes of use are:

1. Residential
2. Commercial
3. Agricultural
4. Industrial
5. Special purpose

Subclasses are then developed for each general class. As an example, in the residential class a municipality can have areas zoned for high density use, such as high-rise apartment buildings, or low-density use, such as a single-family residence on a five acre tract, or any combination or mix between these extremes. In the residential classification, land use could be restricted to cluster zoning, senior citizen housing, mobile-home courts, townhouses, or large estates. There are as many variations as there are planners or planning boards desiring to control the growth of the community.

Generally a municipality develops a zoned plan of its area and creates an ordinance defending each area zoned. The ordinance sets limits on the amount of land a structure may cover, its height, its set-back and side-yard distances from adjoining lots, and its use. Any parcel of land that is already being used differently from the use developed by the map and ordinance is known as a preexisting non-comforming use. In most areas of this country, that non-conforming use may exist as long as it is never abandoned.

VARIANCES

All ordinances permit an appeal from a zoned use. The process is known as "seeking a variance." A *variance* is a request from a private land owner to use his property in a manner not permitted by the zoning ordinance. A person who has a house in a residential zoned area and wishes to convert the house to an office may seek a variance. Before the building inspector issues a permit to allow the owner to convert, the owner must go before a Zoning Board of Adjustment and get a variance. If denied, the owner cannot convert. Variances are usually granted if there is a public need for the new use plan, or if the planned use does not harm the purpose or intent of the zoning ordinance or adjacent property values.

BUILDING PERMITS

A building permit is generally issued by the *building inspector* of a community upon the request of a land owner, provided the owner has followed certain guidelines and regulations. Among the first requirements for getting a building permit is that the improvement shall conform to the zoned plan of the community. Other requirements could be the proper submission of building plans and the payment of proper fees for inspection and surveys. The intent of the building code or ordinance of a community is to control the type of development or improvement and insure that the improvement (whether new or renovated) meets minimum standards of safety and health. It should be pointed out that all public regulations, including building codes, are designed to protect the general public and not to insure a specific owner that a contractor is abiding by the owner's specific wishes.

MASTER PLAN

A *master plan* is a general design of the projected growth of an area. It is a long-term concept of future economic and social needs of a community. It is conducted by all levels of government—federal, state, county, city, township, or borough—but is generally administered at the local level. Federal or state laws may require a local district to have a master plan and may even require that district to have certain standards within its plans of projected growth, but they (federal and state governments) rarely get directly involved in the planning process.

The concept is to have a blueprint of the future of a community and to then devise zoning ordinances and zoned districts to achieve that long range goal.

SUBDIVISION REGULATION

A subdivision is normally defined as the division of land into more lots, usually for resale. Most communities have specific subdivision regulations that require the submission of plans by a certified engineer indicating the exact subdivision desired. Some communities have classifications of subdivisions into major or minor classes, and some even require environmental impact studies prior to approvals. Some states have a full disclosure law on the sale of lots within the state, and all developers must abide by the Interstate Land Disclosure Act. This law requires a developer to register all subdivided land sold interstate with the *Office of Interstate Land Sales Registration (OILSR)*, a division of HUD of our federal government, and to provide the purchaser with a copy of a *property report* before the sale. The purchaser has a *right of rescission* within 48 hours after the receipt of this property report. The report must be a factual account of the subdivided property with emphasis on what must be considered its shortcomings. It must include the following information:

1. Date of report
2. Name and address of subdivider
3. Name and location of subdivision
4. Financing terms
5. Distances between subdivision and adjacent communities
6. Protection for buyer against developer's default
7. Information on mortgages, liens, taxes, and special assessments
8. Escrow, leasing, and title arrangements
9. Restrictions on title
10. Available recreational facilities, schools, hospitals, and medical centers
11. Available utilities and services
12. Transportation services

The penalty for misrepresentation or failure to distribute the property report may be a five-year jail sentence or a $5,000 fine plus a possible civil suit by the buyer.

HEALTH REGULATIONS

To insure that public accommodations are safe and that the conveyance of private property meets certain standards, health regulations are passed to protect the water we drink, the air we breathe, and the places in which we live or work. These regulations come directly from the police power of government to regulate the proper use of private property to protect us from ourselves.

FAIR HOUSING LAWS

Federal Fair Housing legislation includes the Civil Rights Acts of 1866 and 1964, Title VIII of the Civil Rights Act of 1968 (known as the Federal Fair Housing Act), the Housing and Community Development Act of 1974, and the Fair Housing Amendments Act of 1988. This legislation upholds the position that discrimination in the sale or leasing of housing in the United States is unlawful and against public policy. Many states have passed their own laws against discrimination which enforce and in many cases expand upon the federal restrictions. Some municipalities have extended the coverage of Fair Housing protection even beyond the laws of their own states. In answering questions on national real estate licensing exams, you must be aware of which groups of persons are protected by federal legislation; for the state portions, you must be thoroughly conversant with your own state's restrictions.

Real estate salespersons and brokers licensed by the state are strictly forbidden from practicing any form of discriminatory action. Among prohibited practices are blockbusting and steering. *Blockbusting* is the solicitation of properties for sale based upon the scare tactic that certain ethnic groups are moving in and affecting land values adversely. *Steering* is the direction of people of a certain race, religion, color, or creed to specific neighborhoods only. A licensed real estate salesperson cannot refuse to show a qualified prospect a listing, regardless of where the property is located. Furthermore, a licensee cannot participate in a discriminatory act at the direction of a principal. The obligation of an agent is to refuse to place either his principal or himself in the position of committing an unlawful act and consequently of facing possible prosecution.

Compliance with Fair Housing Laws is an absolute obligation of real estate salespersons and brokers. At the same time, the topic is one of the most sensitive ones that real estate professionals must deal with. A firm restatement of the law will serve the agent better than an emotional response to the seller who would like to engage in discriminatory practices. Likewise, the agent must keep the law in mind when tempted to show prospects properties that they would "feel most comfortable with." Remember: *Anyone has the right to live anywhere.*

The following is a summary of the provisions of Title VIII of the Civil Rights Act of 1968 as amended by the Housing and Community Development Act of 1974 to include prohibition against discrimination based on sex and by the Fair Housing Amendments Act of 1988 to include handicapping conditions and familial status. (Familial status refers to the presence of children under the age of 18, not to marital status.)

Legal Bases, Coverages and Enforcement of Fair Housing Requirements

Law

The Fair Housing Law provides protection against the following acts, if they are based on race, color, religion, sex, handicap, familial status or national origin:
• Refusing to sell or rent to, deal or negotiate with any person.
• Discriminating in terms or conditions for buying or renting housing.
• Discriminating by advertising that housing is available only to persons of a certain race, color, religion, sex, or national origin.
• Denying that housing is available for inspection, sale, or rent when it really is available.
• "Blockbusting"—For profit, persuading owners to sell or rent housing by telling them that minority groups are moving into the neighborhood.
• Denying or making different terms or conditions for home loans by commercial lenders, such as banks, savings and loan associations and insurance companies.
• Denying to anyone the use of or participation in any real estate services, such as brokers' organizations, multiple listing services or other facilities related to the selling or renting of housing.

Discrimination Prohibited

Race, color, religion, sex, handicap, familial status, national origin.

Coverage

Prohibitions contained in the Fair Housing Law apply to the following types of housing:

Single-Family housing owned by private individuals when:
• A broker or other person in the business of selling or renting dwellings is used and/or;
• Discriminatory advertising is used;
Single-family houses not owned by private individuals;
Single-family houses owned by a private individual who owns more than three such houses or who, in any two-year period, sells more than one in which the individual was not the most recent resident;
Multifamily dwellings of five or more units;
Multifamily dwellings containing four or fewer units, if the owner does not reside in one of the units.

Non-Coverage

The following acts are not covered by the Fair Housing Law:

The sale or rental of single-family houses owned by a private individual of three or fewer such single-family houses if:
• A broker is not used.
• Discriminatory advertising is not used and

• No more than one house in which the owner was not the most recent resident is sold during any two-year period.

☐ Rentals of rooms or units in owner-occupied multi-dwellings for two to four families, if discriminatory advertising is not used.

☐ Limiting the sale, rental, or occupancy of dwellings which a religious organization owns or operates for other than a commercial purpose to persons of the same religion, if membership in that religion is not restricted on account of race, color or national origin.

☐ Limiting to its own members the rental or occupancy of lodgings which a private club owns or operates for other than a commercial purpose.

Enforcement

1. Complaints can be sent to HUD.

If the discriminatory act is covered by the law, HUD will investigate the complaint. If the Secretary decides to resolve the complaint, HUD may attempt informal, confidential conciliation to end the discriminatory housing practice; or, inform the complainant of his or her right to seek immediate court action.

☐ The complaint may be referred by HUD to a State or local agency that administers a law with rights and remedies which are substantially equivalent to those of the Federal law. If the State or local agency does not commence proceedings within 30 days and carry them forward with reasonable promptness, HUD may require the case to be returned.

2. Court action by an individual.

A person may take a complaint directly to the U.S. District Court or State or local court under Section 812, within 180 days of the alleged discriminatory act, whether or not a complaint has been filed with HUD.

3. Court action by the Attorney General.

Information about possible discrimination in housing may also be brought to the attention of the Attorney General. If the resulting investigation indicates that there is a pattern or practice of resistance to full enjoyment of rights granted under Title VIII, or that a group of persons has been denied such rights and the denial raises an issue of general public importance, the Attorney General may bring court action to insure full enjoyment of the rights granted by Title VIII.

IN YOUR OWN WORDS

These are terms you should be familiar with. Check your definitions by referring to the text or to the glossary beginning on page 140.

blockbusting	non-conforming use
building inspector	right of rescission
building permit	steering
Fair Housing Laws	subdivision
health regulations	variance
high-density use	zoning
Interstate Land Disclosure Act	Zoning Board of Adjustment
low-density use	zoning ordinance
master plan	

TEST YOURSELF

1. Which of the following is not a general classification of a zoned area?
   - (a) Residential
   - (b) Industrial
   - (c) Non-conforming
   - (d) Special purpose

2. A variance will usually be granted to a private owner for conversion of his property to a use not permitted by the zoning ordinance so long as
   I. there is a public need for the use
   II. the planned use does not harm adjacent property values
   - (a) I only
   - (b) II only
   - (c) Both I and II
   - (d) Neither I nor II

3. Which of the following statements is (are) correct?
   I. A building permit can be issued even if the improvement does not conform to the zoned plan provided that the owner has applied for a variance.
   II. The improvement must conform to the zoned plan in order for a building permit to be issued.
   - (a) I only
   - (b) II only
   - (c) Both I and II
   - (d) Neither I nor II

4. All of the following are purposes of a building code EXCEPT
   - (a) To control the type of improvement
   - (b) To protect the general public
   - (c) To insure that the improvement meets minimum standards of safety
   - (d) To protect a specific owner in the construction or renovation of his improvement

5. Which of the following statements is (are) true?
   I. A master plan is a general design for the future growth of a community.
   II. The master plan is usually administered by the federal government.
   - (a) I only
   - (b) II only
   - (c) Both I and II
   - (d) Neither I nor II

6. Which of the following are requirements of the Interstate Land Disclosure Act?
   I. The developer must provide a purchaser with a copy of the HUD property report before the sale.
   II. The developer must register all subdivided land sold interstate with the *Interstate Land Sales Registration.*
   - (a) I only
   - (b) II only
   - (c) Both I and II
   - (d) Neither I nor II

7. If a principal requests a real estate agent to participate in discriminatory acts, the agent should
   I. refuse to place either the principal or himself in the position of committing an unlawful act
   II. comply with the request as only the principal would be liable for the unlawful act
   - (a) I only
   - (b) II only
   - (c) Both I and II
   - (d) Neither I nor II

8. Blockbusting is most accurately defined as
    I. directing certain groups to a particular neighborhood based on race
   II. soliciting the sales of properties by using scare tactics involving the entry of certain ethnic groups into a neighborhood
   (a) I only
   (b) II only
   (c) Both I and II
   (d) Neither I nor II

9. Which of the following is not generally included in a zoning ordinance?
   (a) Height of a structure
   (b) Side-yard distance
   (c) Set-back
   (d) Construction materials

10. Public regulations are under the jurisdiction of
    I. local government
   II. federal government
   (a) I only
   (b) II only
   (c) Both I and II
   (d) Neither I nor II

ANSWERS: 1. c   2. c   3. b   4. d   5. a   6. c   7. a   8. b   9. d   10. a

Chapter Eleven

Real Estate Mathematics

The mathematics included on real estate license examinations throughout the country normally involves seven areas of computation. The principal purpose of these test questions is to insure to the licensing agency that a broker or salesperson candidate for licensure (1) understands basic arithmetic functions; (2) knows certain business math formulas; and (3) can interpret and solve problems of a general nature. It may be necessary for candidates who have been out of school for some time to brush up on general business math or to take advantage of the more complete discussion of real estate mathematics offered by Arco's *Math Review for Real Estate Licensing Examinations*, by Susan A. Shulman.

In this chapter, the major concentration will be on understanding the types of questions posed on real estate exams and on only that knowledge the student *must* possess in order to answer them.

The seven areas normally covered in licensing examinations include:

1. Commissions and Sales Price
2. Depreciation and Appreciation
3. Measurements (Area Computations)
4. Interest Calculations (Mortgages, etc.)
5. Prorations (Closing)
6. Investment and Appraising
7. Taxes and Assessments

A word of caution is necessary as we begin our short discussion of each of the math areas covered on the examination. A professional tester is not restricted by common practice; i.e., he can structure any question in any manner consistent with proper testing techniques. A student should always remember that a question is just that—a question. It doesn't have to conform to the real world; it is just a problem to be solved. The student's objective is to read, understand, and answer the question given and nothing more.

As an example a commission is normally paid on the gross sales price; i.e., if a property sells for $50,000 and the commission rate is 7 percent, the indicated commission would be $50,000 × .07 = $3,500. Regardless of the other expenses a seller may have, the seller normally pays on the gross sales price. It does not mean that a commission problem on an examination could not be written so the student applies the commission rate to a net sales price. If, for example, in the preceding problem the seller had expenses totalling $10,000, the problem could be structured to read:

What is the rate of commission a seller would pay in the net proceeds of a sale if the selling price was $50,000 and the commission was $3,500? Seller's expenses, including mortgage payout, were $10,000.

(a) 14.3% (c) 6%

(b) 8.75% (d) 11.4%

The answer is (b). $50,000 less $10,000 = $40,000. $3,500 divided by $40,000 = .0875. Check: $40,000 times 8.75% = $3,500.

COMMISSION PROBLEMS

A *commission* is usually thought of as a percentage of the selling price and an expense to the seller. Most real estate brokers have listing agreements with owners of properties that stipulate a certain percentage will be paid to the broker when he consummates a sale satisfactory to the seller. This charge is purely a negotiated rate and can vary greatly throughout the country on the type of services offered by the broker, class of property being handled, time length of the listing contract, or even the geographic region of the country. Practically speaking, there is no standard rate of commission. The broker could even have the commission stated in his contract on a flat dollar basis. Regardless of who pays the commission, buyer or seller, it is a service charge to the incurring party.

All commission problems involve three quantities:

Rate of commission (expressed as a %)

Selling price (in dollars)

Amount of commission (in dollars)

The relationship among these quantities can be expressed as follows:

$$\text{Amount of Commission} = \text{Rate of Commission} \times \text{Selling Price}$$

$$\text{Rate of Commission} = \frac{\text{Amount of Commission}}{\text{Selling Price}}$$

$$\text{Selling Price} = \frac{\text{Amount of Commission}}{\text{Rate of Commission}}$$

The simplest kind of commission problem is one that provides two of the three quantities in the commission formula and asks you to find the third quantity. For example:

An agent sells a property for $60,000. What is the agent's commission on this sale if the commission rate is 6%?

Since the Selling Price ($60,000) and the Rate of Commission (6%) are given, you simply substitute these figures in the Amount of Commission formula to solve this problem.

$$\text{Amount of Commission} = \text{Rate of Commission} \times \text{Selling Price}$$
$$= .06 \qquad\qquad \times \$60,000$$
$$= \$3600$$

On the Real Estate License Exam, the same straightforward commission problem might appear as follows:

An owner lists his property for sale at $80,000 with the XYZ Realty Company. A 6 percent commission fee is agreed upon and the listing period is for five months. The buyer's first offer is for $50,000. The parties negotiate and the property is sold within the listing period for $60,000. At closing the broker would receive a commission of
(a) $3,000   (c) $3,600
(b) $4,800   (d) $4,200

The answer to this problem is (c), and the solution is exactly the same as given in the previous problem (.06 × $60,000 = $3600). However, the problem is complicated by the inclusion of more facts than are necessary (the listing price, the listing period and the initial offer). All you really have to know to solve this problem is that a commission rate is applied to the final selling price.

Unless otherwise stated, if more than one broker participates in a sale the commission rate is split between each *equally*. In the preceding problem, the tester could add another dimension, i.e., a co-broker, and present the problem as follows:

An owner lists his property for sale at $80,000 with the XYZ Realty Company. A 6 percent commission is agreed upon and the listing period is for five months. The buyer's first offer through the ABC Realtors is for $50,000. The parties negotiate and the property is sold within the listing period for $60,000. At closing the listing broker would receive a commission of
(a) $2,100   (c) $2,400
(b) $1,800   (d) $1,500

The answer is (b). Commission rates are always charged against the *selling price*, not the listed price or offer. Furthermore, since there are two brokers, one is considered the listing broker and the other is known as the selling broker. Since the problem is silent on the amount of a cooperative agreement, it should be assumed that an equal share would be paid to each. Therefore: $60,000 times .06 = $3,600; times 50% = $1,800.

This problem, because it includes an additional fact, could be classified as a middle-difficulty problem. It requires not only general arithmetic skills (multiplication), but also specific knowledge about the manner in which commissions are determined and sufficient reasoning power to decipher a word problem.

A still more difficult variation on a commission problem might ask the same question as the previous problem, but backwards. For example:

What was the total selling price of a property if the listing broker received $1,800 and the gross listing commission was 6 percent?
(a) $54,000   (c) $60,000
(b) $30,000   (d) $108,000

The answer is (c). Because the problem specifies that the *listing* broker received $1,800, the student is expected to recognize that there were two brokers involved in the transaction, and, therefore, the gross listing commission of 6% must be divided between them. In the absence of information about the agreement between the brokers, the student must assume that they share equally in the commission, thus receiving 3% each. Referring to the commission formula,

$$\text{Selling Price} = \frac{\text{Amount of commission}}{\text{Rate of commission}}$$

Therefore, Selling Price = $1,800 / .03 = $60,000.

On a multiple-choice examination with only four possible answers, many students have discovered that they can work backwards from the answers to solve a problem. In this case, knowing that the cooperative shared rate is 3%, you can simply multiply each answer choice by .03 until you find the one that equals $1,800. Using this method can double check your division and sometimes help you to solve a problem more quickly.

From this short discussion on commissions, a student with basic mathematical skills should be able to solve the following problems.

Which of the following sales will yield the seller exactly $23,402?

	Sales Price	Broker's Fee	Other Expenses
(a)	$25,700	6%	$400
(b)	25,000	6%	98
(c)	24,800	6%	15
(d)	24,900	6%	107

The answer is (b). All you have to do to solve this kind of problem is to work out each answer choice. Multiply sales price times broker's fee to find the broker's commission, subtract this commission from the selling price and then subtract other expenses. At answer (b) you will discover that $25,000 × .06 = $1,500. $25,000 − $1,500 = $23,500 − $98 = $23,402.

A quicker way, by use of a hand-held calculator, would be to multiply $25,000 times .94 (100% − 6% = 94%) and see $23,500 appear in the display; then just subtract $98 to yield the seller exactly $23,402.

Other students may take the number in the problem ($23,402) and add the expenses and commission to it to see if they arrive at the sales price; i.e., $23,402 plus $98 = $23,500, plus $1,500 commission = $25,000. Again, this is a good check and a sometimes valuable tool. Another example:

A house sold for $86,480, which was 8 percent under the original list price. The broker's commission fee was 5 percent. What was the original list price?

(a) $94,000 (c) $99,400
(b) $93,398 (d) $91,032

The answer is (a). In this problem the broker's commission is *unnecessary* information. The only facts you need to know are that the property sold for $86,480 and that this figure is 8 percent under the original list price. The question asks "What was the original list price?" Since the selling price was under the list price, you know that the original list price was greater, not less, than the eventual sales price. You could then say that $86,480 represents 92 percent (100% − 8%) of the original list price. By dividing $86,480 by 92% you discover that the answer is $94,000.

Again you could use each of the answers to solve the problem. Simply multiply each answer choice by .92 until you find the one that equals $86,480. This happens with the first answer choice ($94,000 × .92 = $86,480). Another example:

An agent who sells for a residential development receives a 6 percent commission on the first $90,000 of sales per month plus 2 percent on all sales over that amount. If, in one month, he sold houses for $42,000, $41,500, and $48,900, approximately how much more could he have earned had he worked on a straight 5 percent commission?

(a) $300 (c) $500
(b) $400 (d) $600

The answer is (b). The real answer is $372, but note the use of the word *approximately* in the problem. Many students complete this type of problem and get hung-up over the fact that the *right* answer is nowhere to be found, when in truth the right answer is in front of them, if they will read the problem carefully and round their figures as instructed.

The solution to this class of problem is just a lot of arithmetic. If you put your figures down in an orderly fashion, the problem solves itself.

```
 $42,000
  41,500
  48,900
 132,400 × 5% =        $6,620
 −90,000 × 6% = $5,400
 $42,400 × 2% = +  848
                    −6,248
                  $   372,   or $400
```

PRACTICE PROBLEMS   (See answers on p. 127.)

Here are five simple types of commission problems. See how well you answer them.

1. A property was listed at $70,000. It sold for $3,200 under the listing price. What was the actual sales price of the property?
   (a) $73,200 (c) $63,600
   (b) $70,000 (d) $66,800

2. An agent sells exclusively for a residential developer and receives 7 percent commission on the first $80,000 and 3 percent for all sales over that amount. If in one month he sold development houses for $37,000, $55,400, $40,800, and $43,200, how much more could he have earned had he worked on a straight 6 percent commission?
   (a) $2,092 (c) $2,892
   (b) $5,600 (d) The same amount

3. A broker's contract for selling a building called for a fee of 5 percent on the first $350,000 and 2.5 percent of everything over that amount. The broker's fee was $19,312.50. What was the sale price?
   - (a) $386,240
   - (b) $422,500
   - (c) $437,000
   - (d) $403,300

4. If one-quarter of the total commission earned in an office was derived from shared commissions of 3 percent of sales, and the balance from full commissions of 6 percent, what was the average rate of commission for the year?
   - (a) 4.25%
   - (b) 4.5%
   - (c) 4.75%
   - (d) 5.25%

5. A parcel of land sold for $250,000. The seller paid a 10 percent commission fee plus an additional $200 for miscellaneous expenses. How much will the listing person receive if his portion is 30 percent of the broker's commission fee?
   - (a) $8,333
   - (b) $7,494
   - (c) $7,560
   - (d) $7,500

DEPRECIATION/APPRECIATION PROBLEMS

Generally, it can be said that *depreciation* is a loss in value, price, or cost, and *appreciation* is a growth or increase in value, price, or cost. The rate of decline or growth can be expressed as a percentage per year (compounded) or as an overall rate for the total holding period (simple rate), or it can be expressed in dollar amounts on the same two bases.

Depreciation takes into account the *useful life*, or *economic life* of an asset. That means the period of time in which an asset is anticipated to remain economically feasible to the owner.

The annual rate of depreciation will always be a fraction with 1 over the number of years of useful life. Thus an asset with a useful life of 50 years depreciates at 1/50 = 2 percent per year. An asset with a useful life of 20 years depreciates at 1/20 = 5 percent per year. An asset with a useful life of 10 years depreciates at 1/10 or 10 percent per year.

Most real estate math problems involve *straight-line depreciation* which assumes that a property depreciates an equal amount each year. For example, according to the straight-line method, a $90,000 building that depreciates at 2 percent a year depreciates at $90,000 × .02 = $1,800 each year, or $1,800 × 3 = $5,400 for the first 3 years.

Occasionally, a problem specifies the use of *declining balance depreciation*. That means that the depreciation is deducted each year from a declining balance. For example, the same $90,000 building depreciated at 2 percent a year by the declining balance method would depreciate as follows:

1st year: $90,000 × .02 = $1800
2nd year: $90,000 − $1,800 = $88,200 × .02 = $1,764
3rd year: $88,200 − $1,764 = $86,436 × .02 = $1,728.72

$1800 + $1,764 + $1,728.72 = $5,292.72 for the first 3 years.

As with commission problems, depreciation problems on the real estate license examinations usually entail both computation and real estate knowledge. For example:

An owner wishes to sell his investment property after two years. The original purchase price was $120,000 of which $30,000 was the estimated land value. The annual maximum rate of depreciation allowed by the government on this property is 2 percent. Upon the sale, the owner's basis of capital gain would be
(a) $91,800
(c) $88,200
(b) $86,400
(d) $115,200

The answer is (b). Depreciation is only allowed or taken against improvements. For general purposes, the rate is computed each year against the original amount on a straight-line basis. Therefore, $120,000 less land value of $30,000 equals improvement value of $90,000. Therefore, $90,000 times 2% = $1,800 per year, or $3,600 total allowed depreciation. Capital gains basis would be $90,000 less $3,600 hence $86,400.

Appreciation is the reverse of depreciation; i.e., it expresses the growth of a property's value. Whereas depreciation is generally concerned only with improvement cost, price, or value, appreciation is usually expressed against the *entire* property; i.e., both land and improvements. Also, remember that what we think of these terms in the real world or how we apply them in practical situations does not restrict a tester from structuring an exam problem differently. Always read, understand, and *then* solve the problem.

Jim Jones purchased a tract of land ten years ago for $25,000. He was recently offered a price of $137,500, provided the purchaser could acquire a variance for commercial use. What would be the annual appreciation rate for this property if Mr. Jones accepts the offer?
(a) 18%
(c) 25%
(b) 55%
(d) 45%

Most students miss this problem because they forget that the tester is trying to discover if they know how to read. The question asks what the annual appreciation rate is. Since the purchase price is $137,500, many students believe they can make a direct correlation (without tables) to solve the problem. You *could* find a factor of 5½ times by dividing $137,500 by $25,000. All this states is that *over 10 years* the property's value has grown by 5½ times. You do *not* then divide by 10 and say the property has appreciated 55 percent each year. You can divide $25,000 by $137,500 and note a compounded rate of .1818. All this states is that a compounded rate, *not* an average rate, is approximately 18 percent; or, if you multiply 18 percent by $25,000, then add that number to $25,000 and multiply it by 18 percent, each succeeding time, you will over 10 years reach $137,500. This is like the compounded rate expressed in savings accounts or certificates. It might be nice to know, but doesn't solve the problem at hand.

The answer is (d). The solution is in *reading* the problem. Since the owner originally paid $25,000 and has been offered $137,500 ten years later, the quickest solution is to find out how *much* money the seller received each year. Therefore, $137,500 less $25,000 = $112,500; divided by 10 = $11,250 each year. *Now* this sum of money divided by $25,000 = 45%, the rate of the annual dollar increase to the original purchase price.

A real estate investor purchased two lots, one of which cost $8,000. This was 40 percent of the cost of the second lot. What was the cost of the second lot?

    (a) $13,300   (c) $20,000

    (b) $11,200   (d) $24,000

The answer is (c). The problem is relatively basic; i.e., it states that lot number one is 40 percent of lot number two. Multiply each answer by 40 percent, until you find the one that gives you $8,000 ($20,000 × 40%); that one is answer (c). Alternatively, you can divide $8000 by 40% to arrive at the answer ($8000 ÷ .40 = $20,000).

NOTE: Appreciation and depreciation problems can have a number of variations. You must read each word and translate the problem into a proper answer.

If it cost a subdivider $18,000 to build a house several years ago, and prices rose to 35 percent above original cost and then decreased to $7\frac{1}{2}$ percent below this high point, approximately what would it cost to build today?

    (a) $20,500   (c) $22,500

    (b) $22,950   (d) $26,100

The answer is (c). This is a mixed problem of appreciation and a form of depreciation in price lost, but not of value. Many students believe they can mix the percentages by taking 35 percent and subtracting from it the $7\frac{1}{2}$ percent to achieve an overall growth rate of 27.5 percent. But this is *wrong!* The problem states $7\frac{1}{2}$ percent below the high point, and you must know the high point first. You can multiply these rates, but you must change them to factors first. The easiest way to solve the problem is to do what the problem tells you to do; i.e., take $18,000 and add 35% or $6,300 ($18,000 × .35) to find an appreciated price of $24,300, and then deduct $7\frac{1}{2}$ percent from it or $1,822.50 ($24,300 × .075) to compute a balance of $22,477.50, which is approximately $22,500.

Using your hand-held calculator, take $18,000 and multiply it by 1.35 to find $24,300; then multiply again by 92.5% (100% − $7\frac{1}{2}$%) to calculate $22,477.50.

Or, if you know factors, you can multiply the appreciation rate of 1.35 by .925 to find an overall factor of 1.24875, and multiply this by $18,000 to arrive at $22,477.50.

There are many ways to solve these problems. Pick the one that works best for you and use it. However, if you get stuck, just do what the problem tells you to do (diagram it) and the problem will cease to give you difficulty.

PRACTICE PROBLEMS
(See answers on p. 128)

1. The value of a house at the end of 8 years was $189,000. What was its original cost, to the nearest $100, if the house appreciated in value at a rate of 6 percent per year of the original cost?

    (a) $132,800   (c) $127,700

    (b) $128,000   (d) $127,800

2. A property purchased for $560,000 depreciates at the rate of 5 percent per year over the previous year's value. What is its approximate value at the end of the third year?

    (a) $481,000   (c) $480,100

    (b) $505,400   (d) $465,500

3. Mr. Jones paid $28,000 for a property that he later offered for sale at a 15 percent profit. When the property did not sell at this price, he reduced his price by 5 percent. The property sold at the reduced price. How much did he gain on the sale?

   (a) $2,590

   (b) $2,400

   (c) $2,800

   (d) $1,250

4. If a $140,000 building depreciates at twice the rate of its useful life of 40 years, its first-year depreciation would be

   (a) $3,500

   (b) $14,000

   (c) $7,000

   (d) $6,000

5. A man sold a property for $15,000 losing 15 percent of his original purchase price. Approximately what did the property cost him originally?

   (a) $16,250

   (b) $17,650

   (c) $12,750

   (d) $17,250

MEASUREMENTS
(AREA COMPUTATIONS)

Anyone and everyone involved in real estate must know how to estimate or express the size of land or buildings. The student must bring to the test center (1) some knowledge of formulas for calculating area; (2) the ability to convert the various units of measurement; e.g., 43,560 square feet equals one acre; and (3) a grasp of basic terms; e.g., *area*, which is the total surface within the boundaries of a figure.

Following are the *basic formulas* a student must know in order to answer questions on the examination. **Know them!**

1. Area of a rectangle: $A = 1 \times w$.
   Area (in square units) equals length times width.
2. Volume of a rectangle: $V = 1 \times w \times h$.
   Volume (in cubic units) equals length times width times height.
3. Area of a triangle: $A = \dfrac{b \times h}{2}$.
   Area (in square units) equals base times height divided by two.

These are the *basic units of measurement a student must bring to the test center*. **Memorize them!**

1 foot = 12 inches

1 yard = 3 feet

1 mile = 5,280 linear feet

1 square foot = 144 square inches

1 square yard = 9 square feet

1 cubic yard = 27 cubic feet

1 square mile = 640 acres

1 acre = 43,560 square feet

These are the *basic terms* students must know when they take the examination. **Learn them!**

AREA: The total surface within the boundaries of a figure.

PERIMETER: Total distance around the boundary of an object or parcel of property.

FRONTAGE: Measurement along a street or streets.

VOLUME: The amount of space any three-dimensional shape contains.

A typical problem that demonstrates why knowledge of formulas is required is as follows:

Mr Jones sold one-fourth of an acre to his neighbor. Mr. Jones was asking $1.25 per square foot. Approximately how much money did Mr. Jones receive for this sale?
(a) $21,780   (c) $13,600
(b) $5,445   (d) $6,806

The answer is (c). The first thing you must know is that 43,560 square feet equals one acre. Therefore, one-fourth (25%) of it is 10,890 square feet (43,560 × .25); then multiply 10,890 square feet by $1.25 to arrive at $13,612, which is approximately $13,600. We can take the same type of problem and make a diagram out of it and require the student to make some further calculations. For example:

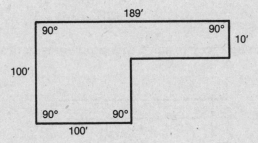

At what price did Mr. Jones sell this tract of land if he sold it at $54,450 per acre?
(a) $21,780   (c) $13,600
(b) $5,445   (d) $6,806

The answer is (c). First you must know that 43,560 square feet equals an acre. Dividing $54,450 by 43,560 = $1.25 per square foot. Now you must find the size of the figure above. By breaking the figure down into areas (as shown in the following diagram), you learn that the area of section 1 is 100 feet times 100 feet = 10,000 square feet; the area of section 2 is 10 feet times 89 feet = 890 square feet. Together they equal 10,890 square feet and this, multiplied by $1.25, equals $13,612, rounded to $13,600.

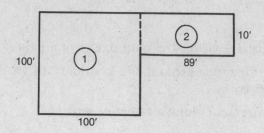

A room measured 16' × 24'. In a rectangular scaledown, the same room measured 4" × 6". What would an 8" square room measure in square feet?

(a) 384   (c) 32

(b) 64   (d) 1024

The answer is (d). The first step is to discover the relationship between the scaledown and the actual room. Note that the scaledown relationship is in the form of a ratio; i.e., 4 inches to 16 feet is equivalent to 1 inch for 4 feet, and 6 inches to 24 feet yields the same ratio. Therefore, by using the ratio of 1 inch for 4 feet, we multiply the 8 inch scaledown times 4 to arrive at a square room 32 feet on each side. 32 feet times 32 feet = 1024 square feet.

NOTE: Similar problems could relate to maps; i.e., 1 inch = 1 mile, or to blueprints; i.e., 1/4 inch = 1 foot. The purpose is to test your reasoning power. Look for any relationship between two numbers in the problem and then relate them to the solution.

How many square feet of concrete would be required to build a 6-foot wide sidewalk around a pool measuring 25' by 40'?

(a) 780   (c) 924

(b) 980   (d) 1124

The answer is (c). The best way to solve this problem is to draw the pool and the sidewalk around it.

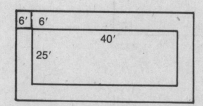

Now you can see that you have two rectangles:

1. The pool which measures 40 × 25 and therefore has an area of 1000 square feet (40 × 25 = 1000)
2. The pool plus the walk which measures (40 + 6 + 6) × (25 + 6 + 6) and therefore has an area of 1924 square feet (52 × 37 = 1924)

The area of the walk is the area of the pool plus the walk minus the area of the pool: 1924 − 1000 = 924 square feet.

NOTE: Other similar problems may involve finding the area of a parking lot that surrounds a building or a yard that surrounds a house. In each case, draw a picture first, then solve the problem.

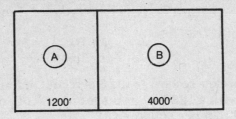

In the diagram above, if lot "A" contains 55 acres, how many acres does lot "B" contain?

(a) 165 acres   (c) 183 acres

(b) 110 acres   (d) 150 acres

The answer is (c). You will note that there is no depth given for either lot. You must know that 43,560 square feet equals one acre. To solve the problem, convert 55 acres of lot "A" into 2,395,800 square feet, and then divide by 1200 feet to arrive at the lot's depth of 1,996.5 feet. Once you know this, it is a simple problem of multiplying 4000 feet by 1996.5 feet to find the area of lot "B" or 7,986,000 square feet. Then divide by 43,560 square feet to discover that the lot is 183.33 acres.

NOTE: There are many problems a tester may give you in which you have to determine depths and areas before you can seek or apply a solution. Understand the concept and you can solve any of these problems.

Some students might work the previous problem by developing a ratio between 1200 feet and 55 acres, knowing that the lot depth is constant. By dividing 55 acres by 1200 feet you find a ratio of .0458. If you take all the answers and divide them by 4000 feet, only one will give you .0458, and that is (c) (183 ÷ 4000 − .04575). Since the ratio of apportionment is the same, the answer has to be (c). Again, we have used the answers to solve the problem.

Although it is important to know certain concepts or formulas, it is more important to *understand* these concepts. Measurement problems can be so varied on any examination that it is virtually impossible to cover them all by example. The following is an array of problems to aid you in understanding the various concepts employed.

As stated earlier, test-wise students do not worry about a few problems on an examination. A good rule is to answer all the easy questions on an examination first, then attack the more difficult or time-consuming problems at the end of the examination.

PRACTICE PROBLEMS   (See answers on p. 128.)

1. A broker is subdividing a 4½ acre tract into 50′ × 100 ′ lots. After allowing 71,020 square feet for the necessary streets, into how many lots can the tract be divided?

   (a) 39   (c) 14

   (b) 25   (d) 8

2. Find the number of square feet in a plot of ground with a frontage of 80 feet 6 inches and a depth of 150 feet 9 inches. (Round your answer.)
   (a) 8,512
   (b) 10,000
   (c) 12,135
   (d) 12,153

3. Mr. Klink was contracted by Mr. Katz to build a sidewalk 4 feet wide and 90 feet long. Mr. Klink charges $2.45 per square yard. How much will Mr. Katz have to pay?
   (a) $294
   (b) $98
   (c) $198
   (d) $249

4. How much will a broker receive as his 6 percent commission fee for the sale of a triangular lot with a 122-foot frontage and a depth of 124 feet if the sales price is based at $2.25 per square foot?
   (a) $1,701.90
   (b) $1,004.67
   (c) $2,042.28
   (d) $1,021.14

5. Mr. Lyons is purchasing 4/5 of a piece of land measuring 2,178,000 square feet at $2,500 per acre. What is the total price he will pay?
   (a) $100,000
   (b) $54,450
   (c) $43,560
   (d) $400,000

6. Find the area of the following diagram. This diagram is not drawn to scale.

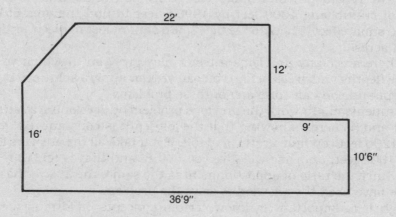

   (a) 945 square feet
   (b) 1,640.19 square feet
   (c) 495 square feet
   (d) 700.19 square feet

7. What is the cost of constructing a 6 foot, 6 inch high fence around a property with a frontage of 90 feet and a depth of 175 feet if the cost of erecting the fence is $.75 per foot and the cost of material is $.625 per square foot?
   (a) $2,153
   (b) $2,550
   (c) $397
   (d) None of these

8. A room measures 9 feet × 12 feet. In a scaledown of the same room the measurements are 3 inches × 4 inches. What would the width be, in feet, of a similarly scaled down 5 inch square room?
   (a) 10 feet
   (b) 15 feet
   (c) 12 feet
   (d) 20 feet

9. If a lot with a frontage of 72 feet and a depth of 127 feet sold for $13,716, what was the price per square foot?
   (a) $1.50
   (b) $9.14
   (c) $1.91
   (d) $6.89

10. What would be the total listing price for 116 acres listed at $.05 per square foot?
    (a) $246,848
    (c) $252,648
    (b) $505,296
    (d) $580,000

INTEREST CALCULATIONS

Interest is a charge for the use of money over a period of time. It is usually expressed in a common formula:

$$I = P \times R \times T$$
$$\text{Interest} = \text{Principal} \times \text{Rate} \times \text{Time}$$

Time is usually an annual period. If you were asked what the interest would be on $1,000 at 6 percent for 1 year, you would compute it as follows:

$$I = \$1,000 \times .06 \times 1$$
$$I = \$60$$

If you know the formula, you can compute interest for a partial year, a full year, or many years just by changing the time factor.

Regardless of the length of the loan, interest is usually stated in terms of an *annual percentage rate (APR)*. To find the interest rate for a single month, simply divide the annual rate by 12. Thus an annual interest rate of 12% is 12%/12 = 1% per month. An annual rate of 9% = 9%/12 = .75% (or 3/4%) per month. An annual rate of 6% = 6%/12 = .50% (or 1/2%) per month.

The simplest kind of interest problem is one like this:

What is the total interest due on a $5,000 note at 8 percent for 18 months?
    (a) $400
    (c) $600
    (b) $800
    (d) $1,000

The answer is (a). First change 18 months to years. 18 months = 1 year 6 months or 1.5 years. Next substitute the given figures in the Interest formula.

$$\text{Interest} = \text{Principle} \times \text{Rate} \times \text{Time}$$
$$= \$5000 \times .08 \times 1.5$$
$$= \$600$$

Alternatively, you can compute monthly interest by finding the dollar amount of yearly interest and dividing by 12. Thus to find the monthly interest on the same $5,000 note at 8 percent for 18 months, you would simply multiply the principal times the annual interest rate and then divide the result by 12.

$$\$5000 \times .08 = \$400 \text{ (interest per year)}$$
$$\$400 \div 12 = \$33.33 \text{ (interest per month)}$$
$$\$33.33 \times 18 = \$599.94 \text{ (interest for 18 months)}$$

The same problem becomes a bit more difficult when presented in reverse as illustrated below:

Mr. Brown paid $600 interest for a note to be held for 18 months. The original note was in the amount of $5,000. What was the percentage of annual interest charged?

(a) 6%   (c) 10%

(b) 8%   (d) 12%

The answer is (b). Remembering that interest problems are calculated in terms of a year, the first step in solving this problem is to find the amount of interest Brown paid for one year. To do this, divide the 18 month interest payment by 1.5 years: $600 ÷ 1.5 = $400. Next, divide the yearly interest by the principal to find the rate of interest: $400 ÷ $5,000 = .08 = 8%.

The same formula is also the basis for mortgage payments, the only difference being that a portion of the principal is included in the payout period. In this way a mortgage becomes self-liquidating (amortized).

As an example, if we know that the monthly payments on a $1,000 mortgage for 25 years at 9 percent interest are $8.39, then the annual payment is $8.39 times 12 months or $100.68. We know that this sum of money ($100.68) is greater than the pure interest of 9 percent on $1,000 (or $90). The difference then is the payoff of the money borrowed over 25 years. Thus in the first year the difference between $100.68 and $90, or $10.68, is going toward the reduction of the original $1,000 indebtedness. Of course, this is only a generalized example and only explains the difference between an indebtedness that is reduced (amortized) and one that is not. Most mortgages are direct reduction loans; many short-term loans charge interest only with lump-sum repayment.

Mortgage problems may ask for the interest payable in any given month or the loan balance at some point during the life of the loan. The following problem illustrates how a self-amortizing, equal payment loan works.

The Moores take a $40,000 mortgage at 12% for 30 years. Their mortgage payments are $412 per month. After making 3 monthly payments, what is the balance of the Moore's loan?

(a) $38,764.00   (c) $39,963.64

(b) $38,800.36   (d) $41,200.00

The answer is (c). To solve this problem, you must first determine the monthly interest rate:

12% per year = 12%/12 = 1% per month

First Month   Amount of loan = $40,000
Payment = $412
Interest = $40,000 × .01 = $400
$412 − $400 = $12 Amount applied to reduce loan

Second Month   Amount of loan = $40,000 − $12 = $39,988
Payment = $412
Interest = $39,988 × .01 = $399.88
$412 − $399.88 = $12.12 Amount applied to reduce loan

Third Month   Amount of loan = $39,988 − $12.12 = $39,975.88
Payment = $412
Interest = $39,975.88 × .01 = $399.76
$412 − $399.76 = $12.24 Amount applied to reduce loan

Fourth Month   Amount of loan = $39,975.88 − $12.24 = $39,963.64

On a house valued at $60,000, a $15,000 loan was obtained to add a garage. The payments are to be $150 per month plus 9 percent interest on the decreasing balance. The loan was made on October 15th, and all interest and principal payments are due on the 15th of each month thereafter. What amount will be due on November 15th?

(a) $112.50
(b) $150.00
(c) $262.50
(d) $487.50

The answer is (c). The first thing to determine is the monthly interest. $15,000 times 9% = $1,350 annual interest. Divide $1,350 by 12 to find the monthly interest of $112.50. Add this to the principal payment of $150 to obtain a total first payment of $262.50 ($150.00 + $112.50).

Using the previous example as the basis, what amount will be due on December 15th?

(a) $150.00
(b) $259.41
(c) $261.38
(d) $262.50

The answer is (c). Now the problem asks what the balance is before you compute interest. In this case only one principal payment of $150 was made. Therefore, the original principal of $15,000 is reduced by $150 to $14,850; times 9% = $1,336.50 annual interest; divided by 12 = monthly interest of $111.375, or $111.38. Add this to the principal payment of $150, which gives you $261.38.

Mortgage problems may also require certain calculations concerning discount points. When answering these questions it is important for you to keep in mind which party is paying the points. In the case of an FHA or VA guaranteed mortgage, the seller pays the points. The seller pays these points directly to the buyer's lender at the closing. Most mortgages are neither FHA nor VA guaranteed but are rather conventional mortgages. Points charged with a conventional mortgage loan are charged against the buyer or borrower. In the case of a conventional mortgage loan, the sum of the points is deducted from the loan itself. The buyer must make up the difference at closing from his own funds. In calculating "point problems" remember that a point represents 1 percent of the loan, not 1 percent of the purchase price.

Thus if you must pay 2 points on a $10,000 loan, you actually get the use of $9,800, yet you pay interest on the full $10,000. Here's how discounting works:

$$2 \text{ points} = 2\% = .02$$
$$\$10,000 \times .02 = \$200 \text{ (discount)}$$
$$\$10,000 - \$200 = \$9,800 \text{ (cash advance from lender)}$$

PRACTICE PROBLEMS

(See answers on p. 129.)

1. During the life of variable rate loans, a bank always charges 140 percent of the rate it pays on savings accounts. If the rate paid on savings varies during the life of the loan from 2.5 percent to 6 percent, then the interest on the loan varies from

(a) 2.00 to 4.80
(b) 2.80 to 8.50
(c) 3.25 to 8.00
(d) 3.50 to 8.40

2. In preparation for acquiring a property, Ben Wilson obtained a mortgage loan of $35,490, which was 70 percent of the total sales price. He also deposited a 15 percent earnest money deposit with the broker. What was the amount of the earnest money deposit?

    (a) $5,070.00 (c) $7,605.00
    (b) $5,323.50 (d) $2,282.00

3. Mr. Abbott borrowed $7,200 from the bank at 14 percent interest so that he could modernize his home. If he repaid the principal and the interest in one payment at the end of 7 months, what was the total amount he paid the bank?

    (a) $8,288.00 (c) $7,788.00
    (b) $7,200.00 (d) $7,588.00

4. Ms. Long borrowed $2,400 at the going annual interest rate of 18 percent. The terms of the loan stipulate that she is to repay the loan with semiannual payments of $600 plus interest. What will her first payment be?

    (a) $600 (c) $1,032
    (b) $432 (d) $816

5. If a lending company wishes to earn $288.00 interest in one year on a loan of $1,800, what interest rate should it charge?

    (a) 16% (c) $17\frac{1}{4}$%
    (b) $15\frac{1}{2}$% (d) $16\frac{3}{4}$%

6. To purchase a house at the price of $172,000, Brown obtained a mortgage for $108,000 for 20 years at a rate of 10.75% plus $2\frac{1}{2}$ points. At signing of contract of sale, Brown paid $17,200. What is the balance that he must pay at closing?

    (a) $2,700 (c) $108,000
    (b) $49,500 (d) $154,800

PRORATIONS (CLOSING)

Proration, as applied to real estate, is best defined as sharing of costs between two or more parties. All a student needs to know is that the problem usually states all the facts necessary for its own solution. The student must read the problem and then decide on the division necessary to apportion the costs or expenses stated. Here are some examples:

> An office building is listed at $175,000. One offer received by a prospective buyer was the assumption of the $85,000 mortgage and $80,000 in cash. If the seller accepts this deal and authorizes the broker to deduct $577 for the transfer tax, $650 for title insurance, and a 10 percent commission fee, how much will the seller receive from a 20 percent earnest money deposit?
>
> (a) $15,273 (c) $17,273
> (b) $14,273 (d) $16,273

The answer is (a). Reading, as stated earlier, is the biggest problem for students on this examination. In this problem the question is what the seller will receive from a deposit of 20 percent held by his broker after certain deductions. The first computation is to determine how much that deposit was; therefore $165,000 times 20% = $33,000. Subtracted from that is a 10 percent commission on

$165,000 (selling price) and two miscellaneous costs of $577 and $650, which leaves the amount of $15,273.

NOTE: It makes no difference whether or not this procedure is used in actual practice; all that is required is to read, interpret, and solve the problem.

> Title insurance on a property is $232.70. In addition, the following costs are incurred: title search fee—$65.00; cost of preparing the papers—$20.00; appraisal fee—$40.00; and miscellaneous fees—$8.30. If the seller pays 70 percent of the total charges and the buyer pays the rest, how much more does the seller pay than the buyer?
> (a) $109.80   (c) $146.40
> (b) $366.00   (d) $256.20

The answer is (c). The first step is to add up all the costs, which total $366. The seller absorbs 70 percent of this, or $256.20, and the buyer $109.80. The difference between these two numbers is $146.40.

> How much cash will a buyer need at the closing after he has deposited with the broker a $7,000 earnest money deposit and after he has acquired a mortgage loan for 65 percent of the $48,500 sales price on a property that he is purchasing?
> (a) $9,975   (c) $41,500
> (b) $16,975   (d) $24,525

The answer is (a). This is a typical proration problem. On the sale price of $48,500 the buyer has a mortgage of 65 percent, or $31,525. If you deduct this plus the $7,000 deposit from the sales price, you will see that the buyer owes $9,975.

> Closing is set for April 20. School taxes at the rate of 3.60 per thousand assessed value are levied on a tax year of February 1 to January 31 and are payable March 1. Town taxes at the rate of 1.20 per thousand are payable on May 1 for a tax year of April 1 through March 31. The assessed value of the property is $60,000. At the time of closing all tax payments are current as of date payable. For tax purposes, 1 month = 30 days. At closing
> (a) buyer pays seller $480 school tax
>   buyer pays seller $40 town tax
> (b) seller pays buyer $1,680 school tax
>   seller pays buyer $00 town tax
> (c) buyer pays seller $1,680 school tax
>   buyer pays seller $00 town tax
> (d) seller pays buyer $480 school tax
>   seller pays buyer $40 town tax

The answer to this complicated problem is (c). At closing, taxes must be prorated so that the seller pays all taxes up to and including the day of closing, and the buyer takes responsibility for all taxes after that date. If the seller has already paid taxes, the buyer must refund to the seller tax monies beginning with the day after closing. If the seller has not yet paid taxes which were assessed for a period during which he held title to the property, he must advance to the buyer the portion of the taxes that buyer will pay which include that time. In this illustration, the annual school tax rate is $2,160 (60 × 3.6) which means $180 per month. The seller has paid taxes for the full year but is responsible for only 2 and

2/3 months (Feb., March, and 2/3 April). The buyer must remit to seller school taxes for nine and 1/3 months. $180 × 9⅓ = $1,680. The town tax, on the other hand, while assessed has not yet been paid. The town tax year begins April 1 but taxes are not due until May 1. On May 1, buyer will have to pay a town tax bill of $720 (60 × 1.2) which will include town taxes for the first 20 days of April. An annual bill of $720 means a monthly charge of $60. Since the buyer will pay the seller's taxes for 2/3 of one month, the seller must advance to the buyer $40. Reread the four answer choices to confirm that only choice (c) is a totally correct statement.

PRACTICE PROBLEMS

(See answers on p. 130.)

1. Louis Townsend agreed to assume a $15,000 mortgage on a property he was purchasing for $35,000. He also deposited 15 percent earnest money. If the seller authorized the broker to deduct his 7 percent commission, title insurance expenses of $195, and the transfer tax fee of $70, how much will the broker owe the seller at closing?

    (a) $3,300   (c) $3,247
    (b) $3,450   (d) $2,535

2. The tax year in a community begins each July 1. On July 1, Mr. Jones paid $745 as his full property taxes. On January 1 he had paid a total premium of $126 on a 3-year fire insurance policy, effective immediately. Using the above information, determine the prorated amount to be returned to Mr. Jones when he sells his property on October 28.

    (a) $592.00   (c) $279.00
    (b) $244.00   (d) $220.00

3. When J. Sutherland sold his house, the buyer assumed the unpaid balance of the mortgage. The monthly mortgage payment had been paid on August 10. The unpaid balance of Mr. Sutherland's 8 percent interest mortgage was $11,500. What was the amount of the accrued interest if the closing was held on September 2?

    (a) $168.67   (c) $51.11
    (b) $58.88   (d) $20.44

4. A house is sold on August 6 (settlement date). The yearly taxes on this house amount to $361.20 and had been paid in advance by the seller of the house earlier in the year. Find the amount due back to the seller, as a credit on the tax he paid, on the day of settlement. (Assume taxes paid on January 1.)

    (a) $361.20   (c) $145.50
    (b) $215.70   (d) $185.35

5. An apartment building contains 7 apartments that rent for $250 each per month. When the building was sold, the January rents had been collected before the January 27 closing date. Each tenant had also placed a security deposit on his apartment in the amount of one month's rent. What was the rent proration for this transaction? NOTE: rents are only prorated for amounts already collected. Security deposits are not prorated, but the amounts will be transferred to the new owner.

    (a) $1,524.15   (c) $225.80
    (b) $169.35   (d) $233.32

INVESTMENT AND APPRAISING

This type of problem determines what a parcel of real property or personal property is worth. The purpose is not only to test math skills and reasoning ability but to see if the student knows the various approaches to value and how to apply them.

Refer to Chapter 8, "Appraising," in conjunction with the following problems.

COST APPROACH TO VALUE PROBLEMS

An appraiser has been hired by the state to estimate the value of a property being taken for public use. The house was built two years prior to the date of taking. The house has a total floor area of 2,374 square feet, and the estimated current replacement cost of $18 per square foot has been established. If the land value is $11,000 and the annual depreciation charge is $2,500, what is the estimated value of the real estate? (Round your answer to the nearest hundred.)

    (a) $32,200   (c) $51,200
    (b) $48,700   (d) $54,700

The answer is (b). To solve this problem the student has to know that the steps in the cost approach to value are as follows:

1. Compute land value
2. Compute cost new
3. Compute depreciation
4. Deduct depreciation from cost new
5. Add land value to depreciated building or improvement value

In step one of this problem, the land value has been given at $11,000. In step two of this problem, the cost new is 2,374 square feet at $18 per square foot, or $42,732. In step three, annual depreciation is given at $2,500, and the residence is two years old; therefore, $2,500 times 2 = $5,000 total depreciation. In step four, cost new of $42,732 less $5,000 depreciation equals current value of $37,732. Step five is to add together the land value and the building value ($11,000 + $37,732 = $48,732, or $48,700).

When you have a problem regarding the cost approach to value, use these steps. You will note that everything flows easily and the problem solves itself.

Remember that land value may have to be computed and that depreciation may be expressed as a percentage, but that depreciation is taken only against cost new of the improvements and not against the land value.

MARKET APPROACH TO VALUE PROBLEMS

These problems usually relate to unit value measurements like "so much per front foot," "so much per acre," or "so much per square foot," and may involve a comparison with a similar property, with or without adjustments.

What is the probable value of a two-story, seven room residence if a similar residence of eight rooms just sold for $82,000?

    (a) $71,750   (c) $70,000

    (b) $82,000   (d) None of the above

The answer is (a). The only unit given is "per room." Therefore, if you divide $82,000 by 8 rooms you note the per-room price of $10,250, and this price times the 7 rooms of the subject property equals $71,750.

Of course, there is an infinite number of units that a tester can employ in comparison or market value problems. These units will be clear, however, if the student recognizes what is being asked and knows that some logic must be applied to his response.

The owner of a block of 14 building lots, each with a frontage of 75 feet, desires to realize $33,750 from the sale of said lots, while withholding 2 lots for himself. What must the sales price be per front foot on the lots sold?

    (a) $45.00   (c) $90.00

    (b) $32.14   (d) $37.50

The answer is (d). If the owner is going to hold two lots, then he is only going to sell twelve. These 12 lots, 75 feet each, equal 900 front feet (12 lots $\times$ 75'). Therefore, his desired price of $33,750 divided by 900 feet = $37.50 for each front foot.

INCOME APPROACH TO VALUE PROBLEMS

Also known as *investment problems,* this approach to value has to do with computing net incomes, yield, and final values. Net income from any investment is the money that is left after all expenses have been met. Net income and expenses are computed on an annual basis. Yield is computed *only* on the net income and is usually expressed as an annual interest or capitalization rate of return. The value of an income stream of money from property, savings accounts or bonds is based upon the investor's expected yield calculated by dividing the net annual income by the yield (capitalization) rate.

An office building produces an annual gross income of $200,000. What would be the capital value of this building if the expenses were 50 percent of the gross income and the investor expected a 10 percent return on his money?

    (a) $2,000,000   (c) $1,500,000

    (b) $1,000,000   (d) None of the above

The answer is (b). Structuring this simple problem is the best way to reflect the principle stated earlier.

1. Net Income = Gross Income − Expenses

       Gross Income $200,000

       Expenses (50% of $200,000)   − 100,000

       Net Income $100,000

2. Capital Value = $\dfrac{\text{Net Annual Income}}{\text{Yield (Capitalization) Rate}}$

                = $100,000 ÷ .10 = $1,000,000

NOTE: The point to remember is that even though the answer is very obvious here, because the problem is basically easy, this method would work no matter how unusual the numbers were. Always refer to a simple problem when you are presented with a difficult one and know that if the "steps" work there, then they will work equally well on the more difficult problem.

What would a dry cleaning business be worth if it earns a net profit of $975 per month and produces a return of 1 percent per month on the total investment?

(a) $81,250   (c) $9,750

(b) $97,500   (d) $1,404

The answer is (b). The average student has been taught that an annual net return divided by an annual overall rate equals value. You can take $975 per month and multiply it by 12 to obtain the annual net income of $11,700. This is then divided by 12% (1% per month times 12) to find the correct answer of $97,500.

However, you can divide monthly net income ($975) by the monthly net rate of return (1%) to achieve the same answer of $97,500. The key to this type of problem is to learn *not* to mix monthly rates with yearly income and/or expenses. You must be consistent with your use of rates, income, and expenses and not mix unlike quantities.

PRACTICE PROBLEMS
(See answers on p. 130.)

1. Find the estimated replacement cost of a building 65 feet by 40 feet if the estimated cost is $12.95 per square foot.

(a) $26,000   (c) $51,800

(b) $33,670   (d) $54,714

2. Each of 12 apartments can be rented thusly:

(1) At $120 per month with utilities

(2) At $90 per month without utilities

If the cost of utilities for each of the 12 apartments averages $15 per month, the net annual income under option (1) is

(a) $2,160 more than under option (2)

(b) $4,320 more than under option (2)

(c) $2,160 less than under option (2)

(d) $4,320 less than under option (2)

3. If a business property has been valued at $100,000, and a prospective buyer wishes to earn 15 percent annually on his total investment, what should the net monthly income be?

(a) $1,250   (c) $6,667

(b) $1,500   (d) $5,556

4. Mr. Sinclair wishes to buy an income property that grosses $300 per month. If the total annual expenses on this property are $1,200, and Mr. Sinclair wants a 12 percent return on his investment, how much should he offer for this property?

(a) $36,000   (c) $28,800

(b) $24,000   (d) $20,000

5. An appraiser has estimated the current replacement cost of a one-year-old building to be $57,000. The building is situated on a plot of land valued at $13,000. If the depreciation has been calculated to be $7,000 annually, what is the estimated value of this property?

    (a) $50,000   (c) $77,000

    (b) $63,000   (d) $56,000

TAXES AND ASSESSMENTS

A *tax* is a charge or lien placed against property or income. A tax rate is usually expressed in a relationship to an assessment levied, such as 3 dollars per hundred or 30 cents per thousand. What the student needs to know in this type of problem is something about decimals.

A decimal is essentially a fraction. The numerator consists of the numbers following the decimal point, and the denominator is 1 followed by a zero for each number in the numerator. Thus:

$$.1 = \frac{1}{10}, \quad .02 = \frac{2}{100}, \quad .003 = \frac{3}{1,000}, \quad .0004 = \frac{4}{10,000}$$

Each is expressed thusly:

.1 is one-tenth

.02 is two-hundredths

.003 is three-thousandths

.0004 is four-ten-thousandths

When a problem states "the tax rate is $3.00 per $100 of assessment," this rate can be expressed in decimal form as .03, by moving the decimal point two places to the left.

$$\$3.00 \text{ per hundred} = \frac{3}{100} \text{ or } .03$$

NOTE: Some students will quickly note that this is the same as 3% and is therefore mathematically correct.

A tax rate per thousand can be expressed as a decimal by moving the decimal point three places to the left; therefore

$$\$3.00 \text{ per thousand} = \frac{3}{1000} \text{ or } .003$$

REMEMBER: Rule #1 on tax problems is know the basis of the tax rate and express it in a proper decimal structure.

The second part of a tax problem is the basis of the assessment. Assessment can be based on an entire income or a property's value or a portion of income or value. Again, the secret here is to read the problem presented and know what the tax rate is being applied to.

REMEMBER: Rule #2 is know the basis of the assessment.

> The county tax rate is $3.20 per $100 of assessed value. The county assessor has placed a true value of $40,000 on Mr. Jones' residence. What are the annual taxes on this property if the assessment is 50 percent of the true value?
>
> (a) $320   (c) $1,280
>
> (b) $640   (d) $6,400

The answer is (b). The tax rate is *always* applied to the assessment, not to the basis of the assessment. *Rule # 2*—multiply $40,000 true value (or tax basis) by 50 percent to find $20,000, the tax assessment. *Rule # 1*—by moving the decimal point on the assessment rate two places to the left, the tax rate is structured properly. Now the tax rate can be applied directly to this assessment to determine the annual taxes. Therefore, $20,000 times .032 = $640.

NOTE: Some math books state that when you have a tax problem you can move the decimal point in your answer. This is correct, but you may forget this important step when choosing your answer. Professional testers know this and will give you probable incorrect answers such as answer (d) in the sample problem. Also, some math books state that you can divide by 100 after you have completed the problem. This is also true, but again may be forgotten if not done at the outset. The best procedure is to convert your tax rate to a proper decimal and your value to a proper assessment *before* you proceed to solve a tax problem.

Tax assessment problems may be structured in a manner completely different from that with which the student is familiar in his or her own area. Again, tax problems on an examination need not be practical. They are only designed to test your skills and reading comprehension.

Tax problems may ask you to find annual, semiannual, quarterly, or monthly tax payments on income or property, or they may ask you to solve for assessments, rates, or ratios. If you know the concept—tax rate times tax assessment = taxes—you can solve any problem.

> George Brown just purchased a new house for $54,000. He was informed that his taxes would be $1,958.04 per year, based on the township's tax rate of $3.70 per $100 of assessed value. What is the assessed value of his property?
>
> (a) $45,465   (c) $52,920
>
> (b) $46,755   (d) $54,000

The answer is (c). You know that the rate ($3.70) times the assessment equals $1,958.04 in annual taxes. What you don't know is the assessment. You can therefore multiply the rate times each of the answers, and only one is going to give you $1,958.04; that is (c) or $52,920. Or you can divide $1,958.04 by .0370 and discover that the answer is $52,920, which is answer choice (c).

> A house is currently assessed at $47,200. It was formerly assessed at $20,000. The tax rate was $6.50 per $100. Due to a recent revaluation, the tax rate is decreased by $3.40 per $100. What is the new monthly property tax payment?
>
> (a) $108.33   (c) $133.73
>
> (b) $121.93   (d) $146.32

The answer is (b). There is a lot of unnecessary information given in this problem. All you need to know is the current assessment, given at $47,200, and the current tax rate. The current tax rate is *not* $3.40, but $6.50 less $3.40 or $3.10. Then just use your formula, tax rate times assessment equals annual taxes, and divide by 12 (for 12 months in the year), and your answer is $121.93.

Using the previous problem, what is the difference in the new annual property taxes compared to the old taxes?
(a) $163.20 less
(b) $304.80 more
(c) $163.20 more
(d) $304.80 less

The answer is (c). The annual taxes prior to the revaluation were $20,000 times $6.50 per $100 or $1,300. The annual taxes after the revaluation were $47,200 times $3.10 per $100 or $1,463.20. The difference is $163.20, and you can see it is greater than the preceding year's taxes.

In the municipality of Hope the local tax has been increased from $0.023 per dollar to $0.031 per dollar. What is the increase in local tax that must be paid on a house that has an assessed value of $20,000?
(a) $1,120
(b) $16
(c) $640
(d) $160

The answer is (d). Since you have learned to read an entire problem, you can see here that the question is really very simple. The tester wants you to give the difference in total tax dollars. Your first step is to discover the difference between the two rates, which is .008 per dollar (.031 − .023). If you multiply this by $20,000 you obtain a difference of $160 ($20,000 × .008 = $160).

Note that the problem reads *per dollar,* which means that the rate is directly applied to the full dollar expressed without a change for per hundred or per thousand dollars.

Some students take the long way and multiply $20,000 by each rate and then subtract to find the difference. This is acceptable but slow. Remember to read an entire problem before attempting to answer it. This will save you test time!

The Piersons went overseas for the summer and forgot to pay their annual real estate taxes of $1,200 due on June 1. When they returned, they paid the amount in full on October 1. What was their total payment if there was a penalty of 1 percent per month on the overdue taxes?
(a) $1,212
(b) $1,260
(c) $1,248
(d) $1,152

The answer is (c). The penalty is for four entire months—June, July, August, and September—and therefore 4 percent. $1,200 times 4% or .04 = $48. This sum added to the tax payment of $1,200 is $1,248. However, be careful when reading such problems. They could be on a compounded basis, and you might have to compute the interest on each month's balance owed. As an example, the first month's interest would be $12 ($1,200 × .01), the second month's interest would be $12.12 or $1,212 times .01, etc. Read, understand, and then solve the problem.

PRACTICE PROBLEMS

(See answers on p. 131.)

1. A property with a market value of $75,000 is assessed at 90 percent of that value. If the tax rate is $4.20 per $100 of assessed value, what will the taxes be on this property for one year?
   - (a) $2,835
   - (b) $3,150
   - (c) $3,780
   - (d) $315

2. Juan Rivera just purchased a new house for $96,000. He was informed that his taxes would be $1,958.04 per year, based on the township's tax rate of $3.70 per $100 of assessed value. What is the assessed value of this property?
   - (a) $46,755
   - (b) $45,465
   - (c) $54,000
   - (d) $52,920

3. A discount of 3¼ percent is allowed if taxes are paid before June 1 of each year. What could you save if you paid your taxes on May 20, assuming that the assessed value of your property is $52,000 and the tax rate is $31 per $1,000 of assessed value?
   - (a) $161.20
   - (b) $52.39
   - (c) $16.12
   - (d) $59.62

4. The current market value of Craig Moon's property is $72,700, according to a recent revaluation. The township assessed at 60 percent of current value plus an equalization factor of 1.5. The tax rate was $3.10 per $100 of assessed value. What would Craig's taxes be under this system?
   - (a) $3,380.55
   - (b) $2,028.33
   - (c) $1,352.22
   - (d) $2,008.80

5. Referring to problem 4, after the revaluation was completed the township assessed at 100 percent of market value, eliminated the equalization factor, and lowered the tax rate by $.60 per $100 of assessed value. What will the difference be in Mr. Moon's taxes under the new arrangement as compared to the old system?
   - (a) $210.83 less
   - (b) $465.28 more
   - (c) $191.30 less
   - (d) $210.83 more

ANSWERS TO PRACTICE PROBLEMS

COMMISSION PROBLEMS

1. (d) $70,000 − $3,200 = $66,800

2. (a) $37,000
       $55,400
       $40,800
       $43,200

   $176,400 × .06 = $10,584 earned on straight 6% commission.
   − 80,000 × .07 = $5,600
   $ 96,400 × .03 = $2,892.

                 −8,492
                 $2,092

3. (b) $350,000 × 5% = $17,500
$19,312.50 − $17,500 = $1,812.50 ÷ 2½% = $72,500
$350,000 + $72,500 = $422,500.

4. (d) .25 × 3 = .75
.75 × 6 = 4.50
5.25

5. (d) $250,000 × .10 = $25,000 broker's fee
$25,000 × .30 = $7,500 listing person's share

DEPRECIATION/APPRECIATION PROBLEMS

1. (c) 6% per year × 8 yrs = 48% appreciation for 8 yr period
Therefore, $189,000 represents 148% (148% = 1.48)
$189,000 ÷ 148% = $127,702.70

2. (c) $560,000 × 95% = $532,000 value at end of 1st year
$532,000 × 95% = $505,400 value at end of 2nd year
$505,400 × 95% = $480,130 value at end of 3rd year

3. (a) $28,000 × 1.15 = $32,200 original price
$32,200 × .95 = $30,590 final price
$30,590 − $28,000 = $2,590

4. (c) Useful life = $\frac{1}{40}$; = .025 = 2.5%
2.5% × 2 (twice) = 5%
$140,000 × 5% = $7,000

5. (b) $15,000 = 85% of original purchase price
Therefore, $15,000 ÷ .85 = $17,647, or $17,650

MEASUREMENTS (AREA COMPUTATIONS)

1. (b) 4.5 acres × 43,560 sq. ft. = 196,020 sq. ft.
−71,020 sq. ft.
125,000 sq. ft.
50 × 100 = 5,000 sq. ft.
125,000 ÷ 5,000 = 25 lots

2. (c) 80 ft. 6 in. × 150 ft. 9 in. = 80.5 ft. × 150.75 ft. = 12,135.38, or 12,135 sq. ft.

3. (b) 4 ft. × 90 ft. = 360 square feet ÷ 9 (9 sq. ft. = 1 sq. yd.) = 40 sq. yds.
40 sq. yds × $2.45 = $98.00

4. (d) AΔ = 1/2 (b × h) = 1/2 (122 × 124) = 7.564 sq. ft.
7.564 sq. ft. × $2.25 = $17,019 × .06 = $1,021.14

5. (a) 2,178,000 × .80 = 1,742,400 square feet
1,742,400 sq ft. ÷ 43,560 = 40 acres
40 acres × $2,500 = $100,000

6. (d) First divide the total area into 3 rectangles and 1 triangle as shown:

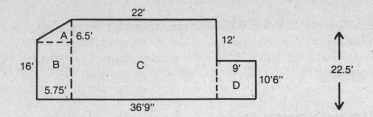

Next change all measurements to feet (because all answers are in square feet).

$$36'9'' = 36.75' \qquad 10'6'' = 10.5'$$

Find the missing dimensions by adding to or subtracting from known dimensions.

Calculate the areas of each figure and add to find area of entire figure;

A = ½ (6.50 × 5.75) = 18.69
B = 5.75 × 16   = 92.00
C = 22 × 22.50   = 495.00
D = 9 × 10.5   = 94.50

Total Area   = 700.19 square feet

7. (b) Labor—2(175 + 90) = 530 feet × $.75 = $397.50
Material—530 ft. × 6.5 ft. = 3,445 sq. ft. × $.625 = $2,153.13
$397.50 + $2,153.13 = $2,550.63, or $2,550

8. (b) 9 ft. × 12 ft. scales down to 3 in. × 4 in.
With a factor of 3, 5 in. × 3 = 15 ft.

9. (a) 75 ft. × 127 ft. = 9,144 square feet
$13,176 ÷ 9,144 sq. ft. = $1.50 per square foot

10. (c) 116 acres × 43,560 sq. ft. = 5,052,960 sq. ft. × $.05 = $252,648

INTEREST CALCULATIONS

1. (d) 2.5 × 1.40 = 3.5, 6.0 × 1.40 = 8.4

2. (c) $35,490 ÷ .70 = $50,700 total sales price
$50,700 × .15 = $7,605 deposit

3. (c) $7200 × 14% = $1,088 annual interest
$1088 ÷ 12 = $84 monthly interest
$84 × 7 = $588 total interest for 7 months
$7200 + $588 = $7,788 total payment

4. (d) $2400 × 18% = $432 annual interest
$432 ÷ 2 = $216 semiannual interest
$216 + $600 = $816 first payment

5. (a) $288 \div $1,800 = .16 = 16\%$

6. (b) $172,000 - $17,200 = $154,800$ balance due at closing
$108,000 - $2,700$ (2½ points discounted from loan) = $105,300.
$154,800$ balance due $- $105,300$ paid by bank at closing = $49,500$ due
from buyer

PRORATIONS (CLOSING)

1. (d) $35,000 \times .15 = $5,250$ deposit
$35,000 \times .07 = $2,450$ commission
$2,450 + $195 + $70 = $2,715$
$5,250 - $2,715 = $2,535$

2. (a) property taxes = $745.00/yr., $62.08/mo., $2.07/day
July 1–October 28 = 3 month, 28 days
$62.08 \times 3 = 186.24
$2.07 \times 28 = \underline{$\ 57.96}$
244.20

$745.00 - $244.20 = 500.80 taxes to be returned to seller

fire insurance = $126/3 yrs., $42/yr., $3.50/mo., $.12/day
January 1–October 28 = 9 months, 28 days
$3.50 \times 9 = 31.50
$.12 \times 28 = \underline{$\ 3.36}$
34.86

$126.00 - $34.86 = 91.14 insurance to be returned to seller

Therefore, $500.80 + $91.14 = 591.94

3. (b) $11,500 \times .08 = $920/year, $76.67/mo., $2.56/day
August 10–September 2 = 23 days
2.56×23 days = $58.88

4. (c) $361.20/year, $30.10/mo., $1.00/day
January 1–August 6 = 7 months, 5 days
$30.10 \times 7 = 210.70
$1.00 \ \times 5 = \underline{$\ \ 5.00}$
215.70

$361.20 - $215.70 = 145.50

5. (d) $250 \times 7 = $1,750/month, $58.33/day
January 27–31 = 4 days
$58.33 \times 4 = 233.32

INVESTMENT AND APPRAISING

1. (b) $65 \times 40 = 2,600$ sq. ft. $\times $12.95/sq. ft. = $33,670$

2. (a) (1) 120×12 apts. = $1,440 \times 12$ months = $17,280$ gross income
15×12 apts. = 180×12 months $= \underline{$\ 2,160}$ cost of utilities
$15,120$ net income

      (2) $90 × 12 apts. = $1,080 × 12 months = $12,960 net income
         Difference between (1) and (2)   = $ 2,160

3. (a) $100,000 × .15 = $15,000/year
      $15,000 ÷ 12 months = $1,250

4. (d) $300 × 12 months = $3,600 gross income
     Less $1,200 expenses
                 $2,400 net income ÷ .12 = $20,000

5. (b) $57,000 − $7,000 depreciation = $50,000
     Land Value at $13,000
                          $63,000

TAXES AND ASSESSMENTS

1. (a) $75,000 × .90 = $67,500 assessment × .042 = $2,835

2. (d) $1,958.04 ÷ .037 = $52,920
     (Remember that the price actually paid for a property has no bearing upon the tax assessment.)

3. (b) $52,000 × .031 = $1,612 × .0325 = $52.39

4. (b) $72,700 × .60 = $43,620 × 1.5 = $65,430
     $65,430 × .031 = $2,028.33
     New tax rate = $3.10 − $.60 = $2.50 per $100

5. (a) $72,700 × .025 ($3.10 − $.60) = $1,817.50
     $2,028.33 − $1,817.50 = $210.83 less

Chapter Twelve

Closings

The *closing* of a real estate transaction implies a settlement of all charges, obligations, and liens between the seller and purchaser. Each state, and even areas within a state, has various rules or procedures developed by custom for closing out a transaction. On most examinations, students are requested to forget local procedures and adopt uniform rules set by the examiner. The closing guide used in this book is not a total listing of all items one might encounter in a real estate transaction, but it includes the items normally taught in classrooms as examples and used on uniform examinations. Furthermore, the closing statement used in this chapter, is not a normally used closing statement from the real world, but it is used in various examinations and contains bookkeeping items (debits and credits) for both the seller and buyer. In real life closings, these seller and buyer statements are usually separate settlement sheets.

In solving a closing problem on an examination, the student should apply the following rules:

1. Read the instructions for closing and filling out forms (if necessary) carefully. The examiner will present certain rules that must be followed, such as a 30-day "pro ratio" rule. If this rule varies from local custom, remember you are taking an examination—not conducting or attending an actual closing. Accept the rules given to you by the examiner.
2. Read the narrative completely, underscoring all pertinent facts, such as location, size, parties, variances, closing date, commission costs, etc.
3. Study the listing form and contract of sale carefully. Be sure they agree with the facts in the narrative. If they differ, remember that the contract of sale prevails, since it is the controlling closing statement.
4. Fill out the forms and/or answer the questions presented. Do not attempt to balance the two statements between buyer and seller. They are individual statements and should be treated as separate statements even though they are on one sheet.
5. In the closing statement, a double-entry accounting system, known as "debits and credits," is used. The term *debit* is something *owed*. Remember, "d and o" (down and out) to remember debit means obligation. The term *credit* is something receivable, such as the purchase price to the seller. It is something earned or due to *that* person because a sale has been made.

CLOSING GUIDE

The order in which items are set down on a settlement sheet is immaterial. The only caution to a student is to be sure that nothing is left off the statement that is given in the problem. The following is a guide to those items found on uniform examinations and the method in which they are handled.

Purchase Price: The amount to be paid for the property by the purchaser at settlement is entered as a debit to the buyer. Since it is received by the seller, it is entered as a credit to the seller.

Deposit: The earnest money amount paid by the purchaser, which is to be used as part of the purchase price, should be entered as a credit to the buyer. There is no entry to the seller since the deposit was paid earlier and is not a debit at this time.

Sales Commission: The commission charged by the broker for the sale of the property is an expense to the seller and should be debited. No entry is made on the buyer's statement.

New First Mortgage: If the buyer is obtaining a mortgage to purchase the property, enter this amount as a credit to the buyer. It is the means by which the purchaser is to pay the sales price.

Assumed Mortgage: If the mortgage of the seller is being assumed by the buyer, enter this amount as a credit to the buyer and a debit to the seller. The amount is being used by the buyer to pay for the property and reduces the amount owed.

Paying Existing Mortgage: This amount is debited to the seller in order that the property may be transferred free and clear.

Second Mortgage: If a second loan is needed by the buyer to meet the purchase price, enter the amount of the second loan as a credit to the buyer. There is no entry to the seller.

Purchase Money Mortgage: If the seller takes a purchase money mortgage for a portion of the sales price, enter this amount as a credit to the purchaser against the sales price and a debit to the seller.

Taxes in Arrears, Prorated: If the taxes are not yet due and payable, prorate the annual amount of taxes, including the day of closing. Credit the purchaser and debit the seller.

Taxes in Advance, Prorated: If the taxes have been paid in advance, prorate the amount, including the day of closing, and subtract it from the amount already paid. The remainder should be debited to the buyer and credited to the seller.

Delinquent Taxes: If the taxes are delinquent, this amount should be charged to the seller. There is no entry to the buyer.

Fire Insurance, Cancelled: Credit the remaining premium balance to the seller. Be careful of the term. Often charges on fire insurance are for three-year terms.

Fire Insurance, New Policy: Enter the cost of the new policy as a debit to the purchaser if payable at closing. Many purchasers acquire their fire insurance policy prior to closing and prepay it themselves.

Fire Insurance, Assigned Policy: If the seller assigns the existing policy to the purchaser, prorate the premium and enter the remaining amount as a debit to the purchaser and a credit to the seller.

Interest in Arrears: If the mortgage loan is assumed or paid by the seller and interest is calculated in arrears, prorate the monthly interest to the date of settlement and enter it as a debit to the seller. If the mortgage loan is assumed, enter the prorated amount as a credit to the purchaser.

Rent in Advance: Enter the prorated amount as a credit to the purchaser and a debit to the seller.

Rent in Arrears: If rent is collected in arrears, enter the prorated amount as a debit to the purchaser and a credit to the seller.

Attorney's Fee: Debit either party for any legal fees charged.

Loan Origination Fee: Debit the purchaser for the cost of originating the new loan. In the case of an assumption, a loan assumption fee may be charged.

FHA or VA Discount Points: As required by law, they are debited to the seller.

Conventional Discount Points: Negotiable. You must read the problem to determine who you are to debit.

Prepayment Penalty: Debit to the seller for prepaying balance.

Balance Due From the Purchaser: The amount owed by the purchaser at closing after subtracting the credits from the debits. Enter as a credit, since it is needed to balance the double-entry system.

Balance Due Seller: The amount received by the seller at settlement after subtracting the debits from the credits. Enter as a debit if the credits exceed the debits as a balancing item. Enter as a credit if the debits exceed the credits.

Settlement Fees: Usually all are negotiable items. However, custom in your area may differ from general practice. In any problem solving, the narrative given to you must be followed even though it may differ from custom in your area. Do not add or subtract any charge not stated in the problem. Some other settlement charges are as follows:

Abstract continuation—Normally a debit to the seller.
Appraisal fee—A negotiable item, but normally a debit to the buyer.
Credit report—Normally a debit to the buyer.
Deed preparation—Normally a debit to the seller.
Escrow charges—Negotiable. Usually a debit to the purchaser.
Interest—To purchaser as a debit.
Opinion of title—Normally a debit to the buyer.
Recording deed or mortgage—Normally a debit to the buyer.
Survey—May be negotiable, but generally a debit to the purchaser.
Special assessment—Negotiable.
Title insurance—Normally a debit to the purchaser.
Transfer tax—Normally a state charge against the previous owner and therefore a debit to the seller.

CLOSING PROBLEM

The following is a typical example of a closing problem used in examinations. It begins with a hypothetical sales transaction, followed by a listing agreement, contract of sale, a settlement sheet, and a series of questions about the closing. Your ability to read and to reason is being tested in this problem.

Mr. and Mrs. Joseph E. Smith decided to sell their six-room frame ranch-style house at 452 Meadow Road, Rural County, Anyplace, USA. On June 12 they listed the property with the ABC Realty Company. The listing was an exclusive agency for three months at an asking price of $42,000.

The house covered 1600 square feet of a 100-foot by 200-foot rectangular lot. The lot enjoyed all public utilities. The residence was built in 1969 and was in good physical condition with few items of deferred maintenance. It contained a small foyer, living room, dining room, kitchen, three bedrooms, and a full bath on the first floor. The roof was gabled and contained only a storage attic, fully insulated. The basement had a small laundry area, an outside entrance, a small panelled den, and a powder room. It also housed the heater and domestic hot-water plant, both of which were gas-fired. Included in the sale would be venetian blinds, a gas stove, and a refrigerator. The property is legally known as Block 4, Lot 16, Meadowland Subdivision, Rural County, USA. The tax rate in this county for this year is $4.00 per $100 of assessed valuation. Most assessments were at 50 percent of true value.

On June 25 an offer was received on the property by Happy Realty Inc., who presented it to the ABC Realty Co. The offer was for $38,000, subject to a $28,500 conventional first mortgage at 9 percent interest for 20 years or better. ABC Realty Company presented the offer to the Smiths, who rejected same. The purchasers then counter-offered with $40,000, all other terms to remain the same. The Smiths accepted the counter-offer, subject to a 15 percent deposit and closing within 60 days. The purchasers, Mr. and Mrs. Philip Newcamp, accepted on June 30.

At the time of closing, taxes were paid to March 31, and the tax assessment for this property was $25,000, land and buildings. Fire insurance coverage included a three-year policy and was to expire as of December 31 of that year. Purchasers decided to accept this policy assignment from the sellers. The original cost was $168. Title insurance would cost $2.00 per $100 and would include purchaser's closing charges. Costs to the sellers included a termite inspection of $60, a survey costing $150, and drawing of a deed costing $30. The real estate commission would be split equally by both brokers at 3 percent each. Appraisal, credit report, and loan-origination fee to the purchasers would be 1 percent of the mortgage. The purchaser was to prepay taxes to end of year.

On the above, complete the closing statement on page 136. Use a 30-day method of computation. Assume that the tax year is the same as the calendar year. Closing to take place on August 31.

SETTLEMENT STATEMENT WORKSHEET

NOTE: A completed copy of this worksheet appears at the end of this chapter.

Settlement Date	Buyer's Statement		Seller's Statement	
	Debit	Credit	Debit	Credit

CLOSING PROBLEMS TEST

1. Which of the following correctly describes the lot?
   - (a) Square
   - (b) Rectangular
   - (c) Triangular
   - (d) Parallelogram

2. Utilities not available to the site would include
   I. electricity and telephone
   II. sewers and telephone
   - (a) I only
   - (b) II only
   - (c) Both I and II
   - (d) Neither I nor II

3. In the listing, ABC Realty promises to
   I. sell the property for $42,000
   II. exclude other agents from the sale
   - (a) I only
   - (b) II only
   - (c) Both I and II
   - (d) Neither I nor II

4. The residence is best described as
   I. approximately 1600 square feet on one floor
   II. seven rooms on two floors
   - (a) I only
   - (b) II only
   - (c) Both I and II
   - (d) Neither I nor II

5. Which of the following statements is (are) true concerning the property?
   I. The residence covers 8 percent of the total lot area.
   II. The frontage is approximately one-half of the depth of the lot.
   - (a) I only
   - (b) II only
   - (c) Both I and II
   - (d) Neither I nor II

6. Tax rates in this county are based upon which of the following?
   - (a) True value
   - (b) Market value
   - (c) Assessed value
   - (d) Sales price

7. The true value ratio of assessments would indicate the property is based upon a value of
   - (a) $40,000
   - (b) $35,000
   - (c) $62,500
   - (d) $50,000

8. The layout of the residence would suggest that the property could suffer from
   - (a) physical depreciation
   - (b) functional obsolescence
   - (c) locational obsolescence
   - (d) none of the above

9. Property taxes on the property would represent a monthly payment of
   - (a) $104.16
   - (b) $116.66
   - (c) $83.33
   - (d) $208.33

10. The selling broker's commission is
    - (a) $1,140
    - (b) $1,260
    - (c) $1,200
    - (d) none of the above

11. Personal property in the sale includes
    I. blinds and carpets
    II. refrigerator and freezer
    - (a) I only
    - (b) II only
    - (c) Both I and II
    - (d) Neither I nor II

12. The latest date that the closing would take place should be
    - (a) August 25
    - (b) July 1
    - (c) August 31
    - (d) September 30

13. The first-offer mortgage contingency represented a
    I. 75% loan-to-price ratio
    II. 71% loan-to-price ratio
    - (a) I only
    - (b) II only
    - (c) Both I and II
    - (d) Neither I nor II

14. The fire insurance assumption represents a
    I. debit to the seller
    II. debit to the buyer
    - (a) I only
    - (b) II only
    - (c) Both I and II
    - (d) Neither I nor II

15. The seller's expenses at closing are
    - (a) $3,075.32
    - (b) $1,856.65
    - (c) $3,056.65
    - (d) $2,640.00

16. The buyer's expenses (debits) at closing, exclusive of purchase price, are
    - (a) $1,418.32
    - (b) $1,436.99
    - (c) $1,103.67
    - (d) $1,020.34

17. At the closing the sellers receive
    - (a) $40,018.67
    - (b) $36,962.02
    - (c) $40,435.32
    - (d) $35,762.02

18. The mortgage of $28,500 is
    I. a credit to the buyer
    II. a debit to the seller
    - (a) I only
    - (b) II only
    - (c) Both I and II
    - (d) Neither I nor II

19. The cooperating broker's total commission is
    I. a sharing of $1200 total commission
    II. an obligation of both parties
    - (a) I only
    - (b) II only
    - (c) Both I and II
    - (d) Neither I nor II

20. The total due from the buyer at closing is
    - (a) $936.99
    - (b) $520.34
    - (c) $6,520.34
    - (d) $6,187.02

ANSWERS: 1. b 2. d 3. d 4. a 5. c 6. c 7. d 8. a 9. c 10. c
11. d 12. c 13. a 14. b 15. c 16. b 17. b 18. a 19. d
20. c

SETTLEMENT STATEMENT WORKSHEET

Settlement Date: 8/31	Buyer's Statement		Seller's Statement	
	Debit	Credit	Debit	Credit
Purchase Price	$40,000.00			$40,000.00
Deposit		$ 6,000.00		
Mortgage		$28,500.00		
Taxes		$ 416.65	$ 416.65	
Insurance	$ 18.67			$ 18.67
Title Insurance	$ 800.00			
Termite Inspection			$ 60.00	
Survey			$ 150.00	
Deed			$ 30.00	
Commission			$ 2,400.00	
Mortgage Processing Fee	$ 285.00			
Pre-Paid Taxes	$ 333.32			
Balance due from the Purchaser		$ 6,520.34		
Balance due seller			$36,962.02	
TOTAL	$41,436.99	$41,436.99	$40,018.67	$40,018.67

Chapter Thirteen

Glossary of Real Estate Terminology

Terminology is the language of a business or profession. Of all the areas outlined in this text, none is as vital as this for successfully passing the examination. It is a valid and important source of test questions in any field.

There are as many ways to learn as there are students willing to learn. We have tried throughout this book to help you learn these terms in various ways: (1) by reading; (2) by tests; (3) by having you define the terms yourself. In this section we have defined these terms for you. Here are some suggestions you might try to aid you in your studies.

1. Record these terms on a tape and listen to them at your leisure. By reading the terms aloud and listening to them you will aid your learning process.
2. Write each term on an index card and put the definition on the backside of the card. Like a game, you can mix up the cards, look at the term, and try to define it. You can do this in small groups or carry the cards with you and refer to them during idle times of the day.
3. Research each term by referring to the pertinent part of the text. You will note that we have placed a number after most terms. This number corresponds to the chapter in which this term is further explained.
4. Talk about each term in a study group. If you keep the group small, no more than four, each would then add to the others' understanding of the individual term as discussed because each individual student brings a different background to the study session.
5. Read the entire glossary and commit it to memory. This is probably the hardest way to master real estate terminology. The list is as short as we could make it; but these are the common terms used by most professional testmakers, and they must be known and understood.

At the end of each term we have placed in parentheses the chapter number where this term is used. You should refer to that chapter for a greater understanding of the term. There are some terms that are not designated by a chapter number. In those cases, the terms are self-explanatory.

ABANDONMENT: The act of letting property remain unused. (6)

ABSTRACT OF TITLE: A complete summary which sets forth in chronological order all grants, conveyances, encumbrances, and liens that affect the title of a parcel of real estate. (2)

ACCELERATION CLAUSE: The clause in a mortgage or deed of trust that gives the lender the right to declare all unpaid sums due immediately upon default of the mortgagor. (5)

ACCEPTANCE: A statement of the intent of a person receiving an offer to take said offer and be bound by its terms. (4)

ACCESS RIGHT: The right of an owner to get off and onto his property. This gains special importance in the case of a landlocked parcel.

ACCRETION: The gradual increase or addition of land resulting from the action of streams, lakes, and rivers.

ACCRUED INTEREST: Interest which remains in an account instead of being immediately remitted to the depositor.

ACKNOWLEDGMENT: A formal statement made before an officer (usually a notary public) by a person who has signed a document that the execution was a voluntary act and that it is the signer's own signature. (4)

ACRE: An area of land containing 43,560 square feet. (7)

ACTUAL EVICTION: The result of legal action brought against a lessee by the lessor whereby the lessee is physically removed from the leased premises by a court order. (6)

ACTUAL NOTICE: Willful knowledge of a fact; that which is known to be true. (4)

AD VALOREM: "According to value." Generally used in reference to real estate taxes. (2)

ADJACENT: Near or next to, but not necessarily touching.

ADJOINING: Actually touching that which it is next to; abutting.

ADMINISTRATOR: The court-appointed executor of an intestate's estate. (4)

ADMINISTRATOR'S DEED: Deed conveying property of an intestate (person who dies without leaving a will). (4)

ADULT: One who has reached the age of majority (competence) in his state. (4)

ADVERSE POSSESSION: The open, hostile, and continuous use and possession of another's property for a statutory period of time with the intention of acquiring title to the property. (4)

AFFIDAVIT OF TITLE: A sworn written statement in which the seller or grantor attests that since the title examination or the date of contract there have been no bankruptcies, judgments, or divorces; no repairs made to the property which have not been paid for, no defects in the title of which he/she has knowledge, and that he/she is in possession of the premises.

AGENCY: The relationship that exists when a person, known as the principal, contracts to another, the agent, to perform an act in that person's stead. (3)

AGENCY LISTING: A written agreement between an owner and a licensed broker whereby the owner permits the broker to sell his property for a fee, reserving, however, the owner's right to sell without a fee. (3)

AGENT: One who has been given the complete power to act on the behalf of another. (3)

AGREEMENT OF SALE: See *Contract for Sale.*

AIR RIGHTS: The right of the use of the open space above a property. (7)

ALIENATION: The act of transferring ownership to another. Property is transferred by voluntary alienation as in the case of a deed or assignment. Involuntary alienation occurs when property is transferred, by a foreclosure sale or eminent domain, against the owner's will.

ALIENATION CLAUSE: The clause in a mortgage or deed of trust which gives the lender the right to declare all unpaid sums due immediately if the property is transferred by the mortgagor.

ALLODIAL SYSTEM: The method of land ownership in which land is held free and clear with no rent or service due to the government; opposite of feudal system. (2)

ALLUVIUM: Soil deposited by accretion. The alluvium increases the size of a property.

AMORTIZATION: The method of repayment of a loan in which both principal and interest are made payable in monthly or other periodic payments. (5)

ANNUAL PERCENTAGE RATE: The total finance charge to be imposed on the total amount of a loan. Disclosure of the annual percentage rate is required by the Federal Truth-in-Lending Act.

ANTI-TRUST LAWS: Laws that are designed to preserve free enterprise and maintain business competition. Violations of these laws in reference to real estate would include price fixing or brokers' agreeing to limit their areas of trade.

APPRAISAL: The process whereby an estimate is made of the value of a property. An appraisal is usually required when financing, selling, taxing, and insuring property or when a property is being taken for condemnation. (8)

APPRAISER: A person who provides an opinion of value (appraisal) for a fee or salary. (8)

APPRECIATION: An increase in the value or worth of a property due to economic causes; the opposite of depreciation. (11)

APPURTENANCE: Something that is not actually a part of a property but which is an inseparable adjct adding to its value. Appurtenances include such benefits as easements and rights of way.

ASSEMBLAGE: The joining of several small adjoining lots into one large tract to increase the market value.

ASSESSED VALUATION: The value of a parcel of real estate established as a basis for computing real estate taxes. (11)

ASSESSMENT: The process of establishing the value of property for tax purposes; a tax charge imposed according to determined rates. (5)

ASSESSMENT RATIO: The ratio of assessed value to true value. Assessed value is often considerably lower. (11)

ASSIGNMENT: The transfer of any interest of one person (the assignor) to another person (the assignee). Mortgages, bonds, leases, sales contracts, and options are examples of instruments that can be assigned. (5)

ASSUMPTION OF MORTGAGE: The act of acquiring title to a property that has an existing mortgage and agreeing to abide by and be liable for all payments and terms of the existing mortgage. (5)

ATTACHMENT: The process of taking a person's property by judicial order and holding it as a security for the satisfaction of a debt.

ATTEST: To witness and to guarantee said witnessing by signature.

AUTHORIZATION TO SELL: A listing contract in which the seller retains an agent to acquire a buyer for his property. (3)

AXIAL THEORY: A theory of city growth patterns which proposes that growth occurs outward from the central business district along main roads of transportation.

BALLOON PAYMENT: The final payment of a mortgage loan which is considerably greater than the prior required installment payments.

BARGAIN AND SALE DEED: A deed which conveys all of the grantor's interest in a property; however, it does not usually carry warranties against any liens or encumbrances. (4)

BASE LINE: One of a set of imaginary lines which runs from east to west. It is used as a reference point under the rectangular survey system of describing land. (7)

BENCH MARK: A permanent reference point placed for the use of surveyors in measuring elevation.

BENEFICIARY: One who receives or is to receive benefits from another.

BILATERAL CONTRACT: A contract in which each party agrees to perform an act in exchange for the other party's promise to perform. (4)

BILL OF SALE: The written document which passes title of personal property from seller to buyer. May not be used to pass title to real property. (2)

BINDER: An agreement with an earnest money deposit for the purchase of a parcel of real estate to show a purchaser's good faith. (4)

BLANKET MORTGAGE: One mortgage covering more than one parcel of real estate. A "partial release" clause contained in the mortgage guarantees the release of a parcel upon payment of a specified portion of the debt. (5)

BLOCK AND LOT: See *Lot, Block, and Subdivision.*

BLOCKBUSTING: An illegal and discriminatory practice whereby fearful homeowners are induced to sell their homes due to the prospective entry of a minority group into the neighborhood. (10)

BONA FIDE: In good faith. (8)

BOND: The personal contractual obligation of a debtor. (5)

BRANCH OFFICE: A secondary site of business apart from the principal office. Generally run by a licensed real estate broker working on behalf of the broker operating the main office. (9)

BREACH OF CONTRACT: A violation of any covenants or conditions of a contract without a valid reason or nonperformance of one's obligations in a contract. (4)

BROKER: A properly licensed person who for compensation acts as an agent for another in a real estate transaction. The transactions could involve the purchase, sale, or lease of real property. (3)

BROKERAGE: The real estate business concerning itself with bringing together buyers and sellers and completing a transaction for a commission. (3)

BUILDING CODES: Ordinances mandated by local governments to regulate building and construction standards for the protection and safety of the public. (10)

BUILDING LOAN: Also known as construction loan. A variation on the mortgage whereby the lender lends money to a developer or builder with advances of further funding at each stage of completion. The land itself and that which has been completed serves as collateral. (5)

BUILDING PERMIT: A governmental document to permit construction. (10)

BULK TRANSFER: The transfer of a commercial business as a whole, including trade fixtures, goods, and chattels. Regulated by the Uniform Commercial Code.

BUNDLE OF RIGHTS: The method of describing the rights due an owner of real property. These are the rights of quiet enjoyment, possession, control of use of the land, and disposition. (2)

CANCELLATION CLAUSE: A contingency clause in a contract which allows for termination of the contract under certain conditions. (4)

CAPITALIZATION: As commonly used in the income approach to value, a method of converting net income into an estimate of value. (8)

CAPITALIZATION RATE: The rate of return a property will provide on an owner's investment. (8)

CARRYING CHARGES: Unavoidable costs of ownership such as taxes and maintenance. (2)

CAVEAT EMPTOR: "Let the buyer beware." The buyer should inspect the property prior to purchase to be aware of any advantages or defects. (3)

CERTIFICATE OF TITLE: A statement of opinion based on a search of the public records that indicates the status of the title of a parcel of real property. (2)

CHATTEL: An item of personal property. (2).

CHATTEL MORTGAGE: Pledge of personal property to secure a debt.

CLOSING: The point in a real estate transaction when the deed is delivered to the buyer in exchange for the purchase price. (12)

CLOSING STATEMENT: An accounting of funds in a real estate sale. Both buyer and seller must receive separate closing statements prior to closing. In some states closing statements are prepared by brokers; in others by attorneys. (12)

CLOUD ON THE TITLE: A claim or encumbrance not yet adjudicated which, if proven valid, would impair the owner's title. Ordinarily title cannot be passed when it is under a cloud.

CLUSTERING: The grouping of homes within a subdivision on small lots, with remaining land to be used as common areas, such as recreational areas. (10)

COLOR OF TITLE: The instance when title appears to be good but actually is not. This may occur when a person who does not actually own a piece of property deeds it to another. A good title company should not allow one to take possession under color of title.

COMMINGLING: The illegal act by a real estate broker of mixing clients' monies with his personal funds. A broker is required to maintain a separate escrow account for the deposit of clients' funds temporarily being held by him. (9)

COMMISSION: The consideration paid to a real estate broker for services rendered in the sale or purchase of real property. (3)

COMMON ELEMENTS: Portions of a condominium project that are necessary or convenient to the existence of the project and which are used by all residents of the project. Such common elements could include hallways, parking lots, swimming pools, walkways, etc.

COMMON LAW: The basis of English law adopted in all states except Louisiana.

COMMUNITY PROPERTY: A type of property ownership whereby each spouse has an equal interest in property acquired during their marriage.

COMPARABLES: Recently sold properties that are similar to the property being valued. These comparables are used and compared to a specific property to indicate its market value by the market data approach. (8)

COMPOUND INTEREST: Interest paid upon principal plus accrued interest.

CONDEMNATION: A judicial proceeding enforcing the power of eminent domain—the power of government to take private property for a public use for which the owner must be compensated. (2)

CONDITIONAL CONTRACT: A contract which cannot be consummated until all conditions have been fulfilled. Seller retains title until all conditions are met. (2)

CONDOMINIUM: A type of ownership in a multi-unit building in which an owner holds a fee simple interest in his particular unit and owns the common areas of the project as joint owner with the other unit owners. (2)

CONFORMITY PRINCIPLE: The appraisal principle which holds that property values are at their highest when a neighborhood is homogeneous in purpose. The basis of zoning laws which maintain one neighborhood for residential use only while restricting another to commercial uses.

CONSIDERATION: Something that the parties to a contract agree to be of value, such as the purchase price of a property. (4)

CONSTANT PAYMENT LOAN: A loan in which payments remain constant throughout the life of the loan.

CONSTRUCTION MORTGAGE: A straight but short-term mortgage. It is normally paid to a builder during construction as advances for work performed. (5)

CONSTRUCTIVE EVICTION: Because of negligence on the part of the landlord resulting in uninhabitable conditions, a tenant is forced to remove himself from the leased premises with no liability for further rent. (6)

CONSTRUCTIVE NOTICE: Notice which is given to the public by recorded documents. Whether or not a person has actually viewed these documents, he is charged with the knowledge of such recorded instruments. (5)

CONTIGUOUS: Touching or abutting.

CONTRACT: A legally enforceable agreement between two or more parties who agree to perform or not to perform a certain act in exchange for a consideration. (4)

CONTRACT FOR DEED: An agreement between a seller and buyer for the purchase of a parcel of real estate whereby the buyer makes periodic payments to the seller and gains title only after the debt has been satisfied. Also known as an installment contract. (4)

CONTRACT FOR SALE: A contract for the purchase and sale of real property whereby the buyer agrees to a purchase price set by the seller and the seller agrees to transfer title. (4)

CONTRACTUAL CAPACITY: The competency of the parties to enter into a valid agreement. (3)

CONVENTIONAL MORTGAGE: A mortgage loan that is not guaranteed or insured by any government agency. The lender relies solely on the credit of the borrower and the security of the real property to secure payment of the debt. (5)

CONVEYANCE: The actual transfer of title by deed or by will. (4)

COOPERATIVE OWNERSHIP: The ownership as shareholders in a corporation that holds title to an apartment building. In return the owner receives a lease to occupy a specific unit in the apartment building. (2)

CORPORATION: A legal entity created to conduct business with essentially the same rights as individuals. The corporation has continuous existence until dissolved through legal proceedings. (2)

COST APPROACH: An approach to the estimation of value of real property whereby the appraiser determines the reproduction cost of the building, minus any accrued depreciation, and adds the land value. (8)

COUNTER OFFER: A new offer proposed as a reply or rejection of an offer previously submitted.

COVENANT: An agreement between two or more parties in which one or all parties promise to perform or refrain from performing certain acts; also, an agreement which specifies conditions that do or do not exist. (4)

CURTESY: The interest of a husband in the estate of his deceased wife.

DAMAGES: The amount of money recovered by an injured party. In real estate practice, an alternative to demanding specific performance. (4)

DEDICATION: The donation of private property to a governmental body, provided the land is used for public purposes.

DEED: A written instrument delivered to the grantee in which the grantor conveys and transfers ownership and all interest in a parcel of real property. (4)

DEED IN TRUST: A type of mortgage in which title is transferred to a third party (trustee) as security for the repayment of the debt by the borrower to the lender. (5)

DEFAULT: The failure on the part of a party to perform an obligation created in a contract. (5)

DEFEASANCE CLAUSE: The clause in a mortgage which allows the mortgagor to redeem a property upon full payment of the mortgage loan. (5)

DEFICIENCY JUDGMENT: A personal judgment against a borrower when a foreclosure sale produces funds insufficient to satisfy the balance of the mortgage loan.

DENSITY ZONING: A type of zoning ordinance that restricts the number of dwellings which may be built per acre in a particular subdivision. (10)

DEPRECIATION: A loss in value to a parcel of real estate due to physical deterioration or functional or economic obsolescence. (8)

DISCOUNT POINTS: An added fee on a loan charged by the lender to bring a VA or FHA loan up to the competitive interest rates on conventional loans. (5)

DISPOSSESS PROCEEDINGS: The legal means by which a landlord can remove an undesirable tenant. (6)

DOCUMENTATION: A form of proof through observation and recorded facts. (8)

DOMINANT ESTATE: The property that derives the benefit of an easement attached to an adjoining property (servient estate).

DOWER: The interest a wife holds in the estate of her deceased husband.

DUAL AGENCY: The representation of both principals to a transaction by one broker.

DURESS: Forcing a person to perform an act against his will by unlawful means.

EARNEST MONEY: The cash deposit made by a buyer as indication of intent to complete a transaction. (12)

EASEMENT: The right or interest one person has in another's land. (2)

EASEMENT BY NECESSITY: An easement, acquired by law, which is deemed to be necessary for the full use and enjoyment of one's land.

EASEMENT BY PRESCRIPTION: An easement acquired through open, hostile, and notorious use of another's land for a statutory period of time.

EASEMENT IN GROSS: An easement granted personally by an owner but which is not attached to any land owned by the owner; similar to a license.

ECONOMIC LIFE: In appraisal, the period of time within which a piece of real estate yields a profit. (8)

ECONOMIC OBSOLESCENCE: A loss in value that occurs outside the boundary lines of a property, such as residences which are over- or under-improvements, residences located on a heavily traveled street, or located adjacent to a commercial or industrial property. (8)

EMINENT DOMAIN: The right of the government to take private property for a public use for which the owner is compensated. (2)

ENCROACHMENT: The unauthorized use of another's land. (2)

ENCUMBRANCE: An interest or right attached to a parcel of real estate that decreases the value of such parcel but does not prevent a transfer of title. (4)

EQUITABLE TITLE: The interest held by a buyer under a contract for deed or installment contract. (4)

EQUITY: The amount over and above the indebtedness of a parcel of real property. (5)

EQUITY OF REDEMPTION: The right of an owner to redeem a property after a judgment, lien, or foreclosure. (5)

ESCALATOR CLAUSE: A clause in a lease permitting adjustments in rent payments due to changes in expenses, taxes, insurance, and inflation.

ESCHEAT: The reversion of property to the state when the deceased dies intestate with no heirs or when the property is abandoned. (2)

ESCROW: The handling of a transaction through a disinterested third party whereby the escrow agent is responsible for carrying out all terms and instructions as set by the parties to the escrow. (9)

ESTATE: All the interest, in quantity and in quality, that a person has in real property. (2)

ESTATE AT SUFFERANCE: Occupancy of a property by a tenant whose lease has expired, against the will of the landlord. (6)

ESTATE AT WILL: Occupancy of a property by a tenant without a lease with the concurrence of the landlord. With notice, either party may terminate the occupancy at will. (6)

ESTATE FOR LIFE: An interest in property which terminates upon the death of a specified person. (2)

ESTATE FOR YEARS: A lease for more than one year. (6)

ESTATE IN REVERSION: An estate granted by its owner which reverts to the owner upon a specified event. (2)

ESTOPPEL: A legal doctrine that prohibits a person from making assertions inconsistent with previous assertions or actions.

ET AL: Abbreviation for *et alia* "and others."

ET UX: Abbreviation for *et uxor*, "and wife."

EVICTION: A legal action to remove a tenant from the leased premises. (6)

EVIDENCE OF TITLE: Proof of ownership of a parcel of real property. (2)

EXCLUSIVE AGENCY: A listing agreement giving a sole broker the right to sell a property, but which reserves the right of the owner to sell the property personally without paying a commission. (3)

EXCLUSIVE RIGHT TO SELL: A listing agreement which gives a sole broker the right to sell a property. The broker receives a commission even if the owner sells the property personally. (3)

EXECUTED CONTRACT: A contract in which all parties have performed their promises and thus fulfilled the contract. (4)

EXECUTION: The signing and delivery of a contract. (4)

EXECUTOR: Person named in a will to administer a decedent's estate. (4)

EXECUTORY CONTRACT: A contract in which there still remains a promise to be performed.

EXPRESSED CONTRACT: An oral or written contract in which the parties state their terms and intentions in words. (4)

FEE SIMPLE: The most complete and absolute form of ownership in a parcel of real estate. (2)

FHA MORTGAGE: A residential mortgage that is insured by the Federal Housing Administration. (5)

FIDUCIARY RELATIONSHIP: An obligation of trust imposed on an agent toward his principal. The agent is known as the fiduciary. (3)

FIRST MORTGAGE: The mortgage with priority over all other liens (except taxes) and which will be satisfied first. (5)

FIXTURE: An article, once classed as personal property, which has become affixed to the real estate and is now classed as real property. (2)

FLEXIBLE-PAYMENT MORTGAGE: A loan in which the payment schedule is such that smaller payments are made in the early years of the loan and payments increase in the later years as the income of the borrower increases. (5)

FNMA: Federal National Mortgage Association, also known as Fannie Mae. Buys and sells residential mortgages. (5)

FORECLOSURE: In the event of default by the borrower, a legal process whereby a property pledged as security for a debt is sold to satisfy the debt. (5)

FORFEITURE: A loss of value or money due to lack of performance under a contract. (6)

FREEHOLD ESTATE: An estate which is for an indeterminate length of time, such as fee simple or life estate. (2)

FRONT FOOT: Measurement of land along the street line. (11)

FUNCTIONAL OBSOLESCENCE: See *Obsolescence.*

GENERAL AGENT: One who is authorized to perform any and all acts on behalf of the principal. (3)

GOVERNMENT SURVEY METHOD: A method of land description utilizing principal meridians and base lines to create squares called townships and sections. (7)

GRACE PERIOD: Time allowed to perform an act or to make a payment before default is declared.

GRADUATED LEASE: A lease where the rental payments will change during its existence by a prescribed schedule. (6)

GRANT DEED: A deed which includes three warranties. The owner warrants (1) that he has the right to convey the property; (2) that there are no encumbrances to the property except as noted in the deed; (3) that the grantor will convey any future interest he may acquire. (4)

GRANTEE: The person who receives a conveyance of real estate from a grantor. (4)

GRANTOR: The person who conveys real property, or an interest in real property, to another. (4)

GROSS INCOME: The total income received from an investment property before deducting any expenses. (8)

GROSS INCOME MULTIPLIER: A number derived by dividing the selling price of a comparable property by its monthly gross income. This number is then multiplied by the gross income of the subject property in order to obtain an estimate of value for the property being appraised. (8)

GROSS LEASE: A lease whereby the lessee pays a fixed rental fee to the lessor. The lessor pays all taxes and insurance. (6)

GROUND LEASE: A lease on the land only. The tenant usually is required to build or already owns the building and any improvement to the land. (6)

GUESSTIMATE: A valuation opinion without documentation. (8)

HABENDUM CLAUSE: The part of a deed following the granting clause which defines the extent of ownership; for instance fee simple, life estate, etc. (4)

HEIRS AND ASSIGNS: Beneficiaries of wills and deeds.

HIGHEST AND BEST USE: In appraisal, that use to which a property may be physically and legally put that will yield the greatest return. (8)

HOLDOVER TENANT: A person who remains on the leased premises after the expiration of his lease. The landlord may elect to evict the tenant or permit him to stay and pay rent. (6)

HOMESTEAD: Land which is used and occupied as the family home.

IMPLIED CONTRACT: An agreement created by the actions of the parties, neither in words nor writing. (3)

IMPROVEMENTS: Any structure erected on a parcel of land enhancing its value, known as improvements to land; improvements of land would consist of streets, sewers, curbing, sidewalks, etc. (2)

INCOME APPROACH: An approach to the valuation of real property that utilizes the amount of net income the property will produce over its remaining economic life. (8)

INCORPOREAL RIGHTS: Nonpossessory rights in real estate such as easements.

INDEPENDENT CONTRACTOR: One who is retained to perform a specific act, but is subject to a limited amount of control in the performance of such act. An independent contractor receives no employee benefits and pays all his own Social Security and income taxes and expenses.

INSTALLMENT CONTRACT: See *Contract for Deed*.

INTEREST: A sum paid or accrued in exchange for the use of another's money. (5)

INTERIM FINANCING: A short-term or construction loan that is made during the building phase of the property.

INTESTATE: To die without a will. (4)

JOINT TENANCY: Ownership of a parcel of real property by two or more persons with equal rights of ownership. The interest of a deceased owner passes to the remaining owners. (2)

JUDGMENT: The formal decree by court action that states that one person is indebted to another as well as the amount of the debt. (5)

JUNIOR MORTGAGE: A secondary mortgage which is subordinate to the first mortgage. (5)

LACHES: A doctrine used by a court to bar legal rights due to an unnecessary delay in asserting those rights.

LAND: The surface of the earth downward to the center, the air above it, and everything permanently attached thereon. (2)

LANDLOCKED: A parcel of property that is entirely surrounded by private property belonging to another. The owner of landlocked property must have access to his property by way of easement or right of way.

LANDLORD: One who rents out property; a lessor. (6)

LEASE: A contract wherein for a consideration a lessor (landlord) gives possession and use of real estate to a lessee (tenant).

LEASE WITH OPTION TO PURCHASE: A lease which includes an agreed upon price at which the tenant may purchase the property by a given date.

LEASED FEE ESTATE: The landlord's interest in property he has leased. Opposite of "leasehold." (6)

LEASEHOLD: A tenant's right to occupy real estate during the term of a lease. Upon expiration of this lease, the property reverts to the owner. (6)

LEGAL DESCRIPTION: A description of land that is specific enough to permit an independent surveyor to locate and identify the parcel. (7)

LESSEE: The person to whom the landlord grants use and possession of real estate for a consideration. (6)

LESSOR: The person who rents or leases property to another. (6)

LICENSE: Authorization to perform a particular act on another's land or property. (2)

LIEN: A claim which one person has upon the real estate of another as security for a debt. (5)

LIFE ESTATE: An estate in real property that is limited in time to the life of the owner or some other person named by the owner. (2)

LIFE TENANT: One who is permitted to use a property for his own lifetime or the lifetime of another specified person.

LIMITED PARTNERSHIP: A partnership that consists of general partners and limited partners. The general partners are fully responsible for the venture. The limited partners are responsible only to the amount of their investment.

LIS PENDENS: Notice that a legal suit is pending upon a particular piece of real property. (5)

LISTING: A written agreement between an owner (principal) and a broker (agent) authorizing the broker to procure a buyer or tenant for his real estate. (3)

LITTORAL: See *riparian rights.*

LOT, BLOCK, AND SUBDIVISION: A method of describing a particular property utilizing a lot number located within a particular block in a subdivision; for example, Lot 10, Block 2, Happy Estate Subdivision as filed and recorded in the office of the Registrar of Deeds in said county. (7)

MANAGEMENT AGREEMENT: An agreement between the owner of an income-producing property and a firm or individual who will manage the property. (6)

MARKETABLE TITLE: A title which is reasonably free and clear of encumbrances and clouds so as to be acceptable to the typical buyer. (2)

MARKET DATA APPROACH: A method of appraisal by which the property under appraisement is compared to other similar properties which have been sold. (8)

MARKET VALUE: The highest price at which a property should be sold given a reasonable exposure period in the market, arrived at by a willing seller and willing buyer, neither being under duress to act. (8)

MASTER PLAN: A plan to guide the long-term development of an area. (10)

MECHANIC'S LIEN: A special lien created for people who have supplied labor and/or materials to the repair or construction of a real estate improvement in order to secure payment for such services. (5)

MEETING OF THE MINDS: See *offer and acceptance.*

MERIDIAN: As used in the rectangular (government) survey method of describing property, a set of imaginary lines which run from north to south. (7)

METES AND BOUNDS: A method of describing land by specifying the shape and boundary measurements using terminal points and angles. (7)

MILL: One-tenth of one cent. Used in some states in the computation of property taxes.

MINOR: One who has not reached his legal majority; not an adult. (4)

MONUMENT: A visible marker used as a reference point to establish the lines and boundaries of a survey. (7)

MORTGAGE: A legal document in which property is conditionally transferred from a mortgagor to a mortgagee as security for the payment of a debt. (5)

MORTGAGEE: The one who receives and holds a mortgage as security for a debt; the lender. (5)

MORTGAGE LIEN: A charge on the property of the borrower that secures the debt obligations. (5)

MORTGAGOR: The one who gives a mortgage as security for a debt; the borrower. (5)

MULTIPLE LISTING: A listing agreement which is distributed by a broker to all other brokers comprising the multiple listing organization. (3)

NET INCOME: Income arrived at after deducting expenses for the gross income received. (8)

NET LEASE: A lease in which the tenant not only pays rent but also maintenance and operating expenses.

NET LISTING: A listing agreement in which the broker receives as his commission all monies over the amount which the owner wishes to realize from the sale of his property. Its use is illegal and/or discouraged in most states.

NONCONFORMING USE: A permitted use of a property which no longer conforms to the current use regulations due to a change in the zoning ordinance. (10)

NOTE: Evidence of a debt, wherein the borrower signs a document stating the amount of the loan, interest rate, method of repayment, and the obligation to repay. (5)

OBSOLESCENCE: A type of depreciation of real property. Functional obsolescence consists of a defect in the structure or design of a property. Economic obsolescence consists of a loss in value due to causes within the neighborhood. (8)

OFFER AND ACCEPTANCE: "A meeting of the minds." Two vital elements of a valid contract. (4)

ON-SITE IMPROVEMENT: Any improvement to property that is contained within the boundaries of the property. (8)

OPEN-END MORTGAGE: A mortgage loan that can be increased back to its original amount. (5)

OPEN LISTING: A listing given to a number of brokers whereby a commission is earned by the broker who is the procuring cause of the sale. (3)

OPINION OF TITLE: An opinion usually made by an attorney as to the status of the title of a parcel of real property; however, it is not a guarantee of title. (2)

OPINION OF VALUE: An appraiser's estimate of the worth of property. Also known as an "appraisal." (8)

OPTION: An agreement to sell or purchase a property for a given period of time and for a given price. (4)

ORAL CONTRACT: A verbal agreement without written form. Normally not used or enforceable in real estate transactions. (4)

OVERIMPROVEMENT: An improvement which is not the highest and best use of the site on which it is located. (8)

PACKAGE MORTGAGE: A method of financing the purchase of items of personal property as well as the real estate involved. (5)

PARTITION: The division of property among joint owners or tenants-in-common when they wish to terminate the co-ownership.

PARTY WALL: A wall separating but shared in common by two buildings.

PENAL SUM: The amount stated in the bond. It is usually greater than the mortgage indebtedness to protect the lender in foreclosure costs. (5)

PERCENTAGE LEASE: A lease whereby the rental is based on a percentage of the gross income received by the tenant; most commonly used in shopping centers. (6)

PERSONAL PROPERTY: Items which are movable and unattached so as to not destroy the real estate if removed. Also known as chattels. (2)

PHYSICAL DEPRECIATION: A loss in value due to the wear and tear of the elements on the physical real property. (8)

PLANNED UNIT DEVELOPMENT (PUD): A concept in housing designed to utilize the maximum amount of open space and produce a high density of dwellings.

PLAT BOOK: A public land record containing maps showing the division of the land into sections, blocks, lots and streets and indicating the measurements of individual parcels. (7)

POINT OF BEGINNING: The first directional point of a survey that legally defines property. (7)

POLICE POWER: The constitutional authority and power of the government to regulate and adopt laws promoting the general safety and welfare of the public. Some examples of police power are the right to tax and the right to regulate land use through master plans and zoning. (2)

POWER OF ATTORNEY: A contract permitting one person to act for another. (4)

PREPAYMENT PENALTY: The amount set by a creditor to be paid by the debtor if he repays the total amount of the debt prior to maturity. (12)

PRIMARY LEASE: Lease between owner and tenant, as opposed to lease between tenant and subtenant.

PRINCIPAL: One who authorizes another to act in his behalf; one of the main parties to a transaction. (3)

PRINCIPAL MERIDIAN: See *Meridian.*

PRIVATE RESTRICTIONS: A limitation of use, stated in a deed or lease, and imposed on the present holder of the title. (2)

PROCURING CAUSE: The effort to bring about the desired result. (3)

PROPERTY MANAGEMENT: The aspect of real estate concerned with the leasing, maintenance, and managing of property for others. (6)

PROPERTY TAX: Money levied by the government against real and/or personal property. (2)

PRORATE: To divide proportionally. (12)

PUBLIC RESTRICTIONS: Restrictions to the use of property imposed by government through its police power. Examples are zoning laws, health regulations, traffic controls, etc. (2)

PURCHASE MONEY MORTGAGE: A mortgage held by the seller for the buyer when there exists a gap between the down payment and the amount of the new mortgage loan. (12)

QUITCLAIM DEED: A deed of conveyance which releases any interest the grantor has in the property without any warranties. (4)

RANGE LINES: On the Government Survey, lines parallel to the principal meridian marking off the land into 6-mile strips known as ranges.

READY, WILLING, AND ABLE: A phrase used to class a prospective purchaser of property, in which the buyer is willing to accept the terms of the seller and enter into a sales contract.

REAL ESTATE: The physical land, below, and the air above it, with everything permanently attached to it. (Also real property, realty, or land.) (2)

REALTOR: A registered trademark to be used only by members of the state and local boards associated with the National Association of Realtors.

RECAPTURE RATE: The rate at which an investor would collect a return on his investment over a period of time. (8)

RECORDED PLAT: A subdivision of lands recorded in the clerk's office for future reference. (7)

RECORDING: Entering into the public records the written documents affecting title to real property. This recording provides constructive notice. (5)

RECTANGULAR SURVEY SYSTEM: A method of legally defining land. This system divides land into squares of six miles called townships. Each township is identified with respect to base lines and principal meridian lines. These are further divided into one mile squares called sections and can even be further divided into smaller squares. Identification of property is then simplified by this grid system. It is not used in all states. (7)

REDEMPTION PERIOD: The period of time in which a property owner can regain title to his property after a foreclosure or tax sale. The owner must pay the sale price, interest, and costs. (5)

REDLINING: The practice of lending institutions of restricting mortgage loans in certain deteriorating areas of a community in order to reduce risks.

REDUCTION CERTIFICATE: Document provided by the lender when a mortgaged property is sold and the buyer assumes the debt. Acknowledges extent of reduction of debt and the sum remaining.

REGULATION Z: A provision of the Federal Truth-in-Lending Act which requires full, complete, and clear disclosure of credit costs as an annual percentage rate. The regulation applies to all those lending money for purchase of residential real property.

RELEASE CLAUSE: A provision in a blanket mortgage by which a specific parcel is released from the mortgage upon payment of a portion of the loan.

REMAINDER ESTATE: A future interest in an estate which is activated upon the termination of a previous estate.

RENT: The consideration (periodic payment) paid by a lessee to a landlord for use and possession of the leased premises. (6)

REPLACEMENT COST: In appraisal, the cost of erecting a building to take the place of an existing structure. (8)

REPRODUCTION COST: The cost of reproducing a similar property based on current prices. (8)

RESCISSION: The act of terminating a contract by which all parties are returned to their original status. (4)

RESTRICTION: A condition or limitation as to the manner in which a property can be utilized.

RETURN RATE: A rate of interest sufficient to attract investors to real estate. (8)

REVALUATION LEASE: A lease that is changed during its term by a reanalysis of market or property conditions. (6)

REVERSION: An interest that exists in the grantor when he gives a limited estate and termination is possible, such as a life estate. (2)

RIGHT OF FIRST REFUSAL: A person's right to have the first choice to either purchase or lease a property.

RIGHT OF SURVIVORSHIP: The automatic right of a surviving joint tenant or tenant by the entirety to acquire the interest of a deceased joint tenant.

RIGHT-OF-WAY: (1) The right to use a particular path for access. (2) The areas of subdivisions dedicated to public use for streets and utilities.

RIPARIAN RIGHTS: The rights of an owner whose land abuts or is adjacent to streams and lakes. Also known as "littoral rights" in some states. (7)

SALE-LEASEBACK TRANSACTION: A method of real estate financing whereby an owner sells his property and leases it back from the new owner.

SALESPERSON: An independent contractor who, under the supervision of a broker, is licensed to perform real estate acts in accordance with state law. (1)

SALVAGE VALUE: The estimated value of an asset at the end of its economic life. (8)

SATISFACTION OF MORTGAGE: A certificate issued by a mortgagee when the mortgagor has repaid his debt in full.

SECOND MORTGAGE: See *Junior Mortgage.*

SECTION: As used in the rectangular (government) survey system, a section contains 640 acres and is one square mile in area. (7)

SECURITY DEPOSIT: Money deposited by the tenant with the landlord to be held in event of damage to the premises, failure to pay rent, or any such costs incurred by the landlord upon the end of tenancy.

SEPARATE PROPERTY: Real property held by a husband or wife in severalty, as opposed to community property.

SERVIENT TENEMENT: The property through which an easement or right-of-way passes to the benefit of the dominant tenement.

SETBACK: A zoning restriction on the amount of land required between the lot line and the building line. (10)

SEVERALTY: Sole ownership of real property. (2)

(IS) SILENT ON: The situation in which a contract makes no mention of certain conditions which might affect interpretation of that contract. When a contract is silent on a subject, the most common arrangement is assumed.

SOLE AND EXCLUSIVE LISTING: A written contract between an owner and broker whereby the owner guarantees a commission

to the broker if the property is sold upon acceptable terms.

SPECIAL AGENT: One who is authorized by a principal to perform a specific act. (3)

SPECIAL ASSESSMENT: A tax levied against specific properties that will benefit from a public improvement, such as sewers or recreational areas. (5)

SPECIAL WARRANTY DEED: A deed in which the grantor warrants against defects that occurred during the period of his ownership but not against defects prior to that time. (4)

SPECIFIC PERFORMANCE: A court action requiring an individual to carry out his obligations in a contract. (4)

STATUTE OF FRAUDS: The law requiring that contracts be in writing in order to be enforceable. (4)

STATUTE OF LIMITATIONS: The law applying to the period of time within which a legal action must be brought to court. (4)

STEERING: The illegal practice of guiding homeseekers into a specific area to either maintain the homogeneity of the neighborhood or to change the area to create panic. (10)

STRAIGHT-LINE DEPRECIATION: The assumption that value decreases at a constant rate. (8)

STRAIGHT-TERM MORTGAGE: A mortgage in which the indebtor pays only interest during its term. No repayment of principal is expected until it terminates. (5)

SUBCONTRACTOR: A contractor who enters into an agreement with the general contractor to perform a special phase of the construction process.

SUBDIVIDER: An owner whose land is divided into two or more lots and offered for sale. (10)

SUBDIVISION: A tract of land that is to be divided into two or more lots and offered for sale. (10)

SUBLEASE: A lease given by a lessee to another party for a portion of the term of the lease. (6)

SUBORDINATION AGREEMENT: An agreement whereby the lender of the first lien gives priority to the lender of a subsequent lien. (5)

SUBROGATION: Substituting a third party in the place of a creditor.

SUBSTITUTION: The principle in appraising that states that the highest value of property is set by the cost of purchasing a similar property with no delay in making the substitution.

SURVEY: The method of measuring boundaries and determining land areas. (7)

SYNDICATION: A group of two or more people who unite for the purpose of making and operating an investment. (3)

TAX DEED: The document used to convey real property when the government (acting as grantor) sells a property for default of tax payments. (4)

TAX LIEN: A general lien imposed against a parcel of real estate for the payment of taxes. (5)

TAX RATE: The rate that is applied to the assessed value to compute the annual real estate taxes. (11)

TAX SALE: Sale of a property by a taxing authority after a period of nonpayment of taxes. (4)

TENANCY AT SUFFERANCE: The tenancy which exists when a tenant continues to possess the leased premises after the lease has expired and against the consent of the landlord. (6)

TENANCY AT WILL: The tenancy that exists when a tenant continues to be in possession of the leased premises after expiration of the lease by permission of the landlord. (6)

TENANCY BY THE ENTIRETY: A joint tenancy between husband and wife with both having an equal, undivided interest in the property. (2)

TENANCY FOR YEARS: A less-than-freehold estate whereby the property is leased for a definite period of time. (6)

TENANCY IN COMMON: A form of ownership between two or more persons whereby they hold an undivided interest in the whole property. Upon the death of a co-tenant, the interest passes to his heirs or devisees. (2)

TESTATE: The status of a deceased person who has executed a valid will. (4)

TIME IS OF THE ESSENCE: A phrase used in a contract setting forth a specific date by which all parties must perform their obligations. (4)

TITLE INSURANCE: A contract in which a title company bears the responsibility of loss arising from defects in a title or any liens or encumbrances affecting the title. (12)

TITLE SEARCH: An examination of the public records to determine any defects to a title or liens and encumbrances that would affect title. (2)

TORRENS SYSTEM: A method of registering land in which ownership is verified and the title status established. This eliminates the need for an additional search of the public records. (2)

TOWNSHIP: A six-mile-square tract of land determined by a government survey. (7)

TRADE FIXTURE: An item of personal property attached to the premises by a tenant as a necessary part of his business. (2)

TRANSFER TAX: Tax stamps that are required to be affixed to a deed at the time of recording.

TRUST: An agreement whereby title to real estate is transferred by the grantor to a third person (trustee) to be held for another (beneficiary).

TRUST DEED: Used in some states that conditionally convey title to the lender until satisfaction of the mortgage. (5)

TRUTH-IN-LENDING LAW: A federal law with the purpose of providing that borrowers can receive information regarding the cost of credit in such a way that they can compare various credit terms. The law requires that all finance charges and interest rates which make up the annual percentage rate be disclosed to the borrower.

UNDIVIDED INTEREST: The rights of possession that a co-owner has in property with the other co-owners. (2)

UNIFORM COMMERCIAL CODE: A law regulating commercial transactions including personal property, pledges, chattel mortgages, and stocks so as to make them uniform throughout the country.

UNILATERAL CONTRACT: A contract in which only one party expresses an obligation to perform with no promise of performance binding on the other party.

USEFUL LIFE: The period of time in which an asset is anticipated to remain economically feasible to the owner. (8)

USURY: The act of charging an interest rate in excess of that which is permitted by law. (5)

VA MORTGAGE: A partially guaranteed mortgage loan for the purchase or construction of a home which is extended to eligible veterans who were honorably discharged. The main purpose is to provide loans with a comparatively low interest rate and no need for a down payment. (5)

VALID CONTRACT: A legally sufficient contract which is binding on all parties. (4)

VALUE: Subject to various interpretations and quite intangible, but defined as the worth of all the rights arising from ownership. (8)

VARIABLE RATE MORTGAGE: A mortgage in which the interest can vary over the term of the loan. (5)

VARIANCE: Permission obtained from government authorities to construct a building or conduct a use that is contrary to the zoning ordinance. (10)

VENDEE: The buyer. (4)

VENDOR: The seller. (4)

VOID CONTRACT: A contract that has no legal force. (4)

VOIDABLE CONTRACT: A contract that appears to be valid but is subject to cancellation by a disabled party. (4)

WARRANTY DEED: A deed which offers the greatest protection. The grantor fully guarantees good clear title to the premises. (4)

WILL: A written instrument disposing of property upon the death of the testator. (4)

WRAPAROUND MORTGAGE: A method of refinancing whereby an additional mortgage with a different lender is secured over the existing prior mortgage amount. The entire loan is then treated as a single obligation and the secondary mortgagee pays the original loan from the total payments received. (5)

YEAR-TO-YEAR TENANCY: A periodic tenancy in which the term of the lease runs from year to year. (2,6)

ZONING: The regulation of the uses of structures in certain areas of a community. (10)

ZONING ORDINANCE: A local law defining the zoned areas of a community. (10)

Chapter Fourteen

Model Real Estate License Examinations

Now that you have built yourself a solid foundation in the many topics tested on real estate examinations, it is time to try your hand at some simulated examinations. This chapter consists of four model examinations. The first exam follows the ASI salesperson format; the second the ASI broker format; the third the AMP format; and the fourth the PSI format. These are not actual examinations but are of about the same general level of difficulty as the exams for which they prepare you. The style, number, and distribution of questions are comparable to those found on actual examinations.

We urge you to take all four exams in this chapter. Set aside a three-hour stretch for each exam, and test yourself under battle conditions. Do not peek at the answers or refer to the text while taking a model exam. When you finish each exam, score yourself. Check your math against the solutions provided and return to the text to review the rationale for those questions you answered incorrectly. If you consistently score 70 percent or higher, you should have nothing to worry about.

We have provided sample answer sheets conforming to the different exams. Tear these answer sheets out of the book and use them as you answer questions in the corresponding exams. If you will be taking a paper-and-pencil exam with a separate answer sheet, it is important for you to get practice not only in answering exam questions but in using the answer sheets accurately. Remember, when you temporarily skip over a question, you MUST skip its answer blank. Conversely, every question must be answered in the proper place. If your examination will be administered by computer or machine, practice with exam sheets will not give you any advantage, but it surely will do no harm.

Finally, we must remind you not to stop studying when you finish this book. No matter which exam you take, you will have to answer from 30 to 75 questions based upon real estate laws in your state. You must study your own state's laws in order to be prepared for the questions based upon state law. Contact your state's licensing authorities well in advance so that you can devote ample time to study. It is not enough to be well versed in real estate principles and practices and in federal regulations; you must also have mastered state law in order to become licensed.

ANSWER SHEET FOR MODEL ASI
SALESPERSON EXAMINATION

1 (A)(B)(C)(D)   26 (A)(B)(C)(D)   51 (A)(B)(C)(D)   76 (A)(B)(C)(D)
2 (A)(B)(C)(D)   27 (A)(B)(C)(D)   52 (A)(B)(C)(D)   77 (A)(B)(C)(D)
3 (A)(B)(C)(D)   28 (A)(B)(C)(D)   53 (A)(B)(C)(D)   78 (A)(B)(C)(D)
4 (A)(B)(C)(D)   29 (A)(B)(C)(D)   54 (A)(B)(C)(D)   79 (A)(B)(C)(D)
5 (A)(B)(C)(D)   30 (A)(B)(C)(D)   55 (A)(B)(C)(D)   80 (A)(B)(C)(D)
6 (A)(B)(C)(D)   31 (A)(B)(C)(D)   56 (A)(B)(C)(D)   81 (A)(B)(C)(D)
7 (A)(B)(C)(D)   32 (A)(B)(C)(D)   57 (A)(B)(C)(D)   82 (A)(B)(C)(D)
8 (A)(B)(C)(D)   33 (A)(B)(C)(D)   58 (A)(B)(C)(D)   83 (A)(B)(C)(D)
9 (A)(B)(C)(D)   34 (A)(B)(C)(D)   59 (A)(B)(C)(D)   84 (A)(B)(C)(D)
10 (A)(B)(C)(D)   35 (A)(B)(C)(D)   60 (A)(B)(C)(D)   85 (A)(B)(C)(D)
11 (A)(B)(C)(D)   36 (A)(B)(C)(D)   61 (A)(B)(C)(D)   86 (A)(B)(C)(D)
12 (A)(B)(C)(D)   37 (A)(B)(C)(D)   62 (A)(B)(C)(D)   87 (A)(B)(C)(D)
13 (A)(B)(C)(D)   38 (A)(B)(C)(D)   63 (A)(B)(C)(D)   88 (A)(B)(C)(D)
14 (A)(B)(C)(D)   39 (A)(B)(C)(D)   64 (A)(B)(C)(D)   89 (A)(B)(C)(D)
15 (A)(B)(C)(D)   40 (A)(B)(C)(D)   65 (A)(B)(C)(D)   90 (A)(B)(C)(D)
16 (A)(B)(C)(D)   41 (A)(B)(C)(D)   66 (A)(B)(C)(D)   91 (A)(B)(C)(D)
17 (A)(B)(C)(D)   42 (A)(B)(C)(D)   67 (A)(B)(C)(D)   92 (A)(B)(C)(D)
18 (A)(B)(C)(D)   43 (A)(B)(C)(D)   68 (A)(B)(C)(D)   93 (A)(B)(C)(D)
19 (A)(B)(C)(D)   44 (A)(B)(C)(D)   69 (A)(B)(C)(D)   94 (A)(B)(C)(D)
20 (A)(B)(C)(D)   45 (A)(B)(C)(D)   70 (A)(B)(C)(D)   95 (A)(B)(C)(D)
21 (A)(B)(C)(D)   46 (A)(B)(C)(D)   71 (A)(B)(C)(D)   96 (A)(B)(C)(D)
22 (A)(B)(C)(D)   47 (A)(B)(C)(D)   72 (A)(B)(C)(D)   97 (A)(B)(C)(D)
23 (A)(B)(C)(D)   48 (A)(B)(C)(D)   73 (A)(B)(C)(D)   98 (A)(B)(C)(D)
24 (A)(B)(C)(D)   49 (A)(B)(C)(D)   74 (A)(B)(C)(D)   99 (A)(B)(C)(D)
25 (A)(B)(C)(D)   50 (A)(B)(C)(D)   75 (A)(B)(C)(D)   100 (A)(B)(C)(D)

MODEL ASI SALESPERSON EXAMINATION

95 questions

1. A leasehold estate may be
   A. a life estate
   B. a remainder estate
   C. an estate for years
   D. an estate *pur autre vie*

2. Along with title to the land, one may also acquire
   A. easements
   B. encroachments
   C. licenses
   D. all of these

3. Once an individual has in his possession a signed contract for purchase of a property, he should be certain that the property is adequately insured because
   A. he has adverse possession
   B. he has a life estate
   C. he has equitable title
   D. he has interest in the property

4. Zoning ordinances are an example of the use of the state's
   A. police power
   B. health regulatory power
   C. right of eminent domain
   D. private restrictions

5. A voidable contract is
   A. never enforceable
   B. always enforceable
   C. subject to rescission
   D. illegal

6. Once a contract has been signed and accepted by both parties
   A. it cannot be changed in any way
   B. it can be changed by a rider signed by the seller
   C. it can be changed by an amendment offered by the buyer and his attorney and signed by both
   D. it can be altered in writing by mutual agreement of buyer and seller

7. The requisites of a valid contract include competent parties, consideration, proper form, and
   A. mortgage provision
   B. legal purpose
   C. general warranty
   D. fair housing statement

8. A salesperson who takes the same prospective customers to a number of properties over a period of time owes first allegiance to
A. the prospective customers
B. his or her broker
C. the offices which list the properties being shown
D. the owners of properties for sale

9. If the principal authorizes his broker to accept good faith deposits, he is appointing his broker
A. fiduciary
B. power of attorney
C. mortgagor
D. executor

10. If a principal wishes to terminate an agency agreement before its specified termination date, he must
A. file a claim with the Board of Realtors
B. pay damages
C. state his wishes in writing
D. withdraw his property from the market

11. The right to "quiet enjoyment" of premises includes all of the following EXCEPT
A. protection from capricious eviction
B. guarantee of friendly neighbors
C. expectation of a sound roof
D. hot and cold running water

12. A parcel of land is assessed at $40,000 and the improvements upon it are assessed at $105,000. In this community, the school tax rate is 8.10 per thousand, the town tax rate is 3.20 per thousand, and the county tax rate is 2.30 per thousand of assessed valuation. What is the total annual tax paid by the owner of the property?
A. $850.50
B. $1,174.50
C. $1,428.00
D. $1,972.00

13. In the community described in problem 12, school taxes are payable semi-annually on January 1 and July 1; town taxes are payable annually on April 1; and county taxes are payable annually on October 1. The property described in problem 12 was sold on June 30, at which time the seller was current in payment of all taxes. How much did the buyer have to pay the seller as payment for prepaid taxes? (The seller is responsible for all taxes up to and including the date of settlement.)
A. $348.00
B. $431.38
C. $587.25
D. $953.37

14. The purchaser of the property described in problems 12 and 13 is financing his purchase with a mortgage. The mortgagee wishes to hold in its escrow account monies sufficient to pay all tax bills which will come due within the next year. At the closing, the purchasers must pay the bank
A. $164.33
B. $1,384.75
C. $1,549.08
D. $1,972.00

15. Under an Exclusive-right-to-sell agency, which of the following scenarios is NOT possible?
   A. Listing broker sells the property and receives commission.
   B. Owner sells property and pays no commission.
   C. Owner sells property and pays reduced commission.
   D. Cooperating broker sells property and receives partial commission.

16. Which approach to value of a property utilizes the competitive market analysis (CMA)?
   A. Cost approach
   B. Market data approach
   C. Income approach
   D. All utilize the CMA

17. The highest and best use of a property must be feasible, possible, and
   A. legal
   B. probable
   C. actual
   D. marketable

18. The purpose of a bridge loan is to
   A. finance bridge and road construction
   B. pay for structural repairs required by the VA
   C. pay the down payment on a property until funds can be collected from the sale of another property
   D. serve as short-term financing until a mortgage can be obtained at a more favorable rate

19. Which of the following may be correctly called a conventional mortgage?
   A. Amortized mortgage
   B. Variable payment mortgage
   C. Wraparound mortgage
   D. All of these

20. Which of the following statements about VA loans is NOT true?
   A. A veteran is not permitted to pay the discount points on the mortgage for the home he is purchasing.
   B. The veteran may prepay the full amount of his mortgage at any time without penalty.
   C. VA-guaranteed loans may be used in the purchase of single-family homes, four-family homes, and cooperative apartments.
   D. The VA must approve the appraiser who values the property.

21. All of the following are considered encumbrances EXCEPT
   A. easements
   B. emblements
   C. mortgages
   D. restrictions

22. An executor's deed warrants title against
   A. acts of the decedent
   B. restrictive covenants
   C. mechanics' liens
   D. the executor's own acts

23. Constructive eviction occurs when
   A. the owner asks the tenant to move out so that he can make repairs
   B. the owner evicts a tenant who makes unauthorized alterations to the premises
   C. premises become uninhabitable
   D. the tenant moves out because nearby construction is so disruptive

24. In order to acquire property through adverse possession, one must occupy it
  A. continuously and secretly
  B. intermittently and openly
  C. continuously and hostilely
  D. visibly and sporadically

25. A purchaser is taking out a $26,000 amortizing mortgage loan at 11¾ percent per annum. If he takes out a 20-year loan, his monthly payments, including principal and interest, will be $281.77. If he takes out a 30-year loan, his payments will be $262.45 per month. If he chooses the 20-year loan, his payments will be
  A. $19.32 less per month
  B. $231.84 more per year
  C. $231.84 less per year
  D. $857.20 greater over the life of the loan

26. Which of the following most accurately describes an assignment of a contract?
  A. The transfer of rights to a third party
  B. The substitution of a new contract for an existing agreement
  C. Transfer of rights from a third party
  D. Sale of the property to someone else

27. What do the following have in common?
  I. The restriction of rentals or occupancies of lodgings owned by a private club that is not operated commercially
  II. The restriction of the rental of rooms in a two-family owner-occupied dwelling
  III. Rental of a one-family house by the owner without the assistance of a broker
     A. All require written leases of at least one year.
     B. All are subject to terms of the Federal Fair Housing Law.
     C. None are subject to the terms of the Federal Fair Housing Law.
     D. All are subject to terms of the Truth-in-Lending Act.

28. A court action that states that one individual is indebted to another and sets the amount of the indebtedness is called
  A. a lien or mortgage   C. an injunction
  B. a devise or will   D. a judgment

29. When a contract for the sale of real property has been signed, the purchaser
  A. has legal title to the property
  B. has the right to possess the property
  C. has equitable title
  D. has nothing until he receives the deed

30. Where must a deed be recorded?
  A. In the office of the registrar of deeds in the county where the grantor resides
  B. In the office of the registrar of deeds in the county where the property is located
  C. In the office of the registrar of deeds in the county in which the grantee resides
  D. In the office of the registrar of deeds in the county in which the attorney for the purchaser maintains an office

31. If the tax rate of a property is decreased by 10 percent and the assessed value is increased by 10 percent, what is the effect on the annual taxes?
- A. Decrease of 1%
- B. Increase of 2%
- C. Increase of 5%
- D. No change

32. What would a business be worth that shows a profit of $275 monthly and is earning 8 percent per year on the total investment?
- A. $33,000
- B. $26,400
- C. $41,250
- D. $22,000

33. A mortgage loan that includes fixtures and appliances located on the property is known as
- A. a wraparound mortgage
- B. a package mortgage
- C. an open-end mortgage
- D. a balloon mortgage

34. Which of the following would prohibit the assignment of a lease?
- A. The lease was not recorded.
- B. The lease was for less than 2 years.
- C. The prospective subtenant is over 65 years of age.
- D. The landlord is not satisfied with the prospective tenant's credit rating.

35. Which of the following is true concerning the requirements of the Statute of Frauds in order to convey clean title?
- A. An agent may sign for a principal if he has power of attorney.
- B. When sellers are co-owners, only one co-owner is required to sign.
- C. Liens against the property must be enumerated.
- D. When the value of the transaction is less than $55,000.00, the contract need not be in writing.

36. Your client's house is on the market at a listing price of $187,000. This client has signed an agreement to purchase a new property, closing date August 30. On June 18, your client receives two offers to purchase. The first offer is for $182,000 with 10 percent down and VA-guaranteed financing. The second offer is for $178,000, 50 percent down, and conventional financing. You should advise your client to
- A. accept the first offer because it was received first
- B. accept the first offer because it is higher
- C. accept the first offer because to reject it would constitute illegal discrimination against a veteran
- D. accept the second offer because the terms offer much greater likelihood of closing before August 30, and, with a possibility of seller's points on the VA mortgage, the price gap is not great

37. Mr. Sinclair wants to buy an income property that grosses $300 per month. If the total annual expenses on this property are $1,200 and Mr. Sinclair wants a 12 percent return on his investment, how much should he offer for this property?
- A. $36,000
- B. $24,000
- C. $28,800
- D. $20,000

38. Tenants in common who wish to terminate their co-ownership of real property may
  A. file a suit for partition
  B. subdivide the real property if possible and agreeable to all parties concerned
  C. sell the property
  D. lease out a portion of the property

39. Liens that take precedence over all other liens are
  A. mortgage liens
  B. tax liens
  C. mechanic's liens
  D. junior liens

40. Mr. Smith's property is valued at $58,000. It is assessed at $51,500 and is taxed at a rate of $3.40 per $100 of assessed value. If the tax rate is increased $.20 per $100 of valuation with the same assessment, how much more will he be required to pay?
  A. $103.00
  B. $301.00
  C. $1,751.00
  D. $1,854.00

41. The wording in a deed "to B for the life of C" creates an estate known as
  A. non-freehold
  B. "pur autre vie"
  C. fee simple determinable
  D. "condition subsequent" fee

42. Proof of ownership of title to personal property is usually evidenced by a
  A. deed
  B. option
  C. bill of sale
  D. chattel

43. When a borrower falls behind in his mortgage payments, the lender can call for the entire balance to be due immediately by virtue of the
  A. acceleration clause
  B. alienation clause
  C. habendum clause
  D. defeasance clause

44. According to the Truth-in-Lending Act, which of the following is not required to be disclosed?
  A. Prepayment penalty
  B. Attorney's fees
  C. Annual percentage rate
  D. Total finance charge

45. The tax assessment is useful to the appraiser using the
  A. income approach
  B. market data approach
  C. both of these approaches
  D. neither of these approaches

46. At which of the following times does title pass in a real estate transaction?
  A. When the buyer completes payment
  B. When the agreement of sale is signed
  C. When the deed is signed by the seller
  D. When the deed is delivered

47. From a seller's point of view, which of the following is a disadvantage of selling to an FHA-insured buyer?
  A. Payment of discount points
  B. The loan may close too quickly
  C. FHA-borrower standards are too lenient
  D. Seller needs to carry a second mortgage or trust deed

48. Which of the following would best be applied to the appraisal of a 20-year-old residence?
   A. Market data approach to value
   B. Cost approach to value
   C. Income approach to value
   D. Engineer's approach to value

49. A remedy that is executed in a court of equity compelling the defendant to carry out the terms of the purchase and sale agreement is called
   A. a breach
   B. specific performance
   C. damages
   D. an attachment

50. A prospective client requests that a broker list a property for sale with certain restrictions that are against the law. The broker should
   A. accept the listing and say nothing
   B. refuse to accept the listing
   C. accept the listing and have the client sign an affidavit accepting all responsibility
   D. accept the listing and report the client to the authorities

51. In estimating the market value of a property, a broker is expected to consider all of the following EXCEPT
   A. special assessments on the property
   B. particular appeal the property might have to a specific type of buyer
   C. appearance of the neighboring properties
   D. age of the roof

52. It is said that "a contract is a mutual agreement to do or not to do some legal thing." Which of the following are NOT considered to be contracts?
   A. Leases
   B. Escrow agreements
   C. Judgments
   D. Listing agreements

53. In common law, which of the following would terminate a lease?
   A. Death of the landlord
   B. Mutual agreement
   C. Death of the tenant
   D. Landlord's need to personally occupy the premises

54. A tenancy in the entirety is
   A. owned by husband and wife
   B. entire property of a corporation
   C. owned by a partnership
   D. owned by one person alone

55. A nonconforming property is one that
   A. in not in agreement with existing zoning laws
   B. is not in agreement with the description as stated in its survey
   C. is not in agreement with building codes
   D. is markedly different in appearance from all others in the neighborhood

56. On a house valued at $130,000, a $15,000 loan was obtained to add a garage. The payments are to be $150 per month plus 16 percent annual interest on the decreasing balance. The loan was made on October 15, and all interest and principal payments are due on the 15th of each month thereafter. What amount will be due on November 15?

A. $150   C. $350

B. $200   D. $550

57. Using problem 56 as a basis, what amount will be due on December 15?

A. $350   C. $348

B. $700   D. $198

58. How much will a broker receive as his 6 percent commission fee for the sale of a triangular lot, with a 122-foot frontage and a depth of 124 feet, if the sale price was based at $2.25 per square foot?

A. $1,004.67   C. $1,701.90

B. $1,021.14   D. $2,042.28

59. An agent who sells for a residential development receives a 6 percent commission on the first $90,000 of sales per month plus 2 percent on all sales over that amount. If, in one month, he sold houses for $42,000, $41,500, and $48,900, approximately how much more could he have earned had he worked on a straight 5 percent commission?

A. $300   C. $500

B. $400   D. $600

60. Regulation Z requires the lender to disclose which of the following to a borrower when a first mortgage is made to finance the purchase of a residence?

A. The appraised value of the residence

B. The total charges required for settlement of a real estate transaction

C. The portion of the charges allocated for mortgage insurance

D. The annual percentage rate of the loan

61. When the interest rate of a mortgage exceeds the legal rate, it is known as

A. equity   C. usury

B. escheat   D. debenture

62. Encroachment is

A. the result from a written easement agreement

B. the unauthorized use of another's land

C. a spotted survey

D. considered as personal property

63. In preparation for acquiring a property, Ben Wilson obtained a mortgage loan of $35,490, which was 70 percent of the total sales price. He also deposited a 15 percent earnest money deposit with the broker. What was the amount of the earnest money deposit?

A. $5,070.00   C. $7,605.00

B. $5,323.50   D. $2,282.00

64. The person who signs a listing agreement authorizing the sale of his property is known as a(n)

A. agent   C. grantor

B. lessee   D. principal

65. In the cost approach, the appraiser makes use of
   A. the owner's maintenance cost of the building including repairs
   B. sales prices of similar buildings
   C. the depreciated value used for insurance purposes
   D. an estimate of the replacement cost of the building new

66. A partially hilly plot of land consisting of 348,480 square feet is to be subdivided and sold. One-fifth of the plot is too steep to be useful and 1 acre is transgressed by streams and unsuitable for development. The remainder of the plot is flat, useable land. If one-fourth of the useable land is reserved for roadways, how many square feet of useable land will be left for development?
   A. 58,806 square feet
   B. 76,230 square feet
   C. 113,256 square feet
   D. 176,418 square feet

67. A contract that involves an exchange of promises between both parties is known as a
   A. unilateral contract
   B. bilateral contract
   C. unitarian contract
   D. dual contract

68. Under an installment land contract, the purchaser does NOT
   A. have the right to rental income
   B. have the right to possession
   C. have legal title
   D. have equitable title

69. A balloon mortgage is best described as
   A. being larger than the owner can afford
   B. having a larger payment due at the end of its term
   C. covering more than one parcel of real property
   D. being increased during the term of the mortgage

70. The Truth-in-Lending Act requires that interest be expressed as
   A. a minimum percentage rate
   B. a maximum percentage rate
   C. a varying percentage rate
   D. an annual percentage rate

71. At which of the following times does title pass in a real estate transaction?
   A. When the deed is signed by the seller
   B. When the buyer completes payment
   C. When the deed is delivered
   D. When the agreement of sale is signed

72. An amortized mortgage loan is one that
   A. is paid in monthly payments with interest in addition
   B. is paid in monthly payments of interest only
   C. is paid in monthly payments of principal only
   D. is paid in monthly payments, which include both principal and interest

73. Which of the following statements is correct?
   A. An unrecorded deed is an invalid deed.
   B. Between two recorded deeds conveying title to the same property, the deed first recorded takes priority over subsequent recordings.
   C. Presence of a mechanic's lien voids a deed.
   D. A quitclaim deed cannot be recorded.

Questions 74–78 refer to the map of Springville Estates, Sheet 2.

74. Which of the following statements is true?
A. Lot 1, Block B is larger than Lot 9 in the same block.
B. Lot 13, Block B has common sides with four other lots.
C. Block A contains eight identical lots.
D. If a building lot must be at least 50' x 100', lot 11 in Block A is unbuildable.

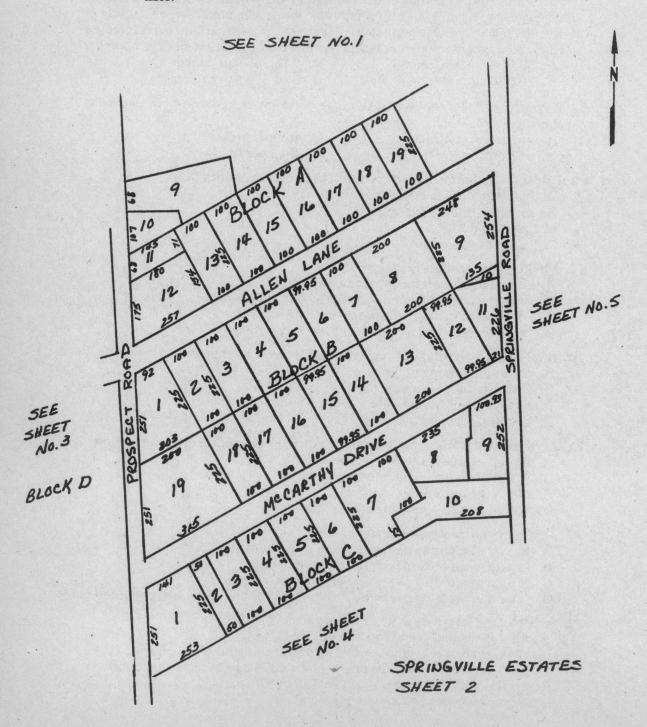

75. Which of the following statements is true?
- A. The lots on the easterly side of Prospect Road should appear on Sheet 3.
- B. Lot 3 in Block C has twice the area of Lot 2 in the same block.
- C. Lot 10 in Block A is the smallest lot on Sheet 2.
- D. Lot 8 in Block B is a perfect square.

76. If the owner of Lot 13 in Block B sold his property for $25,000, what was the cost per acre?
- A. $22,471.85
- B. $23,568.62
- C. $25,000.00
- D. $24,271.84

77. Which of the following lots has the greatest frontage on Allen Lane?
- A. Lot 8, Block B
- B. Lot 12, Block A
- C. Lot 9, Block B
- D. Lot 6, Block B

78. Which of the following statements is NOT true?
- A. Block B has four lots with frontages on two streets.
- B. The lots on the easterly side of Springville Road should appear on Sheet 5.
- C. McCarthy Drive can be found on Sheet 3.
- D. The area of none of the lots 10 can be accurately described on the basis of this map.

79. A young white couple comes into your office and asks to be shown houses in an all-white neighborhood. Your MOST appropriate response is:
- A. "I know just what you are looking for."
- B. "Go to another office. I don't deal with bigots."
- C. "There is no such thing as an all-white neighborhood."
- D. "I don't know the exact makeup of any neighborhood. I will show you a number of houses in your price range, and you may make your own decisions."

80. Which of the following best describes the term "contractual ability"?
- A. That the agreement deliberates a purpose which is legal
- B. That the parties to the contract are competent to enter into a valid contract
- C. That the contract is drawn up by a person legally qualified to do so
- D. That the contract contains all the clauses and covenants necessary to be valid

81. If a salesperson leaves the office of one broker and joins the office of another broker, commissions earned on deals for which contract of sale is completed but final closing has not been accomplished are
- A. payable entirely to the broker through whose office the contract was signed
- B. shared by the original office and the salesperson
- C. paid to the salesperson and that salesperson's new broker
- D. split three ways—among salesperson and both offices

82. Tax levies upon property owners to pay for street improvements are known as
- A. charges
- B. general property taxes
- C. special excise taxes
- D. special assessments

83. Mr. Smith's closing date for the home he recently purchased is May 13. The taxes for the previous calendar year have been paid. If the taxes of $1,250 for the current year began accruing on January 1 and they have not yet been paid, what amount will be credited to the buyer?

A. $416.68
B. $475.67
C. $461.79
D. $523.50

84. What is the estimated value of Mrs. Sycamore's property if the house measures 32 feet by 64 feet and an appraiser has estimated the replacement cost of the house to be $31.25 per square foot? He also valued the land at $14,000 and the depreciation charge at $6,000.

A. $28,000
B. $64,000
C. $72,000
D. $78,000

85. The market approach to value yields which of the following?

A. Lowest indication of value
B. Highest indication of value
C. Range of probable value
D. Indication of future value

86. When estimating the value of a single-family residence, which of the following need the broker not include in the report?

A. Recent comparable sales
B. A statement of how the value was determined
C. A description of the property
D. The total taxes being paid by current residents

87. A deed that contains "warranties against liens" would best be labeled a

A. quitclaim deed
B. bargain and sale deed
C. sheriff's deed
D. title deed

88. A statement made by a person to a qualified official that he freely and voluntarily executed a deed or other instrument is called a(n)

A. acknowledgment
B. authorization
C. authentication
D. execution

89. A valid deed need NOT contain which of the following?

A. A description of the property being conveyed
B. A recital of consideration
C. The name of the grantee
D. The employer tax number of the broker closing the sale

90. A personal property fixture clause is used in a sales contract to insure the inclusion in the sale of which of the following items?

A. A furnace
B. A refrigerator
C. A kitchen ceiling fixture
D. A glass shower enclosure

91. Which of the following statements regarding mortgages is true?

A. All mortgages carry a redemption period determined by the lender.
B. If a mortgagor declares bankruptcy, he is absolved of all debt.
C. If a mortgagee declares bankruptcy, he is absolved of all debt.
D. Mortgage lenders often sell mortgages to other institutions.

92. Which of the following is NOT required before a VA loan is granted for the purchase of a residence?

A. Certification by the borrower that he intends to be the owner-occupier
B. An appraisal of the property to be purchased
C. Payment of equalization points by the veteran
D. Inspection by a qualified termite inspector

93. A written and signed real estate contract can be voided for which of the following reasons?
  A. One of the parties was an unmarried minor at the time he signed the contract.
  B. One of the parties neglected to read the contract before he signed it.
  C. The seller decided to raise the price.
  D. One of the parties changed his mind.

94. Which of the following statements regarding the assignment of sales contracts is true?
  A. Any sales contract may be assigned.
  B. The assignment of rights may be made only by the original seller.
  C. A sales contract may be assigned only to an individual with a current mortgage commitment.
  D. A sales contract may be assigned only to an institution.

95. Which of the following is not recognized as co-ownership rights in property?
  A. Partnership
  B. Corporation
  C. Joint tenancy
  D. Tenancy by the entirety

CORRECT ANSWERS TO MODEL ASI SALESPERSON EXAMINATION

1. C	21. B	41. B	61. C	81. B
2. D	22. D	42. C	62. B	82. D
3. C	23. C	43. A	*63. C	*83. C
4. A	24. C	44. B	64. D	*84. C
5. C	*25. B	45. C	65. D	85. C
6. D	26. A	46. D	*66. D	86. D
7. B	27. C	47. A	67. B	87. B
8. D	28. D	48. A	68. C	88. A
9. A	29. C	49. B	69. B	89. D
10. C	30. B	50. B	70. D	90. B
11. B	*31. A	51. B	71. C	91. D
*12. D	*32. C	52. C	72. D	92. C
*13. B	33. B	53. B	73. B	93. A
*14. D	34. D	54. A	*74. B	94. A
15. B	35. A	55. A	75. B	95. B
16. B	36. D	*56. C	*76. D	
17. A	*37. D	*57. C	77. B	
18. C	38. D	*58. B	78. C	
19. D	39. B	*59. B	79. D	
20. C	*40. A	60. D	80. B	

* Solutions provided

SOLUTIONS TO PROBLEMS REQUIRING MATHEMATICAL CALCULATIONS

12. $40,000 + $105,000 = $145,000 total assessed value
$145,000 × 8.1 per thou = $1,174.50
$145,000 × 3.2 per thou = $464.00
$145,000 × 2.3 per thou = $333.50
$1,972.00 total annual tax

13. The school tax need not enter our calculations.
Town tax $464 × 75% = $348.00 returned to seller
County tax $333.50 × 25% = $83.38 returned to seller
$431.38 returned to seller

14. This is not the usual practice, but read the question carefully and you need not calculate at all. If the bank wants to hold a full year's taxes in advance, the answer is simply the sum of a year's taxes, $1,972.00.

25. 20 yr. loan: $281.77 per mo. × 12 = $3,381.24 per year × 20 yrs. = $67,624.80 over life of the loan
30 yr. loan: $262.45 per mo. × 12 = $3,149.40 per yr. × 30 yrs. = $94,482 over life of the loan
$3,381.24 − $3,149.40 = $231.84 more per year

31. 1.10 × .90 = .99
100 − .99 = 1% change

32. $275 × 12 = $3,300 annual net income
$3,300 ÷ .08 = $41,250

37. $300 × 12 months = $3,600 − $1,200 = $2,400 ÷ .12 = $20,000

40. $51,500 ÷ 100 = $515 × $3.40 = $1,751 old tax rate
$3.40 + $.20 = $3.60 × $515 = $1,854 net tax rate
$1,854 − $1,751 = $103 difference

56. $15,000 × .16 = $2,400 annual interest ÷ 12 = $200 month
$200 + $150 = $350 payment due Nov. 15

57. $15,000 − $150 = $14,850 × .16 = $2376 ÷ 12 = $198
$198 + $150 = $348 due Dec. 15

58. ½ (122 × 124) = ½ (15,128) = 7.564 sq. ft × $2.25/sq. ft. =
$17,019 × .06 commission = $1,021.14

59. $42,000 + $41,500 + $48,900 = $132,400
$90,000 × .06 = $5,400
$43,400 × .02 = $ 848
$6,248
$132,400 × .05 = $6,620 − $6,248 = $372 or approximately $400

63. $35,490 ÷ .70 = $50,700 total sales price
$50,700 × .15 = $7,605 amount of deposit

66. 348,480 × .20 =   69,696 sq. ft. too steep
43,560 sq. ft. transgressed by streams
113,256 sq. ft. unusable land
348,480 − 113,256 = 235,224 × .25 = 58,806 sq. ft. for roadways
235,224 − 58,806 = 176,418 square feet useable land for development

74. Lot 1
A = ½ (225 × 111)   = 12,487.5
B = 92 × 225   = 20,700.0
33,487.5 sq. ft.

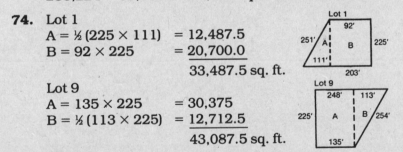

Lot 9
A = 135 × 225   = 30,375
B = ½ (113 × 225) = 12,712.5
43,087.5 sq. ft.

Lot 9 is larger than Lot 1, so statement A is incorrect.
Block A contains seven identical lots.
Lot 11 in Block A exceeds minimum requirements.

76. Lot 13
200 × 225 = 45,000 square feet
45,000 sq. ft. ÷ 43,560 sq. ft. = 1.03 ac.
$25,000 ÷ 1.03 ac. = $24,271.84/ac.

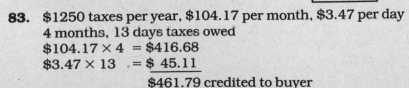

83. $1250 taxes per year, $104.17 per month, $3.47 per day
4 months, 13 days taxes owed
$104.17 × 4 = $416.68
$3.47 × 13 = $ 45.11
$461.79 credited to buyer

84. 32 ft. × 64 ft. = 2048 sq. ft. × $31.25/sq. ft. = $64,000
$64,000 − $6,000 depreciation = $58,000 house value
$58,000 + $14,000 land value = $72,000

ANSWER SHEET FOR MODEL ASI
BROKER EXAMINATION

1 Ⓐ Ⓑ Ⓒ Ⓓ	26 Ⓐ Ⓑ Ⓒ Ⓓ	51 Ⓐ Ⓑ Ⓒ Ⓓ	76 Ⓐ Ⓑ Ⓒ Ⓓ
2 Ⓐ Ⓑ Ⓒ Ⓓ	27 Ⓐ Ⓑ Ⓒ Ⓓ	52 Ⓐ Ⓑ Ⓒ Ⓓ	77 Ⓐ Ⓑ Ⓒ Ⓓ
3 Ⓐ Ⓑ Ⓒ Ⓓ	28 Ⓐ Ⓑ Ⓒ Ⓓ	53 Ⓐ Ⓑ Ⓒ Ⓓ	78 Ⓐ Ⓑ Ⓒ Ⓓ
4 Ⓐ Ⓑ Ⓒ Ⓓ	29 Ⓐ Ⓑ Ⓒ Ⓓ	54 Ⓐ Ⓑ Ⓒ Ⓓ	79 Ⓐ Ⓑ Ⓒ Ⓓ
5 Ⓐ Ⓑ Ⓒ Ⓓ	30 Ⓐ Ⓑ Ⓒ Ⓓ	55 Ⓐ Ⓑ Ⓒ Ⓓ	80 Ⓐ Ⓑ Ⓒ Ⓓ
6 Ⓐ Ⓑ Ⓒ Ⓓ	31 Ⓐ Ⓑ Ⓒ Ⓓ	56 Ⓐ Ⓑ Ⓒ Ⓓ	81 Ⓐ Ⓑ Ⓒ Ⓓ
7 Ⓐ Ⓑ Ⓒ Ⓓ	32 Ⓐ Ⓑ Ⓒ Ⓓ	57 Ⓐ Ⓑ Ⓒ Ⓓ	82 Ⓐ Ⓑ Ⓒ Ⓓ
8 Ⓐ Ⓑ Ⓒ Ⓓ	33 Ⓐ Ⓑ Ⓒ Ⓓ	58 Ⓐ Ⓑ Ⓒ Ⓓ	83 Ⓐ Ⓑ Ⓒ Ⓓ
9 Ⓐ Ⓑ Ⓒ Ⓓ	34 Ⓐ Ⓑ Ⓒ Ⓓ	59 Ⓐ Ⓑ Ⓒ Ⓓ	84 Ⓐ Ⓑ Ⓒ Ⓓ
10 Ⓐ Ⓑ Ⓒ Ⓓ	35 Ⓐ Ⓑ Ⓒ Ⓓ	60 Ⓐ Ⓑ Ⓒ Ⓓ	85 Ⓐ Ⓑ Ⓒ Ⓓ
11 Ⓐ Ⓑ Ⓒ Ⓓ	36 Ⓐ Ⓑ Ⓒ Ⓓ	61 Ⓐ Ⓑ Ⓒ Ⓓ	86 Ⓐ Ⓑ Ⓒ Ⓓ
12 Ⓐ Ⓑ Ⓒ Ⓓ	37 Ⓐ Ⓑ Ⓒ Ⓓ	62 Ⓐ Ⓑ Ⓒ Ⓓ	87 Ⓐ Ⓑ Ⓒ Ⓓ
13 Ⓐ Ⓑ Ⓒ Ⓓ	38 Ⓐ Ⓑ Ⓒ Ⓓ	63 Ⓐ Ⓑ Ⓒ Ⓓ	88 Ⓐ Ⓑ Ⓒ Ⓓ
14 Ⓐ Ⓑ Ⓒ Ⓓ	39 Ⓐ Ⓑ Ⓒ Ⓓ	64 Ⓐ Ⓑ Ⓒ Ⓓ	89 Ⓐ Ⓑ Ⓒ Ⓓ
15 Ⓐ Ⓑ Ⓒ Ⓓ	40 Ⓐ Ⓑ Ⓒ Ⓓ	65 Ⓐ Ⓑ Ⓒ Ⓓ	90 Ⓐ Ⓑ Ⓒ Ⓓ
16 Ⓐ Ⓑ Ⓒ Ⓓ	41 Ⓐ Ⓑ Ⓒ Ⓓ	66 Ⓐ Ⓑ Ⓒ Ⓓ	91 Ⓐ Ⓑ Ⓒ Ⓓ
17 Ⓐ Ⓑ Ⓒ Ⓓ	42 Ⓐ Ⓑ Ⓒ Ⓓ	67 Ⓐ Ⓑ Ⓒ Ⓓ	92 Ⓐ Ⓑ Ⓒ Ⓓ
18 Ⓐ Ⓑ Ⓒ Ⓓ	43 Ⓐ Ⓑ Ⓒ Ⓓ	68 Ⓐ Ⓑ Ⓒ Ⓓ	93 Ⓐ Ⓑ Ⓒ Ⓓ
19 Ⓐ Ⓑ Ⓒ Ⓓ	44 Ⓐ Ⓑ Ⓒ Ⓓ	69 Ⓐ Ⓑ Ⓒ Ⓓ	94 Ⓐ Ⓑ Ⓒ Ⓓ
20 Ⓐ Ⓑ Ⓒ Ⓓ	45 Ⓐ Ⓑ Ⓒ Ⓓ	70 Ⓐ Ⓑ Ⓒ Ⓓ	95 Ⓐ Ⓑ Ⓒ Ⓓ
21 Ⓐ Ⓑ Ⓒ Ⓓ	46 Ⓐ Ⓑ Ⓒ Ⓓ	71 Ⓐ Ⓑ Ⓒ Ⓓ	96 Ⓐ Ⓑ Ⓒ Ⓓ
22 Ⓐ Ⓑ Ⓒ Ⓓ	47 Ⓐ Ⓑ Ⓒ Ⓓ	72 Ⓐ Ⓑ Ⓒ Ⓓ	97 Ⓐ Ⓑ Ⓒ Ⓓ
23 Ⓐ Ⓑ Ⓒ Ⓓ	48 Ⓐ Ⓑ Ⓒ Ⓓ	73 Ⓐ Ⓑ Ⓒ Ⓓ	98 Ⓐ Ⓑ Ⓒ Ⓓ
24 Ⓐ Ⓑ Ⓒ Ⓓ	49 Ⓐ Ⓑ Ⓒ Ⓓ	74 Ⓐ Ⓑ Ⓒ Ⓓ	99 Ⓐ Ⓑ Ⓒ Ⓓ
25 Ⓐ Ⓑ Ⓒ Ⓓ	50 Ⓐ Ⓑ Ⓒ Ⓓ	75 Ⓐ Ⓑ Ⓒ Ⓓ	100 Ⓐ Ⓑ Ⓒ Ⓓ

TEAR HERE

MODEL ASI BROKER EXAMINATION

95 questions

1. In the case of the existence of two or more deeds conveying title to the same property at about the same time, which deed will be enforced?
A. The deed that was signed first
B. The deed that was delivered first
C. The deed that recites highest consideration
D. The deed that was recorded first

2. A metes and bounds description of a parcel of property ALWAYS
A. proceeds in a counter-clockwise direction
B. includes monuments and boundaries
C. ends at the point at which it began
D. is recorded in meters

3. All of the following may serve as legal descriptions of a property EXCEPT
A. street address
B. name of the present owners
C. tax lot
D. plat map location

4. If a homeowner wishes to exclude certain semi-attached fixtures from the sale of his property, he should
A. specify and describe the fixtures in the contract of sale
B. remove the fixtures before showing the property
C. insist that the buyer pay for the fixtures
D. simply remain silent on the subject

5. The order of priorities of liens on real property is
A. mortgage, taxes, mechanic's lien
B. taxes, mortgage, mechanic's lien
C. mechanic's lien, taxes, mortgage
D. mortgage, mechanic's lien, taxes

6. The Board of a cooperative apartment building may reject prospective owners on the basis of
A. race
C. marital status
B. income
D. occupation

7. All of the following are provisions of RESPA EXCEPT
A. limitations upon escrow account requirements by the lender
B. the specified fee which the lender may charge for preparation of RESPA forms
C. the need to disclose the identity of the true borrower to the lender
D. the requirement that the lender permit the borrower to inspect the closing statement one day prior to the closing

8. A broker lists for rent a property at the rate of $2,600 per month for the first year, $2,800 per month for the second year, and $3,000 per month for the third year plus $100 per month for 10 months to be paid to a gardener of the landlord's choosing. The commission is 7 percent of the first year's rent and 4 percent of the second and third years' rents. The property is rented by an agent from another office with a two-year lease at $2,400 per month for the first year and $2,700 per month for the second year plus gardener. Assuming a 50-50 commission split between offices and a 50-50 split between broker and salesperson, what is the total commission earned by the listing salesperson?

A. $828.00
B. $855.50

C. $882.00
D. $909.50

9. In one office, a salesperson receives special consideration for selling properties which are listed by the office. A salesperson sells for full price a property listed by another salesperson in the same office for $132,000. Commission rate is 6 percent. The franchise group receives 6 percent of total commission, the listing salesperson gets 25 percent, and the remainder is shared equally between selling agent and broker. How much does the selling agent earn on this transaction?

A. $1,805.36
B. $1,861.20

C. $2,791.80
D. $3,722.36

10. The manager of a property receives a monthly salary of $680 plus 2 percent of the rent roll plus payment for out-of-pocket expenses. If one month he received a total of $1,156.25 which included expenses in the sum of $226.25, what was the total rent roll?

A. $250.00
B. $1,250.00

C. $12,500.00
D. $125,000.00

11. The effect of taxes upon the value of real estate is
A. to hold the value of the real estate constant
B. to lower the value of the real estate
C. to raise the value of the real estate
D. to have no effect whatsoever upon the value of the real estate

12. A developer who subdivides a large tract into single-family building lots is required to dedicate a portion of the tract to green space. This requirement is based upon
A. building codes
B. zoning
C. property taxation
D. urban planning

13. It is wise for persons who are selling and buying real estate to be advised by attorneys because
A. the law deals uniquely with real estate
B. only attorneys may record deeds
C. a real estate broker may not act as an escrow agent
D. an attorney who represents himself has a fool as a client

14. A client wishes to invest some money into an apartment for rental income and appreciation. He asks your advice as to whether a cooperative apartment or a condominium would be the better investment for this purpose. You should
  A. recommend a cooperative because cooperatives are in more established neighborhoods
  B. recommend a condominium because "better" people live in condominiums
  C. recommend a condominium because a cooperative may change its rules and at some time prohibit the rental of non-owner-occupied units
  D. say that it makes no difference at all

15. The changing of the character of a neighborhood from one or two-family houses to one of rooming houses would have what effect upon residential properties in the neighborhood?
  A. It would have no effect.
  B. It would cause physical depreciation.
  C. It would cause functional depreciation.
  D. It would cause economic depreciation.

16. An appraisal of the value of property is required for all of the following purposes EXCEPT
  A. financing
  B. taxation
  C. condemnation
  D. obtaining a building permit

17. A building is situated on a lot that measures 65,340 sq. ft. The current value of this land is $200,000 per acre. The building itself was built 15 years ago at a cost of $250,000. The building has depreciated at a straight-line rate of 3 percent per year. The improvements to the land are currently valued at $60,000. What is the current appraised value of this property?
  A. $470,500
  B. $472,500
  C. $497,500
  D. $610,000

18. The brokers in an area cannot establish a uniform, inflexible commission rate because of
  A. fair housing laws
  B. truth-in-lending laws
  C. anti-trust laws
  D. Regulation Z

19. A corporation owns property in
  A. severalty
  B. joint tenancy
  C. tenancy in common
  D. tenancy by the entirety

20. Mr. and Mrs. McCabe have purchased the home of Mr. and Mrs. Devine for a total sales price of $120,000. At the time of signing the contract of sale, the McCabes deposited 10 percent of the purchase price with the Devines' attorney to hold in his escrow account. The real estate broker is charging 6 percent of the purchase price as commission. The attorney's fee is 1 percent of the purchase price. Taxes on this property in the sum of $2,200 were paid on June 1. The homeowners' insurance, which the McCabes will assume, in the sum of $418 was paid on December 1 of last year. The Devines have had their oil tank topped off. It holds 275 gallons, and they paid $1.04 per gallon. The sum of $35,000 remains to satisfy the existing mortgage on the Devine property. How much will Mr. and Mrs. Devine be paid at their August 31 closing? (Seller is responsible for all costs up to and including day of sale.)
  A. $65,749.50
  B. $66,640.50
  C. $77,749.50
  D. $78,640.50

21. Private restrictions upon the use of a property are
A. always legal
B. legal if the restriction is not in conflict with private practices in the area
C. never legal
D. legal unless the restriction is against public policy

22. When a real estate broker serves as professional manager of rental proper-ties, he is subject to all laws EXCEPT
A. RESPA
B. fair housing laws
C. Law of Agency
D. building codes

23. Which of the following may the owner of mortgaged property NOT do?
A. Sell the property
B. Pay the taxes
C. Demolish a structure on the property
D. Lease the property

24. The Federal Fair Housing Laws pertain to which of the following?
A. Rentals in a four-family building in which the owner does not reside
B. Sale of a house by its owner, without a broker
C. Rental of rooms in a private club
D. All of these

25. Proof of marketable title may be obtained from
A. a deed
B. a Torrens certificate
C. an affidavit of title
D. a recorded lien

26. Which of the following need NOT be produced at a closing?
A. Proof of ownership
B. Certificate of mortgage insurance
C. Receipt of payment of taxes
D. Certificate of occupancy

27. What do the following terms all have in common?
I. Capitalization rate
II. Dividend rate
III. Equity rate
A. All are terms used by banks to describe the cost of mortgages.
B. All are approaches toward appraisal.
C. All are subject to state regulation.
D. All are synonyms for *rate of return.*

28. In using the income approach in appraising the value of real estate, the number that reflects the ratio between the sales price of a residential prop-erty and its monthly unfurnished rental is known as
A. conversion factor
B. gross-rent multiplier
C. base line
D. annual percentage rate

29. Which of the following statements is NOT true concerning construction loans?
- A. They are considered to be temporary mortgage loans.
- B. Prior to each payment, the lender makes an inspection of the work completed.
- C. They are granted only to holders of building permits.
- D. Their time limits are determined by law.

30. Under the terms of an installment land contract, the deed is delivered to the purchaser
- A. upon signing the contract
- B. when the purchaser performs all of his obligations under the contract
- C. upon payment of the mortgage recording tax
- D. before ground may be broken

31. If a tenant leases the already leased premises to another party for a portion of his lease term, he creates a(n)
- A. waiver
- B. option
- C. sublease
- D. gross lease

32. The income approach used by an appraiser does NOT make use of which of the following processes?
- A. Equalization
- B. Capitalization
- C. Overall rate
- D. Mortgage tables

33. What do the following all have in common?
- I. Closing the transaction according to the terms of the sales contract
- II. Holding the deed and other pertinent documents for the buyer
- III. At closing, writing checks for charges prorated to buyer
  - A. All are responsibilities of seller's attorney.
  - B. All are responsibilities of escrow agent.
  - C. All are responsibilities of buyer's broker.
  - D. All are responsibilities of listing salesperson.

34. In the completion of a printed form of contract of sale, several amendments are made. In order to eliminate any doubt as to whether they were inserted after the contract was signed, the broker should
- A. have each party write a letter approving the changes
- B. have each party initial all changes on the margin of the contract
- C. have each party initial those changes which affect him
- D. attach a dated errata sheet

35. With the proceeds of her late husband's life insurance, Mrs. Smith purchased a house situated on three acres in a neighborhood zoned for one acre per house. She considered the extra two acres to serve as a hedge against inflation. The year after her purchase, the neighborhood was rezoned to one and one-half acres. Mrs. Smith's investment is subject to
- A. appreciation because the neighborhood has become classier
- B. depreciation due to functional obsolescence
- C. no change in value if she maintains the property
- D. depreciation due to economic obsolescence

36. An owner wants to sell his property at a price that will net for him his equity in the property at the present time plus $5,500. He originally purchased the property for $45,000. The mortgage balance at closing will be $22,750. Taxes of $850 for the year are unpaid. The brokerage fee will be 6 percent. The closing date is May 1. Assuming only the above-mentioned expenses, what must the selling price of the property be?

A. $54,627

B. $51,350

C. $55,175

D. $55,735

37. A state law requires that a real estate office located in a home must have a sign that is visible from the street. Broker Hill wishes to open a real estate office in her home. A town ordinance permits home offices but prohibits all signs in residential neighborhoods. Under these circumstances, broker Hill

A. may not operate a real estate office in her home

B. may hang a sign in front of her home

C. may operate her office without a sign

D. may not employ the services of any salesperson

38. Broker Chen holds the license of salesperson Torres. Chen pays Torres no salary but remits to her 50 percent of all revenues that Torres brings into the office. Chen makes no deductions from the payment to Torres. Salesperson Torres is

A. a commissioned employee

B. a licensee

C. an independent contractor

D. a franchisee

39. Alleged violations of the Federal Fair Housing Law should be reported to the

A. Department of Housing Inspections

B. Department of Housing and Urban Development

C. Federal Attorney of the district in which the property is located

D. local police authorities

40. When Broker Flynn agrees to hold the license of salesperson Lyons, he requires Lyons to sign a statement that should Lyons leave Flynn's office he will not work for another office within a radius of one and one-half miles of Flynn's office for a period of six months. This statement is known as

A. restraint of trade

B. price fixing

C. a non-competition clause

D. a defeasance clause

41. Municipal regulations that provide rules for lot areas, setback lines, and areas to be dedicated for public use are known as

A. private restrictions

B. subdivision regulations

C. zoning laws

D. building codes

42. Find the total ground area covered by a building with the measurements as shown below.

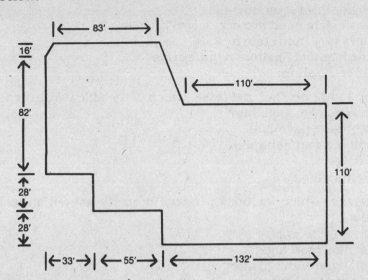

A. 14,520 square feet
B. 18,251 square feet

C. 25,128 square feet
D. none of the above

43. Which is the most appropriate order of steps to take in the cost approach to appraisal?
 I. Add the value of the land to the depreciated value of the improvements.
 II. Estimate the current cost of duplicating the improvements.
 III Deduct the estimated amount of depreciation from the duplication cost.

A. I, II, III
B. II, III, I

C. II, I, III
D. III, II, I

44. A state law says that once an apartment is rent-controlled, it is forever rent-controlled. A rental building converts to cooperative ownership and the owner of one unit wishes to rent out his apartment. On the basis of the law
 A. he may not rent the apartment
 B. he may charge whatever the market will bear
 C. he may charge the previous rental plus 15 percent
 D. he may charge only the official controlled rental

45. In a contract transferring real estate from tenants in the entirety to joint tenants,
 A. one selling party and one buying party must sign
 B. both selling parties and one buying party must sign
 C. one selling party and both buying parties must sign
 D. both selling parties and both buying parties must sign

46. Which of the following is NOT exempted from the Federal Fair Housing Act?
 A. Two rental units in an owner-occupied dwelling
 B. Dwelling units owned by a religious organization and rented to persons of the same religion as long as they do not discriminate against race, color, or national origin
 C. Cooperative apartments
 D. Unimproved land sold by the owner without the services of a broker

47. If a broker who is licensed in one state wishes to conduct business in another state, the broker must obtain a license in the second state. The reason for this requirement is
   A. each state must protect its own brokers
   B. laws vary from state to state
   C. the Board of Realtors requires this
   D. all of the above

48. Under a pure net, net, net lease, which of the following expenses would be the lessor's responsibility?
   A. Mortgage payments
   B. Interior maintenance
   C. Fuel oil
   D. Refuse disposal

49. A mortgage which includes personal property as well as real property is called a
   A. package mortgage
   B. blanket mortgage
   C. non-conventional mortgage
   D. second mortgage

50. Which of the following statements concerning the assignment of sales contracts is NOT correct?
   A. Any sales contract may be assigned.
   B. The assignments of rights may be made only by the original seller.
   C. No consideration need be given to support the assignment of a sales contract.
   D. The services of a broker are not required.

51. Which of the following statements regarding mortgages is true?
   A. All mortgages carry a usury rate determined by the lender.
   B. If FHA, the mortgage cannot be for a term longer than 25 years.
   C. The interest rates carried by VA and FHA mortgages are always the same.
   D. A handyman's special is not eligible for a VA-guaranteed mortgage.

52. A broker's contract with a developer states that he will receive a commission at the rate of 5 percent on the first $200,000 he sells and at the rate of 2.5 percent on all sales over that amount. In one year, the broker received $12,500 commission fees from the developer. What was the total amount of development sales that the broker handled to receive this amount of commission?
   A. $300,000
   B. $145,000
   C. $100,000
   D. $250,000

53. A broker who wishes to purchase a property that is listed in his own office must
   A. forfeit his commission
   B. ask one of his salespeople to negotiate for him
   C. disclose his personal interest to the principal
   D. refrain from this illegal act

54. Which of the following is considered to be a fiduciary?
   A. Executor
   B. Mortgagor
   C. Mortgagee
   D. Grantor

55. A sewer easement would be an example of a(n)
A. easement by necessity
B. easement in gross
C. easement in prescription
D. easement in fact

56. A Power of Attorney automatically terminates with
A. death of the principal
B. completion of the transaction for which it was issued
C. attainment of a specified date
D. any of the above

57. The amount of commission due to a salesperson is determined by
A. state law
B. local Board of Realtors
C. mutual agreement
D. court decree

58. Which of the following points should NOT be included in a property management agreement?
A. Definition of the manager's responsibilities
B. Description of the property involved
C. Manager's compensation schedule
D. Specifications for cleaning supplies

59. A lot was listed at $38,000. The seller received $33,840 after the 6 percent broker's fee of $2,160 was deducted. What was the actual sales price of the lot?
A. $35,720
B. $36,000
C. $36,618
D. $39,480

60. Using problem 59, determine what percent of the original listing price the lot sold for.
A. 94%
B. 95%
C. 96%
D. 104%

61. Which of the following can have the effect of moving the boundary line of a parcel of land?
A. Accretion
B. Attachment
C. Assemblage
D. Annexation

62. The minimum down payment under VA regulations is
A. 3% or greater
B. $17,500
C. 10%
D. none of the above

63. As distinguished from a mortgage, a note creates which of the following?
A. An obligation in rent
B. A personal obligation
C. A perpetual obligation
D. A deed restriction

64. To the owner of a parcel of land who has a recorded easement crossing his land, the easement is
A. an encumbrance
B. an encroachment
C. a contingency
D. a consideration

65. The term "blockbusting" means
A. making telephone calls to seek prospective buyers or sellers
B. offering property for sale only to persons of a certain race
C. prompting homeowners to sell their properties due to the entry of "undesirable" persons in the neighborhood
D. none of the above

66. In a real estate sale, the responsibility of any realty transfer-fee payment is usually borne by
  A. the seller
  B. the broker
  C. the buyer
  D. the mortgagee

67. A broker who enters into a property-management contract is considered to be which of the following?
  A. A lienor
  B. A fiduciary
  C. A contractor
  D. A commissioner

68. The rate charged on adjustable mortgage loans is tied to the rate paid on U.S. Treasury securities. The rate charged by the Eastern Savings Bank on its 5-year adjustable residential mortgage loan is based upon the rate paid on 5-year Treasury securities plus 2.5%. If the treasury rate over the life of the loan varies between 9.5% and 13.65%, the interest rate on the loan will vary roughly between
  A. 9.5% and 13.65%   C. 9.6% and 14.2%
  B. 9.75% and 13.75%   D. 9.75% and 14%

69. Which of the following is not a phrase used to legally describe property?
  A. Metes and bounds
  B. Rectangular survey system
  C. Block and lot
  D. Description by reference

70. When there is a foreclosure sale under a mortgage and the sales price is greater than the amount of the debt, which of the following must bear the expenses of collection?
  A. Lender   C. Attorney
  B. Defaulting borrower   D. Sheriff

71. An appraiser has been hired by the state to estimate the value of a property being taken for public use. The house has a total floor area of 2,374 square feet and an estimated replacement cost of $18 per square foot has been established. If the land value is $11,000 and the annual depreciation charge is $2,500, what is the estimated value of the real estate? (Round your answer to the nearest hundred.)
  A. $32,200   C. $51,200
  B. $40,200   D. $53,700

72. What is the annual depreciation charge on a building 70 feet by 60 feet with a useful life of 40 years if the estimated cost is $14.50 per square foot? (Use straight-line depreciation.)
  A. $1,522.50   C. $4,200.00
  B. $1,050.00   D. $6,090.00

73. If two rival brokers claim a commission under an open listing, to whom should the commission go?
  A. The broker who listed the property
  B. The broker who obtained the first offer
  C. The broker who advertised the property
  D. The broker who was the procuring cause of the sale

74. Which of the following defines a contingency in a contract?
   A. An acknowledgment of an easement to a property
   B. A clause in a contract that limits the validity of the contract until such contingency has been fulfilled
   C. A restrictive covenant as to permitted uses of the property
   D. A codicil

75. Which of the following statements concerning a broker's responsibilities toward monies in his or her possession is NOT correct?
   A. All monies belonging to clients should be deposited in a special separate account.
   B. Personal funds should not be included in any trust account maintained by the broker for real estate clients.
   C. All funds belonging to clients must be deposited in interest-bearing accounts.
   D. Use of the office safe should be strictly limited to short-term storage of undeposited checks.

76. Which of the following practices is prohibited under federal law?
   A. A salesperson's refusal to show a residence, on which he has a listing, to a prospective buyer because of the latter's religion
   B. An owner's refusal to rent a unit in a two-family residence, in which he occupies one unit, to a male boarder
   C. A landlord's refusal to rent a one-bedroom apartment to a family of five adults
   D. A co-op board's rejection of a homosexual couple

77. When real property is sold and there is a lease in existence, that lease
   A. is void
   B. remains binding upon the new owner
   C. expires one month after closing of title
   D. must be renewed with consent of the new owner

78. B leases a store from A and installs shelves, cabinets, refrigerator, and other articles for use in the business that B will conduct in the store. The lease contains no provision regarding this. Which of the following is true?
   A. B must leave said articles for A's benefit when the lease expires.
   B. B can remove said articles at any time after the lease expires.
   C. B can remove said articles he installed before the lease expires.
   D. A must pay B for any articles left when the lease expires.

79. The monthly payment on an $80,000 amortizing mortgage loan for 20 years at 12½ percent interest is $908.92. Assuming that a mortgagor is in an aggregate tax bracket of 55 percent, what is the total cost to the borrower over the lifetime of the loan?
   A. $75,977.44   C. $98,163.36
   B. $62,163.36   D. $119,977.44

80. A broker takes into his office a new salesperson who has taken the licensing exam but has not yet received a license. The broker may permit this person to
   A. take listings
   B. show property
   C. cold canvass
   D. draft advertising copy

81. A prospective client has asked you to take an Exclusive Right To Sell listing of his property with the proviso that the property be shown only to qualified buyers. With this restriction, you
   A. may accept the listing but not advertise the property
   B. must refuse the listing because the restriction constitutes illegal discrimination
   C. may accept the listing with no qualms
   D. may accept the listing but not publish a photo of the property in the multiple listing book

82. The brokers in a community have agreed to divide their commissions so that the listing office receives 40 percent and the selling office 60 percent. This practice is
   A. perfectly legal
   B. illegal because it constitutes collusion
   C. illegal price fixing
   D. illegal restraint of trade

83. A tenant pays 3 percent of his total annual gross sales income for his rental in the Rushmore Mall. However, his minimum base rent must be at least $900 per month. If his annual gross sales volume was $390,000 last year, how much rent did he pay for the year?
   A. $9,000   C. $11,700
   B. $10,800   D. $12,600

84. A mortgage that allows for advances to the mortgagor up to a certain maximum is called
   A. a package mortgage   C. a purchase-money mortgage
   B. a wraparound mortgage   D. an open-end mortgage

85. The GREATEST benefit to be derived from ownership of a second, tenant-occupied house is
   A. tax deductibility of expenses
   B. collection of rent
   C. possibility of a place to move in case of catastrophe
   D. security and growth of investment

86. In the event that a property owner gives an interested party a properly executed option with May 1 as the fixed expiration date, and the property owner dies before that date, which of the following is true?
   A. The option remains valid but must be exercised within a statutory period.
   B. The option remains in effect only if the property owner died intestate.
   C. The option immediately becomes void.
   D. The option remains enforceable.

87. If a 10-year-old building has been estimated by an appraiser to have a current replacement cost of $90,000 and an original estimated useful life of 40 years, what has been the total amount of depreciation for these first ten years? (Use straight-line depreciation.)
   A. $9,000   C. $44,444
   B. $22,500   D. $67,500

88. On the diagram below, 2 acres are to be designated for "Green Acres." What percent of the total area is being reserved for that purpose? (Note: The diagram is not drawn to scale.)

    A. 10%   C. 22%

    B. 20%   D. 33⅓%

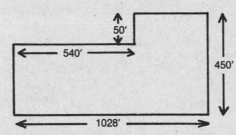

89. The term "highest and best use" can best be defined as which of the following?

    A. That which produces the greatest gross return

    B. That which complies with the building codes of the municipality

    C. That which contributes to the best interests of the county

    D. That which produces the greatest net return on an investment over a given period of time

90. A mortgage is held on three separate parcels of land. If one parcel may be released from a lien while the lien continues to cover the remaining parcels, this mortgage is known as a(n)

    A. package mortgage   C. wraparound mortgage

    B. blanket mortgage   D. open-end mortgage

91. Which of the following terms does not refer to a governmental restriction on property?

    A. Eminent domain   C. Police power

    B. Title closure   D. Taxation power

92. Which of the following is usually NOT included in subdivision regulations?

    A. Installation of sewers and water mains

    B. Building and setback lines

    C. Areas to be dedicated for public use

    D. Construction standards for buildings

93. Five building lots each having 50 feet of frontage and a depth of 120 feet are for sale. Which of the following pricing procedures will yield the highest gross return?

    A. $4,500 per lot   C. $1 per square foot

    B. $100 per front foot   D. $28,000 for the entirety

94. Buyer and seller are only a few thousand dollars apart, and the deal could be consummated if the brokers would agree to reduce their commissions. This action would be

    A. illegal because commissions are set by law

    B. improper because commissions are agreed to by all members of a listing service

    C. acceptable

    D. a breach of contract

95. In the sale of a private home, certain expenses may be added to the cost basis of the house to reduce the capital gains tax. Among these are all EXCEPT

    A. interior painting

    B. the broker's fee

    C. repair of a nonfunctioning oil burner

    D. a new roof

CORRECT ANSWERS TO MODEL ASI BROKER EXAMINATION

1. D	21. D	41. B	61. A	81. C
2. C	22. A	*42. C	62. D	82. A
3. B	23. C	43. B	63. B	*83. C
4. A	24. A	44. D	64. A	84. D
5. B	25. B	45. D	65. C	85. D
6. B	26. B	46. C	66. A	86. D
7. B	27. D	47. B	67. B	*87. B
*8. A	28. B	48. A	*68. D	*88. B
*9. C	29. D	49. A	69. D	89. D
*10. C	30. B	50. B	70. B	90. B
11. B	31. C	51. D	*71. C	91. B
12. D	32. D	*52. A	*72. A	92. D
13. A	33. B	53. C	73. D	*93. C
14. C	34. B	54. A	74. B	94. C
15. D	35. D	55. B	75. C	95. C
16. D	*36. A	56. D	76. A	
*17. C	37. A	57. C	77. B	
18. C	38. C	58. D	78. C	
19. A	39. B	*59. B	*79. B	
*20. D	40. C	*60. B	80. D	

* Solutions provided

SOLUTIONS TO PROBLEMS REQUIRING MATHEMATICAL CALCULATIONS

8. $2,400 × 12 = $28,800 × 7% = $2,016 commission for first year
$2,700 × 12 = $32,400 × 4% = $1,296 commission for second year

$3,312 ÷ 4 = $828 total to listing salesperson

9. $132,000 × 6% = $7,920 less 6% ($475.20) = $7,444.80
$7,444.80 less 25% to a listing agent ($1,861.20) =
$5,583.60 ÷ 2 = $2,791.80 to selling agent

10. $1,156.25 − $226.25 = $930 − $680 = $250 which is 2% of rent roll.
$250 ÷ 2% = $12,500 total rent roll

17. 65,340 sq ft = 1½ acre @ $200,000 = $300,000
3% per yr × 15 yrs = 45% depreciation × $250,000
= $112,500 depreciation
$250,000 − $112,500 = $137,500 depreciated value
$300,000 + $137,500 + $60,000 = $497,500 current value

20. $120,000 less 6% ($7200) to broker = $112,800
less 1% ($1,200) to attorney   − 1,200
             111,600
less mortgage satisfaction   − 35,000
             76,600
plus ¾ yr taxes (¾ × $2,200)   + 1,650
             78,250
plus ¼ yr ins. (¼ × $418)   + 104.50
             78,354.50
plus oil (275 × $1.04)   + 286.00
           $ 78,640.50

(Remember that the escrow money is turned over to the sellers at closing; it should not be deducted for purposes of this question.)

36. $45,000 + $5,500 = $50,500 + $850 =
$51,350 ÷ .94 = $54,627

42.

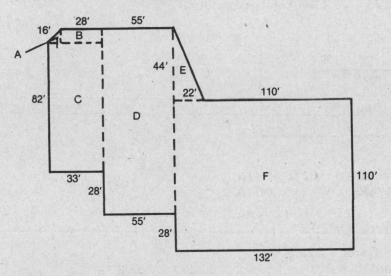

A = 55 + 33 = 88 − 83 = 5
½ (16 × 5) = ½ (80) =   40 square feet
B = 28 × 16 =   448 square feet
C = 33 × 82 =   2,706 square feet
D = 55 × (16 + 82 + 28) = 55 × 126 =   6,930 square feet
E = 132 − 110 = 22,154 − 110 = 44
    ½ (22 × 44) = ½ (968) =   484 square feet
F = 132 × 110 =   14,520 square feet
           Total   25,128 square feet

52. $200,000 × .05 = $10,000; $12,500 − $10,000 = $2,500 ÷ .025 = $100,000
$200,000 + $100,000 = $300,000 total sales

59. $33,840 + $2,160 = $36,000 sales price

60. $36,000 ÷ $38,000 = .947 or 95% of the listing price

68. 9.5 × 1.025 = 9.7375 rounded to 9.75%
13.65 × 1.025 = 13.99125 rounded to 14%

71. 2,374 sq. ft. × $18.00/sq. ft. = $42,732 − $2,500 depreciation = $40,232 house value
$40,232 + $11,000 land value = $51,232 or $51,200

72. 100% ÷ 40% = yearly depreciation rate
1.00 ÷ 40 = .025 or 2.5% yearly depreciation rate
70 × 60 = 4,200 square feet × $14.50/sq. ft. = $60,900 cost of building
$60,900 × .025 = $1,522.50 annual depreciation charge

79. $908.92/mo. × 12 = $10,907.04/yr. × 20 yrs = $218,140.80 total payments
$218,140.80 − $80,000 principal = $138,140.80 interest
$138,140.80 × .45 = $62,163.36 cost

83. $900 × 12 = $10,800
$390,000 × .03 = $11,700

87. 100% ÷ 40% = yearly depreciation rate
1.00 ÷ .40 = 0.25 or 2.5 yearly depreciation rate
.025 × 10 years = 25% total depreciation
$90,000 × .25 = $22,500 total depreciation

88.

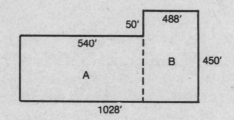

A = 400 ft. × 540 ft. = 216,000 sq. ft.
B = 450 ft. × 488 ft. = 219,600 sq. ft.
435,600 sq. ft. or 10 acres total
2 acres ÷ 10 acres = 20%

93. (a) $4,500 × 5 lots = $22,500
(b) $100/front ft. × 50 ft. = $5,000 × 5 lots = $25,000
(c) 50 × 120 = 6,000 sq. ft. × $1.00 = $6,000 × 5 lots = $30,000
(d) $28,000

ANSWER SHEET FOR MODEL AMP SALESPERSON EXAMINATION

1 Ⓐ Ⓑ Ⓒ Ⓓ   26 Ⓐ Ⓑ Ⓒ Ⓓ   51 Ⓐ Ⓑ Ⓒ Ⓓ   76 Ⓐ Ⓑ Ⓒ Ⓓ
2 Ⓐ Ⓑ Ⓒ Ⓓ   27 Ⓐ Ⓑ Ⓒ Ⓓ   52 Ⓐ Ⓑ Ⓒ Ⓓ   77 Ⓐ Ⓑ Ⓒ Ⓓ
3 Ⓐ Ⓑ Ⓒ Ⓓ   28 Ⓐ Ⓑ Ⓒ Ⓓ   53 Ⓐ Ⓑ Ⓒ Ⓓ   78 Ⓐ Ⓑ Ⓒ Ⓓ
4 Ⓐ Ⓑ Ⓒ Ⓓ   29 Ⓐ Ⓑ Ⓒ Ⓓ   54 Ⓐ Ⓑ Ⓒ Ⓓ   79 Ⓐ Ⓑ Ⓒ Ⓓ
5 Ⓐ Ⓑ Ⓒ Ⓓ   30 Ⓐ Ⓑ Ⓒ Ⓓ   55 Ⓐ Ⓑ Ⓒ Ⓓ   80 Ⓐ Ⓑ Ⓒ Ⓓ
6 Ⓐ Ⓑ Ⓒ Ⓓ   31 Ⓐ Ⓑ Ⓒ Ⓓ   56 Ⓐ Ⓑ Ⓒ Ⓓ   81 Ⓐ Ⓑ Ⓒ Ⓓ
7 Ⓐ Ⓑ Ⓒ Ⓓ   32 Ⓐ Ⓑ Ⓒ Ⓓ   57 Ⓐ Ⓑ Ⓒ Ⓓ   82 Ⓐ Ⓑ Ⓒ Ⓓ
8 Ⓐ Ⓑ Ⓒ Ⓓ   33 Ⓐ Ⓑ Ⓒ Ⓓ   58 Ⓐ Ⓑ Ⓒ Ⓓ   83 Ⓐ Ⓑ Ⓒ Ⓓ
9 Ⓐ Ⓑ Ⓒ Ⓓ   34 Ⓐ Ⓑ Ⓒ Ⓓ   59 Ⓐ Ⓑ Ⓒ Ⓓ   84 Ⓐ Ⓑ Ⓒ Ⓓ
10 Ⓐ Ⓑ Ⓒ Ⓓ   35 Ⓐ Ⓑ Ⓒ Ⓓ   60 Ⓐ Ⓑ Ⓒ Ⓓ   85 Ⓐ Ⓑ Ⓒ Ⓓ
11 Ⓐ Ⓑ Ⓒ Ⓓ   36 Ⓐ Ⓑ Ⓒ Ⓓ   61 Ⓐ Ⓑ Ⓒ Ⓓ   86 Ⓐ Ⓑ Ⓒ Ⓓ
12 Ⓐ Ⓑ Ⓒ Ⓓ   37 Ⓐ Ⓑ Ⓒ Ⓓ   62 Ⓐ Ⓑ Ⓒ Ⓓ   87 Ⓐ Ⓑ Ⓒ Ⓓ
13 Ⓐ Ⓑ Ⓒ Ⓓ   38 Ⓐ Ⓑ Ⓒ Ⓓ   63 Ⓐ Ⓑ Ⓒ Ⓓ   88 Ⓐ Ⓑ Ⓒ Ⓓ
14 Ⓐ Ⓑ Ⓒ Ⓓ   39 Ⓐ Ⓑ Ⓒ Ⓓ   64 Ⓐ Ⓑ Ⓒ Ⓓ   89 Ⓐ Ⓑ Ⓒ Ⓓ
15 Ⓐ Ⓑ Ⓒ Ⓓ   40 Ⓐ Ⓑ Ⓒ Ⓓ   65 Ⓐ Ⓑ Ⓒ Ⓓ   90 Ⓐ Ⓑ Ⓒ Ⓓ
16 Ⓐ Ⓑ Ⓒ Ⓓ   41 Ⓐ Ⓑ Ⓒ Ⓓ   66 Ⓐ Ⓑ Ⓒ Ⓓ   91 Ⓐ Ⓑ Ⓒ Ⓓ
17 Ⓐ Ⓑ Ⓒ Ⓓ   42 Ⓐ Ⓑ Ⓒ Ⓓ   67 Ⓐ Ⓑ Ⓒ Ⓓ   92 Ⓐ Ⓑ Ⓒ Ⓓ
18 Ⓐ Ⓑ Ⓒ Ⓓ   43 Ⓐ Ⓑ Ⓒ Ⓓ   68 Ⓐ Ⓑ Ⓒ Ⓓ   93 Ⓐ Ⓑ Ⓒ Ⓓ
19 Ⓐ Ⓑ Ⓒ Ⓓ   44 Ⓐ Ⓑ Ⓒ Ⓓ   69 Ⓐ Ⓑ Ⓒ Ⓓ   94 Ⓐ Ⓑ Ⓒ Ⓓ
20 Ⓐ Ⓑ Ⓒ Ⓓ   45 Ⓐ Ⓑ Ⓒ Ⓓ   70 Ⓐ Ⓑ Ⓒ Ⓓ   95 Ⓐ Ⓑ Ⓒ Ⓓ
21 Ⓐ Ⓑ Ⓒ Ⓓ   46 Ⓐ Ⓑ Ⓒ Ⓓ   71 Ⓐ Ⓑ Ⓒ Ⓓ   96 Ⓐ Ⓑ Ⓒ Ⓓ
22 Ⓐ Ⓑ Ⓒ Ⓓ   47 Ⓐ Ⓑ Ⓒ Ⓓ   72 Ⓐ Ⓑ Ⓒ Ⓓ   97 Ⓐ Ⓑ Ⓒ Ⓓ
23 Ⓐ Ⓑ Ⓒ Ⓓ   48 Ⓐ Ⓑ Ⓒ Ⓓ   73 Ⓐ Ⓑ Ⓒ Ⓓ   98 Ⓐ Ⓑ Ⓒ Ⓓ
24 Ⓐ Ⓑ Ⓒ Ⓓ   49 Ⓐ Ⓑ Ⓒ Ⓓ   74 Ⓐ Ⓑ Ⓒ Ⓓ   99 Ⓐ Ⓑ Ⓒ Ⓓ
25 Ⓐ Ⓑ Ⓒ Ⓓ   50 Ⓐ Ⓑ Ⓒ Ⓓ   75 Ⓐ Ⓑ Ⓒ Ⓓ   100 Ⓐ Ⓑ Ⓒ Ⓓ

MODEL AMP SALESPERSON EXAMINATION

100 questions

1. Which of the following sets forth that contracts must be in writing to be enforced?
- A. Statute of Limitations
- B. Blue laws
- C. Statute of Frauds
- D. Uniform Contract Act

2. A contract in which a condition is created solely by the actions of the parties involved creates a(n)
- A. expressed contract
- B. implied contract
- C. verbal contract
- D. unilateral contract

3. A contract signed voluntarily by a person who is intoxicated is
- A. void
- B. voidable
- C. valid
- D. none of the above

4. A broker presented a written offer of $53,000 to a seller on behalf of a prospective buyer, a member of a minority group. The seller changed the offer amount to $55,000. This action is known as any of the following EXCEPT
- A. a rejection of the buyer's offer
- B. a new offer by the seller
- C. a discriminatory act
- D. steering

5. Which of the following most accurately describes the term "meeting of the minds"?
- A. All parties to the contract understand and agree to its terms.
- B. All parties to the contract have contractual capacity.
- C. An agreement between competent parties.
- D. Either party has the right to cancel a contract provided that he gives notice.

6. For which of the following reasons may a contract be terminated?
- A. Operation of law
- B. Impossibility of performance
- C. Complete performance
- D. All of the above

7. In most states a broker is required to
- A. submit all offers to the seller
- B. submit only those offers he considers to be reasonable
- C. submit first offers from salespersons in the listing office
- D. submit the best offers first

8. A purchaser of real property that is occupied by a tenant who has recorded his lease
- A. is bound by the terms of the lease for the remaining lease period
- B. may terminate the lease upon taking possession
- C. may refuse to renew the lease only if he or a member of his family intends to occupy the property
- D. need not maintain the property until the lease expires

9. A mortgage lender is least interested in
- A. market value of a property
- B. tax value of a property
- C. insurance value of a property
- D. economic value of a property

10. Regulation Z provides that
- A. real estate agents may prepare mortgage notes
- B. a borrower may change his mind within three days of signing a mortgage commitment for purposes of building a new home
- C. advertising which discloses any costs must disclose all costs
- D. all mortgage lenders must be federally insured

11. Which of the following statements about a purchase agreement for the sale of real property is (are) true?
- I. If the buyer is to take possession after the closing date, a condition should be included in the contract to provide for any rent to be paid by the seller.
- II. If the transaction is to be paid in cash by husband and wife, the wife alone may sign as the buyer and the contract will be valid.
- III. If the agreement is silent on the subject of a closing date, the contract is illegal.

- A. I only
- B. I and III only
- C. I and II only
- D. I, II, and III

12. One is said to be "seized" of his property when he
- A. lawfully owns it
- B. is evicted from it
- C. releases all interest to the property
- D. enters a suit to claim the property

13. Which of the following would be best classified as functional obsolescence?
- A. Exterior needs painting
- B. Property fronts on busy expressway
- C. Very small bedroom closets
- D. Neighborhood is 35 to 50 years old

14. The market analysis approach to value is usually used in the appraisal of single-family homes. The LEAST applicable comparison in this approach to valuation would be that of
- A. a house sold less than six months ago
- B. a house sold by force sale or under stress conditions
- C. houses of approximately the same size but in different neighborhoods
- D. houses that have different square footages but are in the same neighborhood

15. Earnest money deposits
- A. are required in all contracts
- B. may be a source of payment of damages if the buyer breaches the contract
- C. must always be accepted by brokers
- D. must never be accepted by brokers

16. A contract that creates a personal debt in a mortgage loan transaction is
- A. a deed
- B. a mortgage
- C. a note or bond
- D. a contract of sale

17. A plan that enables buyers to make smaller payments in the early years of the loan and larger payments as their income increases is known as

 A. a balloon payment plan   C. a straight payment plan

 B. an amortization schedule   D. a flexible payment plan

18. The "redemption period" usually means

 A. the time after a judgment is entered to clear a debt

 B. the time after a tax sale to sell the tax lien

 C. the time after a foreclosure to regain one's title

 D. none of the above

19. The Federal Fair Housing Act specifically prohibits discrimination in residential sales on the basis of

 A. age

 B. sexual orientation

 C. marital status

 D. religion

20. In arriving at fair value of a property for settlement of a divorce action, the best source of appraisal would be

 A. the listing broker

 B. an independent licensed appraiser

 C. the tax rolls

 D. attorneys for both parties, jointly

21. Which of the following can a life tenant NOT do with his life interest?

 A. Lease it   C. Bequeath it

 B. Mortgage it   D. Sell it

22. If the seller decides not to sell after the contract of sale has been signed

 I. the seller may terminate the contract

 II. the seller may file a suit for specific performance

 III. the broker may collect his commission

 IV. the buyer may sue for damages

  A. I and II only   C. III and IV only

  B. I, II, and III only   D. I, II, III, and IV

23. Broker Teplitzky is called upon to appraise the value of a piece of property. She estimates the value of the land itself, the cost of duplicating the structures, and the depreciation of the structures. The appraisal method being used by broker Teplitzky is

 A. cost approach   C. income approach

 B. market data approach   D. objective approach

24. The tax bill on a property is $490.30. The tax rate is $4.20 per $100. The property is assessed at 58 percent of its value. What is the actual value of the property?

 A. $21,000.00   C. $11,673.80

 B. $20,127.24   D. $27,793.09

25. Which of the following is (are) required to be included in the disclosure statement by the Truth-in-Lending Act?

 I. Annual percentage rate

 II. Finance charges

 III. Name of the organization to which the mortgage is sold

  A. I only   C. I and II only

  B. II only   D. I, II, and III

26. A tenant who continues to occupy the premises after his lease rights have expired, without consent of the landlord, creates
A. tenancy at will
B. tenancy by sufferance
C. an adverse leasehold
D. tenancy by days

27. To which of the following does the chain of title refer?
A. The succession of owners
B. The beneficiaries of the present owner
C. The marital status of the purchasers
D. The amount of the transfer tax

28. Which of the following is received by the mortgagor when he has satisfied his indebtedness to a mortgagee?
A. Trustee's deed
B. Quitclaim deed
C. Deed of correction
D. Deed of release

29. Which of the following may NOT hold and convey a title to real property?
A. A fictitious person
B. A corporation
C. A partnership
D. A person using an assumed name

30. Which of the following is NOT required for a warranty deed to be valid?
A. Competent grantor
B. Covenants
C. Granting clause
D. Restrictions

31. Which of the following statements regarding mortgages is true?
A. All mortgages carry a usury rate determined by the lender.
B. If FHA, the mortgage cannot be for a term longer than 25 years.
C. The lender may set an arbitrary maximum for all mortgage loans.
D. A VA mortgage must be a conventional mortgage.

32. Which of the following is true concerning open-end mortgages?
A. An open-end mortgage may be increased back to the original amount.
B. An open-end mortgage usually occurs when the mortgagor is in default.
C. An open-end mortgage is always terminated by a balloon payment.
D. An open-end mortgage is a reverse mortgage.

33. The Veterans Administration will give a mortgage on a property only if which of the following facts is true?
A. Borrower needs 100% financing.
B. Borrower's use of the property is for a personal residential use.
C. Borrower promises to make structural repairs after taking possession.
D. Borrower has no outstanding debts.

34. The mortgage clause that permits the mortgagee to make the entire debt due immediately upon default of an installment payment is known as
A. a payment clause
B. a prepayment clause
C. an acceleration clause
D. an accretion clause

35. A life estate may become
I. an estate in reversion
II. an estate in remainder
III. an estate in severalty
A. I and II only
B. I and III only
C. II and III only
D. I, II, and III

36. A chain-store firm determining the value of a suburban site is most influenced by

    A. spot zoning   C. traffic count

    B. pedestrian count   D. industrial developments

37. In appraising a property prior to establishing a listing price, a salesperson should consider all BUT which of the following?

    A. Age of the structure   C. Age of the owners

    B. Size of the property   D. Location of bathrooms

38. An executory contract is best described as

    A. one in which all parties have performed their promises

    B. one in which there remains something to be done by one or more of the parties

    C. one in which one of the parties has just died

    D. one in which both parties are represented by proxies

39. In appraising the value of a plot of vacant land, the appraiser must consider all of the following EXCEPT

    A. zoning of the property

    B. current membership on the zoning board of appeals

    C. accessibility of public services

    D. topography

40. Under a net lease, which of the following is the tenant NOT required to pay?

    A. Taxes   C. Utilities

    B. Repairs   D. Mortgage

41. A lease in which the tenant is required to pay 4 percent of his gross sales as rent is known as

    A. a gross lease   C. a net lease

    B. a percentage lease   D. a ground lease

42. Which of the following statements is true regarding a community's zoning laws?

    A. A preexisting property that does not conform to a new zoning regulation as determined by the zoning board must be demolished.

    B. A person wishing to establish a building for a nonconforming use from the existing zoning ordinance must apply for a variance.

    C. Granting of a variance precludes the need for a building permit.

    D. The violator of zoning regulations must pay a surtax.

43. Real estate taxes are based upon

    A. fair value   C. full value

    B. assessed value   D. current value

44. When a real estate broker is retained to perform one specific act for a principal, it is known as a

    A. general warranty   C. general agency

    B. special agency   D. special warranty

45. Which of the following is NOT required of an agent as his responsibility to his principal in real estate sales?

    A. Loyalty   C. Accountability

    B. Broker cooperation   D. Lawn signs

46. The purpose of city planning is most accurately described as

    A. the establishment of a commerce in a city

    B. guiding the future physical development of a city

    C. enacting taxation laws

    D. creating employment

47. A commercial property 240 feet deep is on the market at a price of $400,000. If the cost of this property is $2.78 per square foot, the frontage of this property is most nearly

A. 200 yards   C. 400 yards

B. 300 yards   D. 600 yards

48. A very effective sales agent learns of a two-million-dollar property which may soon come on the market and negotiates its sale to a developer. Since only one office is involved in this very expensive transaction, the negotiated rate of commission is 2.5 percent. The office with which the salesperson works belongs to a franchise group that claims 6 percent of all sales commissions which enter the office. Since this agent is such a good producer, he is entitled to 60 percent of the office's share. What commission does the agent earn on this deal?

A. $27,354   C. $29,100

B. $28,200   D. $29,973

49. An investor purchases a property described for a total sum of $700,000. The property yields a gross monthly income of $27,000. Monthly expenses average $18,200. What is the approximate percent of annual return to this investor?

A. 14.5%   C. 15.25%

B. 15%   D. 15.5%

50. Under an open listing

    I. any number of brokers may attempt to sell the property

    II. only the broker who was the procuring cause of the sale will receive a commission

    III. negotiations are handled by the attorneys

A. I only   C. I and II only

B. II only   D. I, II, and III

51. The value placed upon a property by the tax assessor must be

A. based upon replacement value of the property

B. calculated as a percentage of the price at last sale

C. proportional to the value placed upon similar neighboring properties

D. a percentage of the true value of the property

52. Mr. Smith owns a lot with a house on it (as shown). What percentage of the land is occupied by the house?

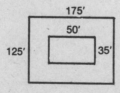

A. 8%   C. 11%

B. 10%   D. 12.5%

53. A balloon mortgage is characterized by

A. constantly increasing size of payments

B. a lump sum payment at the end of the mortgage

C. constant monthly payments with an annual lump sum adjustment

D. annual upward adjustment of monthly payments

54. Which of the following items is not usually prorated between buyer and seller at closing?

A. General taxes
B. Insurance
C. Rents
D. Recording charges

55. By which of the following means may an exclusive agency listing be terminated?

I. Default of principal
II. Mutual consent
III. Death of principal

A. I and II only
B. I and III only
C. II and III only
D. I, II, and III

56. Negative amortization may occur when

A. the mortgagor falls behind in his payments
B. monthly payments consist of interest only with all principal to be repaid at the end of the term
C. interest rates rise higher than the fixed monthly payments on an ARM
D. a loan is subordinated

57. The price of a property has been reduced because neither the dishwasher nor the oil burner is functioning. The condition which has led to this price reduction is known as

A. depreciation
B. economic obsolescence
C. physical deterioration
D. functional obsolescence

58. A clause in a lease which provides for increases in rents due to changes in costs or taxes is known as a(n)

A. escalator clause
B. habendum clause
C. acceleration clause
D. prepayment penalty clause

59. All of the following would be included in a listing agreement, except

A. description of the property
B. expiration date of the listing agreement
C. commission basis
D. an agreement not to sell the property to a member of a minority group

60. How much will the seller net from this sale based on the following: selling price $50,000; buyer to obtain new FHA-insured loan for $48,000; buyer to pay 1 percent loan fee; seller to pay 3 percent discount points, 6 percent broker commission, $400 title insurance, plus $200 in other miscellaneous closing costs; seller to pay off existing loan of $24,250 which includes all principal and interest?

A. $21,270
B. $20,710
C. $27,850
D. $20,770

61. A bilateral contract is one which can best be defined as

A. a restriction placed by one party to limit the actual performance by the other party
B. the promise of one party which requires conduct on the part of the other party
C. the promise of one party is given in exchange for the promise of the other party
D. a contract in which neither party has performed

62. The real estate broker's commission has been earned when

A. a meeting of the minds has been reached
B. contract of sale has been signed by both parties
C. title passes
D. conditions set forth in the agency contract have been met

63. If a lessee wishes to terminate his tenancy before the term of the lease has expired, he must
A. forfeit his security
B. pay rent for the remainder of the term of the lease
C. paint the premises
D. accede to the wishes of the lessor

64. Transfer of title occurs when
A. the deed is signed
B. the deed is delivered
C. the previous owner moves out
D. the new owner moves in

65. Which of the following is NOT required for a deed to be valid?
A. Competent grantor
B. Acknowledgment
C. Granting clause
D. A warranty

66. In recording an instrument, the holder gives notice to the world of his/her interest in property. This recordation is called
A. actual notice
B. constructive notice
C. functional notice
D. written notice

67. If the injured party to a breached contract wishes to file a suit, he must do so within a certain time limit. This is prescribed by the
A. Statute of Frauds
B. Statute of Time
C. Statute of Limitations
D. none of the above

68. Mr. Green has already paid his yearly taxes of $850 and a yearly sewer bill of $100. If settlement on his property is on June 15, how much refund will he receive?
A. $435.41
B. $514.59
C. $950.00
D. none of the above

69. An escrow agreement may be used in closing in which of the following real estate contracts?
I. An exchange of property
II. An installment contract
III. An agency agreement
IV. An option
A I and II only
B. I, II, and III only
C. I, II, and IV only
D. I, II, III, and IV

70. When property reverts to the state due to the lack of heirs, it is called
A. eminent domain
B. equity
C. escheat
D. reversion

71. Which of the following is NOT an essential requirement for a real estate contract?
A. Competent parties
B. Consideration
C. Offer and acceptance
D. Financing contingency

72. Which of the following describes a "rescission of a contract"?
A. The act of substituting a new contract for an existing agreement
B. The act of cancelling a contract by one party when the other party defaults
C. The act of initialing changes by both parties
D. The act of affixing recording stamps.

73. In one community, the real estate taxes are levied for the fiscal year July 1 to the following June 30, and the taxes are payable in two installments—on September 1 and February 1. The owner of a property in this community paid $660 as the first installment on his current taxes but did not pay the second installment. If the property is sold and closing is set for March 25, how much will the seller owe the buyer for taxes?

A. $194.51
B. $201.75
C. $91.75
D. Nothing

74. The American Savings and Loan Association will only give mortgages on 80 percent of the sales price. Mr. Jones purchased a property for $155,000 and obtained the maximum mortgage allowable from the American Savings and Loan at 13¼ percent interest for a 20-year period. If the appropriate rate chart indicates that the monthly loan payment is $11.98 per $1000, what will the monthly payment on this loan be?

A. $1,485.52
B. $1,683.12
C. $983.78
D. $1,212.12

75. The maximum amount guaranteed by the government on a VA loan is

A. the same as conventional loans
B. 60% of the value of the property
C. 60% of the original amount of the loan
D. 60% of the loan or $27,500, whichever is less

76. The value that an owner has in a property over and above any mortgage indebtedness is known as

A. profit
B. equity
C. interest
D. redemption

77. A quitclaim deed properly signed and recorded

A. conveys the interest that the grantee had
B. contains two express warranties
C. conveys the interest that the grantor had
D. guarantees possession of the property

78. An appraiser in his work

A. establishes value
B. estimates value
C. creates value
D. determines value

79. A metes and bounds description must

A. cover an area larger than 15 acres
B. be used in areas not included in the rectangular survey system
C. always use south as the basis for directions
D. commence and finish at the same identifiable point

80. Among the limitations of absolute ownership of land are all of the following EXCEPT

A. the police power, by which governmental agencies control the use to which private property may be put
B. the power of taxation, by which governmental bodies raise funds to operate the community
C. protection of the domicile from Medicaid divestment requirements
D. state fair housing regulations

81. A blanket mortgage usually covers which of the following?

A. Both the mortgaged property and the appropriate mortgage insurance
B. More than one parcel of real estate
C. Property and a developer's construction costs
D. The borrower and his or her heirs

82. Which of the following statements concerning a commission earned by a real estate broker is NOT correct?
A. The amount of the commission cannot exceed 6 percent of the sales price.
B. The amount of the commission can be any amount agreed to by the listing broker and his principal.
C. A broker may expedite closure of a deal by reducing the rate of commission.
D. Commissions may be shared among any number of participating brokers.

83. Which of the following would be the most reliable estimate of the current market value of a 25-year-old single-family residential property?
A. The cost of building a similar dwelling
B. The selling prices of similar properties
C. The condition of the building
D. The rental being paid by current tenants

84. A community's zoning ordinance
A. affects only use, not value
B. should be designed as a part of the overall plan for future development
C. governs placement of skylights in new construction
D. regulates distance between fire hydrants in school zones

85. The owner of an apartment in a condominium may do any of the following EXCEPT
A. sell the interest to another
B. mortgage the interest to secure a debt
C. rent out use of his or her garage space
D. install a bathtub enclosure

86. If a semiannual tax payment on a property currently valued at $100,000 is $820 at an annual rate of $2.05 per $100 of assessed value, what is the ratio of assessed value to current value?
A. 41%
B. 60%
C. 80%
D. 82%

87. Which of the following is NOT contained in a deed?
A. Habendum clause
B. Defeasance clause
C. Acknowledgment
D. Granting clause

88. A property is held by three owners as tenants in common. Upon the death of one owner, ownership of his interest would pass
A. to the remaining owner or owners
B. to the surviving owners and/or his heirs
C. to the surviving spouse
D. to the heirs or to whomever is designated in the will as the devisee

89. If two salespersons from two different offices both show a property to the same customer, and the customer subsequently buys the property, the commission is earned by
A. the agent who showed the property first
B. the agent who finally closes the sale
C. neither
D. both equally

90. The boundaries of a riverside property may be changed by the process of
A. accretion
B. erosion
C. both accretion and erosion
D. neither accretion nor erosion

91. The real estate law of one state makes the statement that "if a broker accepts a good faith deposit he is impliedly being employed by the purchaser for the purpose of conveying the offer to the seller." In this state, a broker
  A. may never accept a binder
  B. may accept a binder only if authorized by the owner to do so
  C. may accept a binder if he immediately turns the check over to the seller
  D. may accept a binder provided that he keeps it undeposited in his office safe

92. The market value approach is most important in determining the value of
  A. an old residence
  B. a new residence
  C. an apartment building
  D. a store building

93. A depreciation schedule that uses an identical amount per year over the economic life of the real estate is known as
  A. straight-line depreciation
  B. sum-of-the-digits depreciation
  C. functional depreciation
  D. declining balance depreciation

94. Which of the following circumstances would release a lessee from his obligation to pay rent?
  A. If he abandons the leased premises
  B. If he is constructively evicted from the leased premises
  C. If the lessor dies
  D. If the property is sold

95. As used in a sales contract, the term "valuable consideration" includes any of the following EXCEPT
  A. expert services for which a fee would be charged
  B. anything movable of monetary value
  C. a right of first refusal to purchase another property
  D. a personal check

96. Which of the following statements concerning a purchase agreement is correct?
  A. The agreement is void if the time of closing is inadvertently omitted from the document.
  B. A check for the earnest money deposit must be made payable to the broker handling the transaction.
  C. Mortgage commitment must be in place before the agreement is valid.
  D. A purchase agreement is always contingent upon satisfactory building inspection.

97. A typical zoning ordinance might include
  A. designation of areas where new commercial structures may be erected
  B. regulations setting standards for fire prevention in a new building
  C. restrictions as to percentage of the property that may be covered by structures or paving
  D. specifications concerning permitted architectural styles

98. Which of the following is true of a lease that contains an escalator clause?
  A. It extends the original term of the lease.
  B. It assures the lessor of an increase in rent under certain conditions.
  C. It guarantees that the rental rate will rise at renewal.
  D. It applies only to commercial properties.

99. Which of the following may the lender not do if the foreclosure sale of mortgaged property yields an amount that is insufficient to pay off the mortgage?
  A. Be satisfied with the proceeds of the sale
  B. Pursue other assets of the borrower
  C. Petition for garnishee of the borrower's wages
  D. Require that the borrower work for him or her until the debt is satisfied

100. As utilized in the cost approach to value, the term "reproduction cost new" means the present cost of reproducing the subject improvement
  A. with one having the same utility
  B. with the same or similar materials
  C. absolutely identical in every way
  D. in another location

CORRECT ANSWERS TO MODEL AMP SALESPERSON EXAMINATION

1. C	21. C	41. B	61. C	81. B
2. B	22. C	42. B	62. D	82. A
3. B	23. A	43. B	63. D	83. B
4. D	*24. B	44. B	64. B	84. B
5. A	25. C	45. D	65. D	85. C
6. D	26. B	46. B	66. B	*86. C
7. A	27. A	*47. A	67. C	87. B
8. A	28. D	*48. B	*68. B	88. D
9. B	29. A	*49. B	69. C	89. B
10. C	30. D	50. C	70. C	90. C
11. C	31. C	51. C	71. D	91. B
12. A	32. A	*52. A	72. B	92. A
13. C	33. B	53. B	*73. B	93. A
14. B	34. C	54. D	*74. A	94. B
15. B	35. D	55. C	75. D	95. C
16. C	36. C	56. C	76. B	96. A
17. D	37. C	57. C	77. C	97. A
18. C	38. B	58. A	78. B	98. B
19. D	39. B	59. D	79. D	99. D
20. B	40. D	*60. B	80. C	100. B

* Solutions provided

SOLUTIONS TO PROBLEMS REQUIRING MATHEMATICAL CALCULATIONS

24. $490.30 ÷ $4.20 = $116.738 × 100 = $11,673.80 ÷ .58 = $20,127.24

47. $400,000 ÷ $2.78 = 143,884.89 sq. ft.
143,884.89 ÷ 240 ft. = 599.52 ft. ÷ 3 = 199.84 yd. = 200 yards

48. $2,000,000 × 2.5% = $50,000 less 6% ($3000) =
$47,000 × 60% = $28,200

49. $27,000 − $18,200 = $8,800 × 12 = $105,600
net return per year ÷ $700,000 = 15%

52. 125 × 175 = 21,875 square feet; 35 × 50 = 1,750 square feet
1,750 square feet ÷ 21,875 square feet = 8%

60.

Sales Price	$50,000	
Less: Old Loan Balance	$24,250	
Broker's Commission	3,000	($50,000 × .06)
3% Discount Points	1,440	($48,000 × .03)
Title Insurance	400	
Miscellaneous	200	
Net	$20,710	

68. $850 ÷ 12 = $70.83 per month × 5.5 months = $389.58
$100 ÷ 12 = $ 8.33 per month × 5.5 months =   45.83
$435.41

$950 − $435.41 = $514.59 returned to seller

73. First installment $660 for 6 months
$110/month, $3.67/day
February 1 to March 25 = 1 month, 25 days
$110 × 1 month   = $110.00
$3.67 × 25 days   = $ 91.75
$201.75

74. $155,000 × .80 = $124, 000
$124,000 ÷ 1,000 = 124 × $11.98 = $1,485.52

86. $820 semiannual × 2 = $1,640 yearly tax
$1,640 x 100 = $164,000 ÷ $2.05 = $80,000 assessed value
$80,000 ÷ $100,000 = 80%

ANSWER SHEET FOR MODEL PSI SALESPERSON EXAMINATION

TEAR HERE

1 Ⓐ Ⓑ Ⓒ Ⓓ   26 Ⓐ Ⓑ Ⓒ Ⓓ   51 Ⓐ Ⓑ Ⓒ Ⓓ   76 Ⓐ Ⓑ Ⓒ Ⓓ
2 Ⓐ Ⓑ Ⓒ Ⓓ   27 Ⓐ Ⓑ Ⓒ Ⓓ   52 Ⓐ Ⓑ Ⓒ Ⓓ   77 Ⓐ Ⓑ Ⓒ Ⓓ
3 Ⓐ Ⓑ Ⓒ Ⓓ   28 Ⓐ Ⓑ Ⓒ Ⓓ   53 Ⓐ Ⓑ Ⓒ Ⓓ   78 Ⓐ Ⓑ Ⓒ Ⓓ
4 Ⓐ Ⓑ Ⓒ Ⓓ   29 Ⓐ Ⓑ Ⓒ Ⓓ   54 Ⓐ Ⓑ Ⓒ Ⓓ   79 Ⓐ Ⓑ Ⓒ Ⓓ
5 Ⓐ Ⓑ Ⓒ Ⓓ   30 Ⓐ Ⓑ Ⓒ Ⓓ   55 Ⓐ Ⓑ Ⓒ Ⓓ   80 Ⓐ Ⓑ Ⓒ Ⓓ
6 Ⓐ Ⓑ Ⓒ Ⓓ   31 Ⓐ Ⓑ Ⓒ Ⓓ   56 Ⓐ Ⓑ Ⓒ Ⓓ   81 Ⓐ Ⓑ Ⓒ Ⓓ
7 Ⓐ Ⓑ Ⓒ Ⓓ   32 Ⓐ Ⓑ Ⓒ Ⓓ   57 Ⓐ Ⓑ Ⓒ Ⓓ   82 Ⓐ Ⓑ Ⓒ Ⓓ
8 Ⓐ Ⓑ Ⓒ Ⓓ   33 Ⓐ Ⓑ Ⓒ Ⓓ   58 Ⓐ Ⓑ Ⓒ Ⓓ   83 Ⓐ Ⓑ Ⓒ Ⓓ
9 Ⓐ Ⓑ Ⓒ Ⓓ   34 Ⓐ Ⓑ Ⓒ Ⓓ   59 Ⓐ Ⓑ Ⓒ Ⓓ   84 Ⓐ Ⓑ Ⓒ Ⓓ
10 Ⓐ Ⓑ Ⓒ Ⓓ   35 Ⓐ Ⓑ Ⓒ Ⓓ   60 Ⓐ Ⓑ Ⓒ Ⓓ   85 Ⓐ Ⓑ Ⓒ Ⓓ
11 Ⓐ Ⓑ Ⓒ Ⓓ   36 Ⓐ Ⓑ Ⓒ Ⓓ   61 Ⓐ Ⓑ Ⓒ Ⓓ   86 Ⓐ Ⓑ Ⓒ Ⓓ
12 Ⓐ Ⓑ Ⓒ Ⓓ   37 Ⓐ Ⓑ Ⓒ Ⓓ   62 Ⓐ Ⓑ Ⓒ Ⓓ   87 Ⓐ Ⓑ Ⓒ Ⓓ
13 Ⓐ Ⓑ Ⓒ Ⓓ   38 Ⓐ Ⓑ Ⓒ Ⓓ   63 Ⓐ Ⓑ Ⓒ Ⓓ   88 Ⓐ Ⓑ Ⓒ Ⓓ
14 Ⓐ Ⓑ Ⓒ Ⓓ   39 Ⓐ Ⓑ Ⓒ Ⓓ   64 Ⓐ Ⓑ Ⓒ Ⓓ   89 Ⓐ Ⓑ Ⓒ Ⓓ
15 Ⓐ Ⓑ Ⓒ Ⓓ   40 Ⓐ Ⓑ Ⓒ Ⓓ   65 Ⓐ Ⓑ Ⓒ Ⓓ   90 Ⓐ Ⓑ Ⓒ Ⓓ
16 Ⓐ Ⓑ Ⓒ Ⓓ   41 Ⓐ Ⓑ Ⓒ Ⓓ   66 Ⓐ Ⓑ Ⓒ Ⓓ   91 Ⓐ Ⓑ Ⓒ Ⓓ
17 Ⓐ Ⓑ Ⓒ Ⓓ   42 Ⓐ Ⓑ Ⓒ Ⓓ   67 Ⓐ Ⓑ Ⓒ Ⓓ   92 Ⓐ Ⓑ Ⓒ Ⓓ
18 Ⓐ Ⓑ Ⓒ Ⓓ   43 Ⓐ Ⓑ Ⓒ Ⓓ   68 Ⓐ Ⓑ Ⓒ Ⓓ   93 Ⓐ Ⓑ Ⓒ Ⓓ
19 Ⓐ Ⓑ Ⓒ Ⓓ   44 Ⓐ Ⓑ Ⓒ Ⓓ   69 Ⓐ Ⓑ Ⓒ Ⓓ   94 Ⓐ Ⓑ Ⓒ Ⓓ
20 Ⓐ Ⓑ Ⓒ Ⓓ   45 Ⓐ Ⓑ Ⓒ Ⓓ   70 Ⓐ Ⓑ Ⓒ Ⓓ   95 Ⓐ Ⓑ Ⓒ Ⓓ
21 Ⓐ Ⓑ Ⓒ Ⓓ   46 Ⓐ Ⓑ Ⓒ Ⓓ   71 Ⓐ Ⓑ Ⓒ Ⓓ   96 Ⓐ Ⓑ Ⓒ Ⓓ
22 Ⓐ Ⓑ Ⓒ Ⓓ   47 Ⓐ Ⓑ Ⓒ Ⓓ   72 Ⓐ Ⓑ Ⓒ Ⓓ   97 Ⓐ Ⓑ Ⓒ Ⓓ
23 Ⓐ Ⓑ Ⓒ Ⓓ   48 Ⓐ Ⓑ Ⓒ Ⓓ   73 Ⓐ Ⓑ Ⓒ Ⓓ   98 Ⓐ Ⓑ Ⓒ Ⓓ
24 Ⓐ Ⓑ Ⓒ Ⓓ   49 Ⓐ Ⓑ Ⓒ Ⓓ   74 Ⓐ Ⓑ Ⓒ Ⓓ   99 Ⓐ Ⓑ Ⓒ Ⓓ
25 Ⓐ Ⓑ Ⓒ Ⓓ   50 Ⓐ Ⓑ Ⓒ Ⓓ   75 Ⓐ Ⓑ Ⓒ Ⓓ   100 Ⓐ Ⓑ Ⓒ Ⓓ

MODEL PSI SALESPERSON EXAMINATION

100 questions

1. If one person wishes to leave a piece of property to another at his death, he must
A. sign and deliver an undated deed
B. sign a deed and leave it in a safety deposit vault
C. state his intentions in his will
D. attach a deed to his will

2. *Condemnation* is the means by which the state uses its power of
A. eminent domain   C. estoppel
B. escheat   D. eviction

3. All of the following are less than freehold estates EXCEPT
A. estate for years   C. estate at sufferance
B. estate at will   D. life estate

4. An Estate in Severalty is owned by
A. a married couple   C. a single person
B. two unmarried persons   D. a partnership

5. The manager of an apartment building
A. must be paid a straight salary only
B. must be paid for specific services according to a published schedule
C. must be paid a percentage of the rent roll
D. may be paid in any way agreed to between owner and manager

6. The legal capacity of a person to enter into a real estate contract is affected by
A. age   C. both
B. sobriety   D. neither

7. An option to purchase differs from a right of first refusal in that it MUST include
A. right of rescission
B. a list of others to whom the option has been offered
C. statement of consideration
D. a habendum clause

8. *Dower* is the term used to describe
A. the property a woman owns in her own right and brings with her into a marriage
B. a wedding gift of real property from the bride's family
C. a gift of real property from husband to wife
D. the rights of a widow to her deceased husband's real estate

9. Under the terms of an open listing,
A. brokers readily cooperate with one another
B. the listing agent handles negotiations for the principal
C. the broker who produces a purchaser must share the commission
D. the owner tends to be personally involved in negotiations

10. The purchaser of a small office building has agreed to a price of $180,000 for the property. The seller has offered to accept a 50 percent straight-term mortgage to be repaid in monthly payments over a term of five years at an annual interest rate of 15 percent. What will be the sum of the first monthly payment on this mortgage?

A. $1,125.00   C. $2,250.00
B. $1,350.00   D. $2,625.00

11. The Statute of Frauds is legislation providing that all agreements affecting title to real estate be in writing in order to be

A. valid   C. enforceable
B. voidable   D. fungible

12. In order to reach his home from his detached garage, a homeowner uses a path which winds across a portion of his neighbor's property. The neighbor's property serves as

A. an easement   C. a dominant tenement
B. an encroachment   D. a servient tenement

13. The owner of a single-family house for rent asks a broker to find a "white" tenant for the house. The broker

A. may take the listing; an owner has the right to specify who lives in his house
B. may take the listing, but should require a written statement from the owner stating his preference
C. may take the listing, but should be sure to have the owner's statement of preference notarized
D. must refuse the listing

14. *Escheat* occurs when

A. the state wishes to build a highway across a portion of one's property
B. a husband inherits his wife's estate
C. a property owner dies leaving no known heirs
D. a debtor cannot pay his bills

15. If more than one broker participates in the sale of a property,

A. the seller must pay two commissions
B. the seller pays commission to the listing broker, and the buyer pays commission to the selling broker
C. the two brokers divide the commission according to a prearranged schedule
D. the seller dictates how he wishes the commission to be divided

16. A real estate salesperson is employed by

A. a real estate broker
B. the owner of property for sale or rent
C. the Board of Realtors
D. a broker's office manager

17. *Satisfaction of mortgage* occurs when

A. the mortgage is duly recorded
B. title passes
C. the borrower defaults
D. the loan is fully repaid

18. The plot below is being sold for $4.25 per square foot. What must the buyer pay for section B?

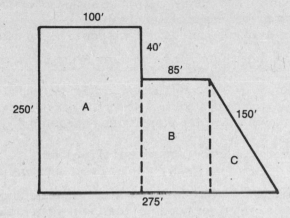

A. $65,112.00 C. $75, 862.50
B. $74,037.50 D. $90,312.50

19. The type of interest a mortgagor holds in a property is known as
A. equitable interest C. redemptive interest
B. security interest D. priority interest

20. A small apartment building consists of 6 units that rent at $550 per month each, 12 units that rent at $375 per month each, and 5 units that rent at $295 per month each. All rents are due on the first of the month, and at the date of closing, April 20, no tenant is in default. At the closing,
A. the buyer must pay the seller $3,091.66
B. the seller must pay the buyer $3,091.66
C. the buyer must pay the seller $6,183.33
D. the seller must pay the buyer $6,183.33

21. A homeowner requests that a broker market her property. The homeowner states that she wishes to realize $140,000 from the sale of this property and signs an agreement with the broker so stating. The homeowner has given the broker
A. an open listing C. a net listing
B. an exclusive listing D. an agency listing

22. Under the terms of Regulation Z, the lender must disclose not only interest charges but also mortgage insurance fees, discount points, origination charges, and
A. appraisal fees C. mortgage recording fees
B. brokers' fees D. principal

23. Which of the following CANNOT serve as a source for mortgage loans?
A. Commercial banks C. Pension funds
B. Private individuals D. None of these

24. An appraisal MUST ALWAYS be
A. written
B. lower than actual market price
C. documented
D. recorded

25. Concerning contract law, which of the following statements is correct?
  A. Contracts may be terminated by complete performance.
  B. Sales contracts generally cannot be assigned by the buyer.
  C. It is best to record a contract of sale.
  D. Signatures on all written contracts must be notarized.

26. Which of the following is true regarding Federal Housing Administration loans?
  A. The loans are made from funds provided by the federal government.
  B. If a property is located in a designated flood area, the FHA will not grant a loan unless the property has adequate flood insurance coverage.
  C. There is a penalty for prepayment of the loan.
  D. FHA loan guarantees will not be granted to veterans.

27. Your purchaser tells you, his sales agent, that he intends to occupy the property he is buying for not more than four years, then intends to trade up. He can obtain an adjustable rate mortgage at 10 percent, adjustable every 6 months with a cap of ½ percent at each adjustment and a lifetime cap of 4 percent or a fixed mortgage at 12½ percent. You should
  A. advise him to take the fixed rate mortgage because a fixed rate mortgage is always preferable
  B. advise him to take the ARM because the ARM will cost him less if he keeps the property only four years
  C. advise him to take the fixed rate mortgage because a fixed rate is better for the lender and your first obligation is to the lender
  D. give no advice; financing is not your province

28. In order to be valid, a mortgage or deed of trust must be
  A. in writing   C. between competent parties
  B. executed by the parties   D. all of the above

29. Which of the following is NOT essential to the validity of a contract?
  A. Legality of object   C. Contingencies
  B. Consideration   D. Meeting of the minds

30. In the negotiation of a difficult sales contract between an experienced seller and a novice buyer, the broker should
  A. employ an attorney for the purchaser
  B. refuse to continue negotiations with the purchaser
  C. suggest to the purchaser that he consult an attorney
  D. have no concern about the purchaser's lack of experience

31. A widow is willed the use of the family home for the rest of her natural life, with the condition that the fee simple title shall go to her children upon her death. She holds
  A. a leasehold
  B. void interest in property
  C. a tenancy in common
  D. a life estate

32. Which of the following is NOT true of a tenancy by the entirety?
  A. A tenancy by the entirety may exist between two unmarried persons.
  B. If one of the parties is involved in a dispute, there is generally no right to partition the land.
  C. The domicile is protected from all creditors.
  D. Parties are heirs to one another.

33. A deed conveys title to X and Y. The intention of the parties is not stated. Which of the following is true?
    A. A joint tenancy is created.
    B. If X dies, his one-half interest will pass to his heirs or according to will.
    C. X and Y own the property in severalty.
    D. A partnership has been created.

34. When title is held by a corporation, it is referred to as
    A. a joint tenancy
    C. tenancy in common
    B. an estate in severalty
    D. tenants by the entirety

35. The provisions of RESPA are directed at
    A. real estate brokers
    C. mortgage lenders
    B. title insurers
    D. attorneys

36. A contract entered into between a minor and an adult would be
    A. bilateral
    C. voidable
    B. void
    D. valid

37. With respect to the signing of the deed, all of the following are true EXCEPT that the signing of the deed by the grantor
    A. executes the deed
    B. automatically passes title to the grantee
    C. must be acknowledged
    D. may be accomplished in the absence of an attorney

38. Which of the following is NOT true of an agency listing?
    A. The owner reserves the right to sell the property and pay no commission to the broker.
    B. The broker receives a commission only if he or another agent is the procuring cause of the sale.
    C. If the owner sells the property himself, he owes the listing broker a reduced commission.
    D. The names of parties who have already seen the property are enumerated in the listing as excluded parties.

39. Which of the provisions below is an unlikely contingency to appear in a real estate contract?
    A. Procurement of financing
    B. Completion of engineer's reports
    C. Obtaining a building permit
    D. Receiving a long-expected inheritance

40. Which of the following statements regarding deeds is NOT true?
    A. A deed must be acknowledged to be recorded.
    B. An unrecorded deed cannot be enforced.
    C. Title passes upon signing of the deed by grantor.
    D. A fee is charged for recording a deed.

41. The term "contractual ability" means which of the following?
    A. The parties to the contract are competent to enter into a valid agreement.
    B. The contract is drawn up by a person legally qualified to do so.
    C. The agreement contemplates a purpose which is legal.
    D. The contract contains all the clauses and covenants necessary to be valid.

42. Money paid upon the signing of a contract of sale is generally known as
  A. rent   C. principal
  B. interest   D. earnest money

43. The sinks, marble slabs, and refrigerated cases installed in a store by a tenant who intends to use the store as a fish market are called
  A. chattels   C. personal property
  B. trade fixtures   D. improvements

44. A condominium is a
  A. method of construction
  B. unique method of ownership
  C. housing complex for adults only
  D. converted apartment house

45. The taxes on a property are $780 per year. The taxes are due January 1 and are paid by the owner. If the owner sold the house and the taxes were prorated as of September 15, what refund would he receive?
  A. $227.50   C. $650.00
  B. $552.50   D. $750.00

46. A property with a market value of $75,000 is assessed at 90 percent of that value. If the tax rate is $4.20 per $100 of assessed value, what will the taxes be on this property for one year?
  A. $3,780   C. $2,835
  B. $3,150   D. $315

47. Blockbusting is most accurately described as
  A. the purchase of a home in a neighborhood by a member of a minority group
  B. directing homeseekers into an area to change its character
  C. directing certain homeseekers away from an area in order to maintain its character
  D. influencing homeowners to sell in advance of movement of minorities into the neighborhood

48. To establish claim to title of a parcel of realty by adverse possession, the claimant must hold the parcel
  A. either exclusively or in common with others, provided he can account for substantial enclosure and improvement or annual cultivation
  B. uninterruptedly for a statutory period, with or without the owner's consent
  C. under any circumstances, provided either a claim or a color of title is filed
  D. under conditions hostile to the owner

49. Which of the following is generally considered to be true?
  A. "Escheat" is the power of government to take private property for public purposes.
  B. Zoning would be a perfect example of the "police power" of government.
  C. Purchase of "riparian rights" would allow a developer to build an apartment house over a highway.
  D. Emblements detract from the value of a property.

50. The money for making a Veteran's Administration loan is provided by
  A. the Veteran's Administration
  B. any qualified lending institution
  C. the seller
  D. a special trust fund

51. The Veteran's Administration will give a mortgage on a property only if the following fact is true.
  A. Borrower needs 100 percent financing.
  B. Borrower's use of the property is for a personal residential purpose.
  C. Borrower has taken advantage of VA education benefits.
  D. Borrower could not qualify for a mortgage without the VA guarantee.

52. The purpose of the Real Estate Settlement Procedures Act is to
  A. reduce legal expenses of closing costs
  B. insure that all parties to a real estate transaction have knowledge of all settlement costs
  C. assure against discrimination in lending
  D. guard against arithmetic errors in apportioning taxes

53. Mr. James wishes to release a right in property he owns as a single person. He can do this with any of the following instruments EXCEPT
  A. deed
  B. option
  C. dedication
  D. eviction

54. Which of the following may convey title to real property?
  A. Title policy
  B. Will
  C. Lease
  D. Contract

55. If a broker purchases business cards for a salesperson, he may compromise that salesperson's status as
  A. a salesperson
  B. a licensee
  C. a franchisee
  D. an independent contractor

56. The type of lease most commonly used in shopping centers is called a(n)
  A. gross lease
  B. percentage lease
  C. net lease
  D. open lease

57. The relationship of the broker to the salespeople in his/her office is that of
  A. supervisor
  B. employer
  C. fiduciary
  D. principal

58. The term "blanket mortgage" is used when a mortgage includes
  A. personal property
  B. more than one parcel of real property
  C. an existing mortgage
  D. projected value of crops already in the ground

59. Which of the following would give a broker the least protection?
  A. An open listing
  B. A net listing
  C. An exclusive agency listing
  D. An exclusive right to sell

60. Laws prescribing the construction requirements or standards for new properties in any locality are known as
  A. subdivision requirements
  B. zoning laws
  C. health ordinances
  D. building codes

61. Property held by two or more persons with right of survivorship describes a

A. tenancy in common   C. corporate property

B. joint tenancy   D. partnership

62. Which of the following would be the best example of functional obsolescence in a single family property?

A. Kitchen cabinets in need of repair

B. Adverse change in zoning

C. Inadequate interior floor plan

D. Close proximity to an industrial park

63. "Equity" is best defined as

A. money included in the monthly mortgage payment

B. an owner's interest in a property over and above all liens

C. a method of apportioning costs at closing

D. apportionment of property among tenants in common

64. When a seller prepays taxes and insurance, he is reimbursed for the unused portion by the method of

A. proration   C. depreciation

B. amortization   D. none of the above

65. Of the following, the VA will only guarantee a mortgage that is to be used for the purchase of

A. a two-family home

B. a cooperative apartment

C. a vacation home

D. a property that will bring in a financial return

66. When a valid contract of sale has been executed by seller and buyer,

A. buyer has legal title

B. buyer has equitable title

C. seller has reversionary rights

D. buyer has reversionary rights

67. The highest and best use of a property means the

A. gross rent of the property

B. use producing the greatest net return over a given period of time

C. difference between the current market value and the assessed value

D. use producing the highest ratio between the land value and the building value

68. Nancy Ames received a mortgage loan of $55,000 at 13¼ percent interest. The loan was amortized over a 20-year period with payments set at $654.19 per month. How much of the first payment was applied to the principal?

A. $46.90   C. $59.40

B. $74.56   D. $86.67

69. How much cash will a buyer need at the closing after he has deposited with the seller's attorney a $7,000 earnest money deposit and after he has acquired a mortgage loan for 65 percent of the $48,500 sales price on a property that he is purchasing?

A. $9,975   C. $41,500

B. $16,975   D. $24,525

70. Which provides the greatest surety that title to real property is as represented?
  A. Title search
  B. Affidavit of title
  C. Certificate of title
  D. Title insurance policy

71. Which of the following can the buyer legally expect from the broker representing the seller?
  A. A copy of the employment contract between broker and seller
  B. An accounting of all monies handled by the broker during the course of the transaction as they pertain to the buyer
  C. A breakdown of commission splits among cooperating brokers
  D. Referral to the best real estate attorney in the area

72. Which of the following statements is true concerning conventional mortgage loans?
  A. They cannot be assumed.
  B. They are made to the borrower with a guarantee by the government.
  C. They cannot be sold.
  D. They may carry an adjustable rate.

73. When an individual owns property in his or her name alone, he or she has
  A. a sole estate
  B. an estate in severalty
  C. an estate in common
  D. none of the above

74. The interest of the deceased spouse under a tenancy by entireties
  A. passes to the surviving spouse
  B. passes to the heirs or devisees according to the laws of descent
  C. passes according to provision in deceased's will
  D. passes by devise

75. Jones enters into a binding contract to purchase Lot 10 in Golden Hills Estates. Before closing, Green receives a higher offer for the lot and refuses to convey it. He instead offers Jones an adjacent, similar lot. What can Jones do now if he wishes Lot 10?
  A. Accept the similar lot and sue.
  B. Sue for specific performance under the contract.
  C. Meet the higher price in order to get the lot.
  D. Nothing—just cancel the contract.

76. A broker who withholds from the client bids from other offices until the client has acted upon bids submitted by agents in the listing office is
  A. protecting the interests of his office
  B. properly screening bids for the client
  C. expediting the sale for the client
  D. behaving in an unethical manner

77. *RESPA* refers to
  A. fair housing laws
  B. truth-in-lending
  C. rent control regulations
  D. closing

78. A buyer is assuming a $21,000 mortgage that has an interest rate of 7 percent annually with payments due the first day of each month. Interest is paid in advance. If the last payment was made on June 1, and closing on the property is set for June 18, what will the buyer owe the seller?
  A. $49.00
  B. $73.49
  C. $134.75
  D. $220.40

79. A discount broker has opened an office in town, and salespersons from full-price, full-service offices refuse to show her listings. This practice is
  A. illegal because it constitutes price fixing among the brokers
  B. illegal because it constitutes discrimination against the discount broker
  C. acceptable because salespersons may show any properties they choose
  D. required because discount brokerage is illegal

80. The tenant is usually liable for which of the following under the terms of a net lease?
  A. Utilities
  B. Property depreciation
  C. Salaries of building managers
  D. Special assessments

81. Which of the following activities describes the term "blockbusting"?
  A. Offering residential property for sale only to persons of the same ethnic background as those present in the neighborhood
  B. Soliciting the sale of residential property on the grounds of alleged change of property value due to the presence of persons of another race in the neighborhood
  C. Refusing to grant mortgages on properties in minority neighborhoods
  D. Pretending to be interested in purchasing specific properties to test compliance with fair housing regulations

82. Which of the following statements concerning VA regulations is NOT true?
  A. In the case of VA loans, prepayment penalty charges are illegal.
  B. The VA requires a down payment be made whenever a veteran agrees to a purchase price in excess of the value estimated by a VA appraiser.
  C. The holder of a VA mortgage may sell his property only to another veteran.
  D. The VA will not grant a mortgage on a property with unrepaired termite damage after termites have been treated.

83. Economic obsolescence can best be defined as a reduction in property value
  A. due to natural wear and tear
  B. as a result of the attachment of liens
  C. as a result of discount points
  D. by causes external to the property and beyond the owner's control

84. The income approach is most important in the value determination of
  A. a condominium
  B. an office building
  C. a residence
  D. industrial vacant land

85. A lease that provides for periodic increases of rent at regular intervals is known as
  A. a percentage lease
  B. a yearly lease
  C. a long-term lease
  D. a graduated lease

86. The "right of first refusal" gives the tenant which of the following rights?
  A. That of placing the first bid if the property is subjected to foreclosure proceedings
  B. That of being given first preference of buying the property should the owner decide to sell
  C. That of refusing access to the apartment to owner or owner's agent
  D. That of turning down an offered paint job

87. Which of the following might be included in a typical building code?
A. Restrictions as to how many acres of the community may be reserved for industrial usage
B. Regulations concerning the number of emergency exits that must be provided in new public structures
C. Specifications for handicapped access to two-family houses
D. Controls over home offices

88. If a person died testate, title to his property would
A. go to the devisees
B. pass to his next of kin
C. escheat to the state
D. be sold by the governmental unit having jurisdiction

89. Which of the following statements regarding FHA mortgage insurance practices is correct?
A. In order to be insured, loans must be made or held by an FHA-approved mortgagee.
B. The FHA will insure both first and second mortgages.
C. A veteran cannot qualify for an FHA-guaranteed mortgage.
D. Only conventional mortgages qualify for FHA insurance.

90. A prospective buyer is considering buying an apartment house containing 15 apartments that rent for $250 per month each. Expenses are $4,200 per year. If the buyer wants a 15 percent return on his investment, how much should he offer for this real estate?
A. $138,667
B. $272,000
C. $387,000
D. $581,000

91. The primary intention of the Statute of Frauds is to prevent which of the following?
A. Clauses included in a title that are contrary to the best interest of the buyer
B. Problems resulting from verbal agreements in land transfers
C. Forged titles
D. Falsehoods that are included in a title and against which the buyer has no protection

92. In order to accurately ascertain the exact metes and bounds of a property, one should obtain
A. an abstract of title
B. a search
C. a survey
D. a title insurance policy

93. All leases must contain which of the following to be enforceable?
A. The amount of taxes on the leased property
B. The name of the institution which will hold the mortgage
C. Statement of the net return expected by the landlord
D. Date of commencement of the lease

94. Which of the following statements best explains why instruments concerning real estate are recorded with the Recorder of Deeds in the county where the property is located?
A. To comply with the terms of the Statute of Frauds
B. The law requires that they be recorded
C. To give constructive notice to the world of the interest in a particular parcel of real estate
D. The broker cannot receive his commission until recording

95. Under federal fair housing regulations, which of the following practices is NOT prohibited?
   A. A broker's refusal to show a residence, for which he has a listing, to a prospective buyer because of the latter's race
   B. An owner's refusal to rent a unit in a two-family residence, of which his nephew occupies one unit, to a member of a certain religious group
   C. A seller's refusal to negotiate with a couple who intends to apply for an FHA mortgage
   D. A landlord's refusal to rent an apartment to a mixed-race married couple

96. The net amount received by Mr. Jackson for the sale of his property was $11,300. If his broker received 5 percent and an allowance of $100 for extra expenses, what was the selling price?
   A. $11,895   C. $12,000
   B. $11,965   D. $11,865

97. A condition or covenant in a real estate sales contract would be legally valid even though it did which of the following?
   A. Limited occupancy of real estate on the basis of religion
   B. Restricted building or architectural characteristics
   C. Required sale to members of specific minority groups in order to maintain neighborhood character
   D. Required buyers to purchase title insurance from a particular company

98. What course of action may a buyer NOT take if the seller defaults in the sale of a parcel of real property?
   A. Sue for specific performance
   B. Rescind the contract
   C. Sue for damages in civil court
   D. Appropriate the property

99. The phrase "time is of the essence" indicates which of the following?
   A. The inclusion of a specific termination date of a listing agreement
   B. A clause in a contract of sale that states the date by which all parties must perform the promises and obligations as set forth in the agreement
   C. Recitation of the statement of penalties for late payment
   D. A discount schedule for prepayment of rents

100. The state condemned the front portion of a lot as indicated below and paid 80¢ per square foot. What did the state pay for the taking?
   A. $3,750   C. $3,600
   B. $3,000   D. None of the above

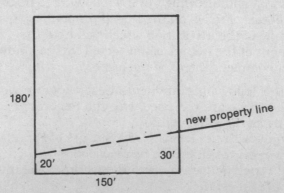

CORRECT ANSWERS TO MODEL PSI SALESPERSON EXAMINATION

1. C	21. C	41. A	61. B	81. B
2. A	22. D	42. D	62. C	82. C
3. D	23. D	43. B	63. B	83. D
4. C	24. C	44. B	64. A	84. B
5. D	25. A	*45. A	65. A	85. D
6. C	26. B	*46. C	66. B	86. B
7. C	27. B	47. D	67. B	87. B
8. D	28. D	48. D	*68. A	88. A
9. D	29. C	49. B	*69. A	89. A
*10. A	30. C	50. B	70. D	*90. B
11. C	31. D	51. B	71. B	91. B
12. D	32. A	52. B	72. D	92. C
13. D	33. B	53. D	73. B	93. D
14. C	34. B	54. B	74. A	94. C
15. C	35. A	55. D	75. B	95. C
16. B	36. C	56. B	76. D	*96. C
17. D	37. B	57. A	77. D	97. B
*18. C	38. C	58. B	*78. A	98. D
19. B	39. D	59. A	79. C	99. B
*20. B	40. C	60. D	80. A	*100. B

* Solutions provided

SOLUTIONS TO PROBLEMS REQUIRING MATHEMATICAL CALCULATIONS

10. $180,000 × 50% = $90,000 mortgage
$90,000 × 15% = $13,500 ÷ 12 = $1,125 monthly interest
Straight-term mortgage is an interest only mortgage with principal repaid in full at the end; therefore all monthly payments are in the sum of $1,125.

18. This problem gives a great deal of extraneous information. The width of section B is 85 ft. The depth of section B is 250 ft. − 40 ft. = 210 ft.
85 ft. × 210 ft. = 17,850 sq. ft. × $4.25 = $75,862.50

20. $550 × 6 = $3,300
$375 × 12 = $4,500
$295 × 5 = $1,475
$9,275 rent roll
1/3 of the month remains, so the seller must give the buyer 1/3 of $9,275 = $3,091.66

45. $780 ÷ 12 = $65 per month × 8.5 months = $552.50
$780 − $552.50 = $227.50 returned to seller

46. $75,000 × .90 = $67,500 ÷ 100 = $675 × $4.20 = $2,835 in taxes

68. $55,000 × .1325 = $7,287.50 ÷ 12 = $607.29 interest per month
$654.19 − $607.29 = $46.90 principal

69. $48,500 × .65 = $31,525 mortgage loan
$ 7,000 deposit
$38,525
$48,500 − $38,525 = $9,975 needed at closing

78. $21,000 × .07 = $1,470 ÷ 12 = $122.50 per month, $4.083 per day
$4.083 × 12 days = $48.996 or $49.00 owed to seller

90. $250 × 15 = $3,750 per month × 12 months = $45,000 rent per year.
$45,000 − $4,200 expenses = $40,800 ÷ .15 = $272,000

96. $11,300 + $100 = $11,400
100% − 5% = 95%
$11,400 ÷ .95 = $12,000

100.

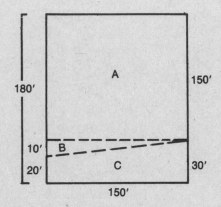

Area of entire lot = 150 ft. × 180 ft. = 27,000 square feet
Area of Section A = 150 ft. × 150 ft. = 22,500 square feet
Area of Section B = 1/2 (150 ft. × 10 ft.) = 750 square feet
22,500 + 750 = 23,250 square feet
27,000 − 23,250 = 3,750 square feet × .80 = $3,000

Chapter Fifteen

Appraiser Licensing and Certification

Federal involvement with real estate appraisal is a fairly new development which has stemmed directly from the savings and loan bank failures of the 1980s. Many factors contributed to the failures of the banks, but one of the major culprits was the gross overvaluation of many properties. The banks were unable to recover the overgenerous sums they had lent when mortgagors defaulted on the loans. To guard against such debacles in the future, Congress passed the Financial Institutions Reform, Recovery and Enforcement Act of 1989 (FIRREA). Title XI of FIRREA provides for state-licensed and state-certified real estate appraisers and mandates that all appraisals done for federally related transactions (FRTs) be done by licensed or certified appraisers. The provisions of this act, after a time extension, became effective uniformly throughout the fifty states, the District of Columbia, Puerto Rico, Guam, and the Virgin Islands on January 1, 1993.

The Appraisal Foundation, a nonprofit, independent organization, was charged by Congress with implementing the provisions of Title XI of FIRREA. Two independent boards serve under The Appraisal Foundation: The Appraisal Standards Board (ASB) and The Appraiser Qualifications Board (AQB).

The Appraisal Standards Board has established and published the Uniform Standards of Professional Appraisal Practice (USPAP). These standards set forth the rules for developing an appraisal and reporting its result. USPAP constitutes a portion of every accredited appraising course.

The Appraiser Qualifications Board has the responsibility of establishing qualifications and criteria for appraisal licensure and certification. The AQB has determined the content that must be included in each state's examinations and approves the examinations that are administered. The AQB has approved three appraiser designations for offering by the states. These three designations are "Licensed Real Estate Appraiser," "Certified Residential Appraiser," and "Certified General Appraiser."

The minimum qualification for the Licensed Real Estate Appraiser designation is successful completion of the AQB-endorsed uniform licensure examination. Before sitting for this examination, the candidate must complete 75 hours of courses in real estate appraising, including coverage of the Uniform Standards of Professional Appraisal Practice, and 2,000 hours of residential appraisal experience gained in a span of two years. Verification of experience credit, educational requirements, and the exam are administered by the state certification/licensing agency. While the standards and requirements are federally mandated, the actual licensure and certification processes are state controlled.

Certified Residential Appraiser credentials may be issued by a state agency upon the applicant's passing the AQB-endorsed residential certification uniform examination. Prerequisite to sitting for the residential certification exam are 105 hours of courses in real estate appraising, including coverage of USPAP, and 2,000 hours of appraisal experience gained over a two-year span.

A state agency may grant Certified General Appraiser credentials upon the candidate's fulfilling the prerequisite 165 hours of courses in real estate appraising, including USPAP, and 2,000 hours of general appraisal experience gained within a two-year span and passing of the AQB-endorsed general certification examination.

The purpose of the three different classifications is to assure adequate appraisal services for different types of properties. A Licensed Real Estate Appraiser is generally approved to value non-complex one-to-four-family residential units having a transaction value of less than $1,000,000 and complex one-to-four-family residential units having a transaction value lower than $250,000. Appraisals of one-to-four-family residential units with a transaction value in excess of $1,000,000 and all one-to-four-family complex appraisals having a value in excess of $250,000 require the services of a Certified Residential Appraiser. A Certified General Appraiser is permitted to appraise all types of real property. All classifications of appraisers are bound by the "Competency Provision" of the Uniform Standards of Professional Practice.

Since, unlike the real estate salesperson and broker licenses, which are entirely state controlled, the content of appraisal license and certification exams is federally mandated, most states use the services of standardized testing services rather than preparing their own exams. Each of the standardized testing services that develops appraisal exams prepares exams at all three levels: licensure, residential certification, and general certification. Obviously, at the higher levels, the questions test both broader and deeper understanding of the principles and practices of appraisal. In general, there are more questions on the higher-level exams. For example, in Maryland the licensure exam contains 100 questions, the exam for residential certification 110 questions, and the general certification exam 120 questions. In some states, the passing score is set at a higher level for the more inclusive certification.

Since the content of appraisal exams is governed by the AQB, the exams prepared by the separate testing services are more similar than different. In some states the exam is customized for that state by the test developer. Most states use a stock standardized exam supplied by the developer. The differences among the exams occur mainly in the question styles, the number of questions, the timing, and the method of administration, i.e., paper-and-pencil or machine administered. The other big difference is in passing scores. While the majority of states require a passing score of 75% on all appraisal exams, passing levels range from 65% to 75%. These variations occur among states and within states according to license or certification level.

The services that develop appraisal exams are:

ASI (Assessment Systems, Inc.)
Appraiser Examination Program
718 Arch Street
Philadelphia, PA 19106
800-274-0999

PSI (Psychological Services, Inc.)
Real Estate Licensing Examination Services
100 West Broadway, Suite 1100
Glendale, CA 91210
800-733-9267

PES (Professional Examination Service)
475 Riverside Drive
New York, NY 10027
212-870-2683

The Psychological Corporation
555 Academic Court
San Antonio, TX 87204-2498
800-228-0752

State control enters into the credentialing process in some very important ways. The states determine which exam is used and what constitutes a passing score. States also set their own standards as to personal background and references. Some states have very strict character requirements. States are free to exceed the federal requirements, and some states do indeed require more hours of classroom training and more years of experience than those set by the AQB. States are also free to change testing services at almost any time. The chart below lists which states utilized which testing service at the time of preparation of this book. Your own state board will direct you to the appropriate service and will give you application information when you have fulfilled all its prerequisites.

STATE UNIQUE	ASI	PES	PSI	PSYCHOLOGICAL CORPORATION
Florida	Alaska	Alabama	Nevada	Arkansas
Mississippi	Arizona	Delaware	Ohio	Georgia
New York	California	Iowa		Maryland
North Carolina	Colorado	Massachusetts		Michigan
Puerto Rico	Connecticut	Missouri		South Carolina
Texas	DC	Nebraska		
	Guam	New Mexico		
	Hawaii	Rhode Island		
	Idaho	Virginia		
	Illinois	West Virginia		
	Indiana	Wisconsin		
	Kansas			
	Kentucky			
	Louisiana			
	Maine			
	Minnesota			
	Montana			
	New Hampshire			
	New Jersey			
	North Dakota			
	Oklahoma			
	Oregon			
	Pennsylvania			
	South Dakota			
	Tennessee			
	Utah			
	Vermont			
	Virgin Islands			
	Washington			
	Wyoming			

STATE REAL ESTATE APPRAISER BOARDS

ALABAMA
Bobbie Eddins
Alabama Real Estate
Appraiser Board
600 Interstate Park Drive
Suite 628
Montgomery, 36109
(205) 242-8747 (Office)
(205) 242-8749 (Fax)

ALASKA
Carol J. Whelan
Department of Commerce
& Economic Development
Division of Occupational Licensing
P.O. Box 110806
Juneau, 99811-0806
(907) 465-2542 (Office)
(907) 465-2974 (Fax)

ARIZONA
Adriane Brown-White
Arizona Board of Appraisers
1700 W. Washington, Suite 133
Phoenix, 85007
(602) 542-1539 (Office)
(602) 542-1599 (Fax)

ARKANSAS
Jim Martin
Arkansas Appraiser
Licensing Board
324 Spring Street, Suite 215
Little Rock, 72201
(501) 324-9815 (Office)
(501) 324-9816 (Fax)

CALIFORNIA
Robert West
Business Transportation &
Housing Administration
1120 N. Street, Room 2101
Sacramento, 95814
(916) 654-5525 (Office)

COLORADO
Stewart A. Leach
Colorado Board of Real
Estate Appraisers
1776 Logan, 4th Floor
Denver, 80203
(303) 894-2166 (Office)
(303) 894-2683 (Fax)

CONNECTICUT
Lawrence Hannafin
CT. Dept. of Consumer
Protection Real Estate Comm.
State Office Bldg., Room G-8A
165 Capitol Avenue
Hartford, 06106
(203) 566-5130 (Office)
(203) 566-7630 (Fax)

DELAWARE
Gayle Melvin
Delaware Real Estate
Appraisal Board
Professional Regulation Division
P.O. Box 1401
Dover, 19903
(302) 739-4522 (Office)
(302) 739-6148 (Fax)

DISTRICT OF COLUMBIA
Patsy Lockett
DCRA/OPLA
614 H. Street NW, Room 913
Washington, DC 20013-7200
(202) 727-7849 (Office)
(202) 727-8030 (Fax)

FLORIDA
Darlene F. Keller
Dept. of Prof. Reg., Div. of Real
Estate/Fl. Real Estate Comm.
400 West Robinson Street
Orlando, 32801-1772
(407) 423-6071 (Office)
(407) 423-6469 (Fax)

GEORGIA
Charles Clark
Georgia Real Estate Comm.
Suite 500 Sussex Place
148 International Blvd. NE
Atlanta, 30303-1734
(404) 656-3916 (Office)
(404) 656-0529 (Fax)

HAWAII
June Kamioka
HI Real Estate Appraisal Board
1010 Richard Street
Honolulu, 96813
(808) 586-2704 (Office)

IDAHO
Duane R. Higer
ID Real Estate Appraiser
Certification Board/Bureau
of Occupation Licensing
2417 Bank Drive, Room 312
Boise, 83705-2598
(208) 334-3233 (Office)

ILLINOIS
Albert M. Suguitan
Dept. of Prof. Regulation
320 W. Washington Street
Springfield, 62786
(217) 785-0890 (Office)
(217) 524-0142 (Fax)

INDIANA
David Carter
Indiana Prof. Licensing Agency
1021 State Office Building
100 North Senate Avenue
Indianapolis, 46204
(317) 232-3997 (Office)
(317) 232-2312 (Fax)

IOWA
William Schroeder
Prof. Licensing & Reg. Div.
Dept. of Commerce
1918 SE Hulsizer Avenue
Ankeny, 50021
(515) 281-7363 (Office)
(515) 281-7372 (Fax)

KANSAS
Jean Duncan
Kansas Real Estate Comm.
900 Jackson Street, Room 501
Topeka, 66612-1220
(913) 296-3411 (Office)

KENTUCKY
James P. Daniels
Kentucky Real Estate Comm.
10200 Linn Station Road, Suite 201
Louisville, 40223
(502) 425-4273 (Office)
(502) 588-3040 (Fax)

LOUISIANA
Anna Kathryn Williams
Louisiana Real Estate Comm.
9071 Interline Avenue
P.O. Box 14785
Baton Rouge, 70898
(504) 925-4771 (Office)
(504) 925-4431 (Fax)

MAINE
Mary Genthner
Dept. of Prof. & Financial
Regulation Div. of Licensing &
Enforcement/Board of Real
Estate Appraisers
State House Station #35
Augusta, 04333
(207) 582-8700 (Office)
(207) 582-5415 (Fax)

MARYLAND
Charles P. Kazlo
Maryland Dept. of Licensing &
Regulation Real Estate
Appraisers Commission
501 St. Paul Place, 9th Floor
Baltimore, 21202
(410) 333-6590 (Office)
(410) 333-1229 (Fax)

MASSACHUSETTS
Ann Collins
Division of Registration
Commonwealth of Mass.
c/o Legal Unit, Room 1508
100 Cambridge Street
Boston, 02202
(617) 727-1738 (Office)
(617) 727-7378 (Fax)

MICHIGAN
Judith A. Dennis
Michigan Dept. of Commerce
Office of Commercial Services
P.O. Box 30018
Lansing, 48909
(517) 335-1686 (Office) or
(517) 335-1688 (Office)
(517) 373-2795 (Fax)

MINNESOTA
Dennis Poppenhagen
Minnesota Commerce Dept.
133 E. 7th Street
St. Paul, 55101
(612) 296-6313 (Office)
(612) 296-4328 (Fax)

MISSISSIPPI
John W. Neelley
Mississippi Real Estate Comm.
1920 Dunbarton Drive
Jackson, 39216-5087
(601) 987-3969 (Office)
(601) 987-4984 (Fax)

MISSOURI
E. Scott Wright
Missouri Real Estate
Appraisers Commission
P.O. Box 202
Jefferson City, 65102
(314) 751-0038 (Office)
(314) 751-4176 (Fax)

MONTANA
Sharon McCullough
Montana Board of Real
Estate Appraisers
111 North Jackson
Helena, 59620
(406) 444-4294 (Office)
(406) 444-1667 (Fax)

NEBRASKA
Marilyn Hasselbalch
Nebraska Real Estate
Appraiser Board
301 Centennial Mall South
Box 94667
Lincoln, 68509-4667
(402) 471-9015 (Office)
(402) 471-4492 (Fax)

NEVADA
Patricia M. Brown
Nevada Real Estate Division
1665 Hot Springs Road, Rm. 155
Carson City, 89710
(702) 687-4280 (Office)

NEW HAMPSHIRE
Sally Sullivan
New Hampshire Real Estate
Appraisal Board
Waverly Square
6 Chenell Drive, Suite 290
Concord, 03301
(603) 271-6186 (Office)

NEW JERSEY
Kevin Earle
Dept. of Law & Public Safety
Div. of Consumer Affairs
P.O. Box 45032
Newark, 07101
(201) 504-6480 (Office)
(201) 648-3536 (Fax)

NEW MEXICO
Lynne Schmolke
New Mexico Real Estate Comm.
1650 University Blvd., NE, Suite 490
Albuquerque, 87102
(505) 841-9120 x 16 (Office)
(505) 841-9120 x 49 (Fax)

NEW YORK
Gail A. Bates
New York Dept. of State Div. of
Licensing Services
162 Washington Avenue
Albany, 12231-0001
(518) 486-6451 (Office)
(518) 474-4765 (Fax)

NORTH CAROLINA
James E. Poole, Jr.
North Carolina Real Estate
Commission
P.O. Box 17100
Raleigh, 27619-7100
(919) 733-9580 (Office)
(919) 872-0038 (Fax)

NORTH DAKOTA
David Campbell
Governor's Office State
Capitol
P.O. Box 1336
Bismarck, 58502-1336
(701) 222-1051 (Office)

OHIO
Tom Goodman
Ohio Div. of Real Estate
77 S. High Street
Columbus, 43266-0547
(614) 466-3411 (Office)
(614) 644-0584 (Fax)

OKLAHOMA
Michelle Shadid
Real Estate Appraisal Board
Oklahoma Insurance Dept.
1901 N. Walnut/P.O. Box 53408
Oklahoma City, OK 73152-3408
(405) 521-6636 (Office)
(405) 521-6652 (Fax)

OREGON
Cal Henry
Oregon Real Estate Appraisal
Board/Commerce Building
158 12th Street NE
Salem, 97310-0240
(503) 373-1505 (Office)
(503) 378-6576 (Fax)

PENNSYLVANIA
Cheryl B. Lyne
PA State Board of Certified
Real Estate Appraisers
P.O. Box 2649
Harrisburg, 17105
(717) 783-4866 (Office)
(717) 787-7769 (Fax)

RHODE ISLAND
Leo McAloon, Jr.
Dept. of Business Regulation
233 Richmond Street
Providence, 02903
(401) 277-2416 (Office)
(401) 277-6098 (Fax)

SOUTH CAROLINA
William B. Tiller, Jr.
South Carolina Real Estate
Appraiser Board
Capitol Center - AT&T Bldg.
1201 Main Street, Suite 1530
Columbia, 29201
(803) 737-0898 (Office)
(803) 737-0848 (Fax)

SOUTH DAKOTA
Jeff Stingley
Commerce/Regulation Dept.
910 East Sioux
Pierre, 57501
(605) 773-3178 (Office)
(605) 773-5369 (Fax)

TENNESSEE
Sandra S. Moore
Real Estate Appraiser Comm.
TN Dept. of Commerce & Ins.
500 James Robertson Parkway
Second Floor
Nashville, 37243-1166
(615) 741-1831 (Office)
(615) 741-6470 (Fax)

TEXAS
Renil C. Liner
Texas Appraiser Licensing &
Certification Board
P.O. Box 12188
Austin, 78711-2188
(512) 465-3950 (Office)
(512) 465-3998 (Fax)

UTAH
Blaine Twitchell
Utah Dept. of Commerce
Division of Real Estate
160 E. 300 S./P.O. Box 45806
Salt Lake City, 84145-0806
(801) 530-6747 (Office)
(801) 530-6650 (Fax)

VERMONT
Rita Knapp
Vermont Real Estate
Appraisers Board
109 State Street
Montpelier, 05609-1106
(802) 828-2808 (Office)
(802) 828-2496 (Fax)

VIRGINIA
Demetra Y. Kontos
Real Estate Appraiser Board
Department of Commerce
Commonwealth of Virginia
3600 W. Broad St., Fifth Floor
Richmond, 23230-4817
(804) 367-2175 (Office)
(804) 367-9537 (Fax)

WASHINGTON
Cleotis Borner
Appraisal Section Prof.
Licensing Services
P.O. Box 9012
Olympia, 98504
(206) 753-1062 (Office)
(206) 586-0998 (Fax)

WEST VIRGINIA
Si Galperin
West Virginia Appraiser
Licensing Board
814 Virginia St. East Suite 212
Charleston, 25301
(304) 348-3919 (Office)
(304) 348-3983 (Fax)

WISCONSIN
Peter Eggert
WI Dept. of Regulation & Lic.
Business & Design Professions
P.O. Box 8935
Madison, 53708
(608) 266-1630 (Office)
(608) 267-0644 (Fax)

WYOMING
Constance K. Anderson
Certification Real Estate
Appraiser Board
205 Barrett Bldg.
Cheyenne, 82002
(307) 777-7141 (Office)
(307) 777-6005 (Fax)

PUERTO RICO
Carlos Gaztambide
Board of Examiners of
Puerto Rico
Banco Popular, Suite 1812
Hato Rey, San Juan 00918
(809) 753-8475 (Office)
(809) 753-1829 (Fax)

VIRGIN ISLANDS
Marylyn Stapleton
Government of the Virgin Islands
Dept. of Licensing & Consumer Affairs
No. 1 Sub Base, Room 205
St. Thomas, 00801
(809) 774-0001 (Office)
(809) 776-0675 (Fax)

GUAM
Joaquin Blaz
Dept. of Revenue & Taxation
Government of Guam
855 W. Marine Drive
Agana, 96910
(671) 477-5144 (Office)
(671) 472-2643 (Fax)

MARIANA ISLANDS
Florence S. Bocago
Commonwealth of the
Northern Mariana Islands
P.O. Box 2078
Saipan, 96950
(670) 234-5897 or 6040 (Office)

AMERICAN SAMOA
Albert Maillo Legal Counsel
to the Governor
American Samoa Government
Pago Pago, 96799
(684) 633-4116 (Office)
(684) 633-2269 (Fax)

The model exam that follows is loosely patterned on the ASI examination for real estate appraiser licensure. It is not a real exam, but it will give you a glimpse at the knowledge that a licensed real estate appraiser must have mastered. Correct answers follow the model exam along with mathematical calculations explaining the answers to questions requiring calculation.

ANSWER SHEET FOR TYPICAL
APPRAISAL LICENSE EXAMINATION

1 Ⓐ Ⓑ Ⓒ Ⓓ	26 Ⓐ Ⓑ Ⓒ Ⓓ	51 Ⓐ Ⓑ Ⓒ Ⓓ	76 Ⓐ Ⓑ Ⓒ Ⓓ
2 Ⓐ Ⓑ Ⓒ Ⓓ	27 Ⓐ Ⓑ Ⓒ Ⓓ	52 Ⓐ Ⓑ Ⓒ Ⓓ	77 Ⓐ Ⓑ Ⓒ Ⓓ
3 Ⓐ Ⓑ Ⓒ Ⓓ	28 Ⓐ Ⓑ Ⓒ Ⓓ	53 Ⓐ Ⓑ Ⓒ Ⓓ	78 Ⓐ Ⓑ Ⓒ Ⓓ
4 Ⓐ Ⓑ Ⓒ Ⓓ	29 Ⓐ Ⓑ Ⓒ Ⓓ	54 Ⓐ Ⓑ Ⓒ Ⓓ	79 Ⓐ Ⓑ Ⓒ Ⓓ
5 Ⓐ Ⓑ Ⓒ Ⓓ	30 Ⓐ Ⓑ Ⓒ Ⓓ	55 Ⓐ Ⓑ Ⓒ Ⓓ	80 Ⓐ Ⓑ Ⓒ Ⓓ
6 Ⓐ Ⓑ Ⓒ Ⓓ	31 Ⓐ Ⓑ Ⓒ Ⓓ	56 Ⓐ Ⓑ Ⓒ Ⓓ	81 Ⓐ Ⓑ Ⓒ Ⓓ
7 Ⓐ Ⓑ Ⓒ Ⓓ	32 Ⓐ Ⓑ Ⓒ Ⓓ	57 Ⓐ Ⓑ Ⓒ Ⓓ	82 Ⓐ Ⓑ Ⓒ Ⓓ
8 Ⓐ Ⓑ Ⓒ Ⓓ	33 Ⓐ Ⓑ Ⓒ Ⓓ	58 Ⓐ Ⓑ Ⓒ Ⓓ	83 Ⓐ Ⓑ Ⓒ Ⓓ
9 Ⓐ Ⓑ Ⓒ Ⓓ	34 Ⓐ Ⓑ Ⓒ Ⓓ	59 Ⓐ Ⓑ Ⓒ Ⓓ	84 Ⓐ Ⓑ Ⓒ Ⓓ
10 Ⓐ Ⓑ Ⓒ Ⓓ	35 Ⓐ Ⓑ Ⓒ Ⓓ	60 Ⓐ Ⓑ Ⓒ Ⓓ	85 Ⓐ Ⓑ Ⓒ Ⓓ
11 Ⓐ Ⓑ Ⓒ Ⓓ	36 Ⓐ Ⓑ Ⓒ Ⓓ	61 Ⓐ Ⓑ Ⓒ Ⓓ	86 Ⓐ Ⓑ Ⓒ Ⓓ
12 Ⓐ Ⓑ Ⓒ Ⓓ	37 Ⓐ Ⓑ Ⓒ Ⓓ	62 Ⓐ Ⓑ Ⓒ Ⓓ	87 Ⓐ Ⓑ Ⓒ Ⓓ
13 Ⓐ Ⓑ Ⓒ Ⓓ	38 Ⓐ Ⓑ Ⓒ Ⓓ	63 Ⓐ Ⓑ Ⓒ Ⓓ	88 Ⓐ Ⓑ Ⓒ Ⓓ
14 Ⓐ Ⓑ Ⓒ Ⓓ	39 Ⓐ Ⓑ Ⓒ Ⓓ	64 Ⓐ Ⓑ Ⓒ Ⓓ	89 Ⓐ Ⓑ Ⓒ Ⓓ
15 Ⓐ Ⓑ Ⓒ Ⓓ	40 Ⓐ Ⓑ Ⓒ Ⓓ	65 Ⓐ Ⓑ Ⓒ Ⓓ	90 Ⓐ Ⓑ Ⓒ Ⓓ
16 Ⓐ Ⓑ Ⓒ Ⓓ	41 Ⓐ Ⓑ Ⓒ Ⓓ	66 Ⓐ Ⓑ Ⓒ Ⓓ	91 Ⓐ Ⓑ Ⓒ Ⓓ
17 Ⓐ Ⓑ Ⓒ Ⓓ	42 Ⓐ Ⓑ Ⓒ Ⓓ	67 Ⓐ Ⓑ Ⓒ Ⓓ	92 Ⓐ Ⓑ Ⓒ Ⓓ
18 Ⓐ Ⓑ Ⓒ Ⓓ	43 Ⓐ Ⓑ Ⓒ Ⓓ	68 Ⓐ Ⓑ Ⓒ Ⓓ	93 Ⓐ Ⓑ Ⓒ Ⓓ
19 Ⓐ Ⓑ Ⓒ Ⓓ	44 Ⓐ Ⓑ Ⓒ Ⓓ	69 Ⓐ Ⓑ Ⓒ Ⓓ	94 Ⓐ Ⓑ Ⓒ Ⓓ
20 Ⓐ Ⓑ Ⓒ Ⓓ	45 Ⓐ Ⓑ Ⓒ Ⓓ	70 Ⓐ Ⓑ Ⓒ Ⓓ	95 Ⓐ Ⓑ Ⓒ Ⓓ
21 Ⓐ Ⓑ Ⓒ Ⓓ	46 Ⓐ Ⓑ Ⓒ Ⓓ	71 Ⓐ Ⓑ Ⓒ Ⓓ	96 Ⓐ Ⓑ Ⓒ Ⓓ
22 Ⓐ Ⓑ Ⓒ Ⓓ	47 Ⓐ Ⓑ Ⓒ Ⓓ	72 Ⓐ Ⓑ Ⓒ Ⓓ	97 Ⓐ Ⓑ Ⓒ Ⓓ
23 Ⓐ Ⓑ Ⓒ Ⓓ	48 Ⓐ Ⓑ Ⓒ Ⓓ	73 Ⓐ Ⓑ Ⓒ Ⓓ	98 Ⓐ Ⓑ Ⓒ Ⓓ
24 Ⓐ Ⓑ Ⓒ Ⓓ	49 Ⓐ Ⓑ Ⓒ Ⓓ	74 Ⓐ Ⓑ Ⓒ Ⓓ	99 Ⓐ Ⓑ Ⓒ Ⓓ
25 Ⓐ Ⓑ Ⓒ Ⓓ	50 Ⓐ Ⓑ Ⓒ Ⓓ	75 Ⓐ Ⓑ Ⓒ Ⓓ	100 Ⓐ Ⓑ Ⓒ Ⓓ

TYPICAL APPRAISAL LICENSE EXAMINATION

1. What term describes the process of estimating value?
A. Analysis
B. Estimating
C. Appraisal
D. Inspecting

2. Typically the term "market value" applies to value to whom?
A. The buyer
B. The market
C. The lender
D. The seller

3. The "highest and best use" of property would generally result in
A. the best value
B. the highest value
C. the market value
D. the lowest value

4. "Investment" value is commonly known as
A. value in the investment market place
B. value to a specific investor
C. value of an investment
D. value to an investment

5. The term "eminent domain" means
A. prominent land
B. dominant estate
C. basic land rights
D. right of condemnation

6. The rights of a landlord are known as
A. Leasehold Estate
B. Fee Simple Estate
C. Leased Fee Estate
D. Tenants Estate

7. In estimating the value of a government building, what type of value would most likely be appraised?
A. Use value
B. Investment value
C. Tax value
D. Insurable value

8. In the cost approach to value, soft costs are generally the following:
A. land costs, building costs, mortgage interest
B. mortgage interest, taxes, insurance
C. land costs, labor, materials
D. inspection fees, builder's profit, land costs

9. Depreciation in real estate valuation for market purposes is generally considered on the basis of
A. difference between cost new and present value
B. a bookkeeper's allowance over time
C. an engineer's estimate of cost
D. Internal Revenue tables

10. A gross rent multiplier is obtained from
A. dividing value by net income
B. dividing net income into value
C. dividing sale prices by gross incomes
D. dividing assessments by tax rates

11. Economic or effective age of a property is generally
   A. shorter than actual life
   B. equal to chronological life
   C. longer than actual life
   D. the same as chronological life

12. In "ad valorem" taxation, the appraiser is generally concerned with
   A. in-use valuation
   B. investment valuation
   C. insurance valuation
   D. assessed valuation

13. Federally related transactions involve appraising for
   A. federal government
   B. insurance brokers
   C. mortgages
   D. auditors

14. Highest and best use of a site is
   A. the use that exists
   B. the same as feasible use
   C. the same as probable use
   D. the use that produces the highest net income

15. Market value is also known as
   A. value in use
   B. value in exchange
   C. value in principle
   D. value in anticipation

16. The term that explains the difference between the value of real estate and the mortgage at any given time is known as
   A. yield
   B. capital
   C. liquidity
   D. equity

17. Reconciliation is generally a process done by
   A. averaging
   B. analysis
   C. capitalization
   D. estimating

18. "Interim" use is generally regarded as the use that
   A. precedes highest and best use
   B. occurs after the best use
   C. is part of highest and best use
   D. is better than the best use

19. The final selector of "highest and best use" is
   A. the seller
   B. the lender
   C. the owner
   D. the buyer

20. The "scope" of the appraisal assignment reflects
   A. the purpose of the appraisal
   B. the fee the appraiser is paid
   C. the extent of research by the appraiser
   D. the feasibility of the value achiever

21. The Cost and Sales Comparison Approach to Value are closely related when the property being appraised is
   A. old
   B. overimproved
   C. new
   D. underimproved

22. The Cost Approach to Value is most meaningful when
   A. the property is unique
   B. the property is old
   C. the property is competitive
   D. the property is conforming

23. A general certified appraiser can appraise
   A. general real estate only
   B. all classes of real estate
   C. commercial and industrial real estate
   D. real estate over $1,000,000

24. A strip center sold for $120,000. It had a gross income of $30,000 and operating expenses of $8,000. The gross income multiplier was
   A. 10.0   C.   .25
   B.   4.0   D.   5.0

25. The cost new of a residence was $192,500. It is 30 years old, but has an effective age of 20 years and an economic life of 80 years. The total amount of depreciation is
   A. $38,500   C. $77,000
   B. $57,750   D. $48,125

26. An identical house sold in a development for $120,000 approximately six months ago. A paired house sold last week for $130,000. The indicated value for the subject property, after adjustments, would be
   A. $110,000   C. $130,000
   B. $120,000   D. $135,000

27. The best way to determine if an encroachment exists on a property is
   A. by a personal inspection   C. by survey
   B. by deed reference   D. by title reports

28. The first step in the appraisal process is to
   A. collect the fee   C. read the survey
   B. inspect the property   D. define the problem

29. Trending is a form of
   A. depreciation   C. behavior
   B. analysis   D. regulation

30. Value can be affected by
   A. individual mores   C. reconciliation
   B. collective mores   D. auctions

31. A legal description of real estate generally does not include
   A. metes and bounds description
   B. title reports
   C. deed reference
   D. street address

32. The most reliable method to estimate land value is by
   A. Land Residual Approach
   B. Sales Comparison Approach
   C. Land Capitalization Approach
   D. Land Extraction Approach

33. A property sold for $150,000 one year ago. Today the same property sold for $160,000. The rate of appreciation is
   A. 6.67% per year   C. 0.67% per day
   B. 5.57% per month   D. 2.22% per quarter

34. The purpose of an appraisal is to
   A. estimate value   C. judge value
   B. create value   D. determine value

35. Forces which affect value, resulting from government regulations, are known as
A. social forces
B. economic forces
C. physical forces
D. political forces

36. The appraisal principle which governs the income approach to value is the
A. Principle of Contribution
B. Principle of Balance
C. Principle of Anticipation
D. Principle of Increasing Returns

37. Adjustments, in the sales comparison approach to value, are a result of
A. Principle of Anticipation
B. Principle of Conformity
C. Principle of Decreasing Returns
D. Principle of Contribution

38. Principle of Substitution is generally reflected in
A. the Cost Approach
B. the Sales Comparison Approach
C. the Income Approach
D. all of the above

39. Highest and best use is always necessary if the appraiser wishes to
A. do a feasibility study
B. estimate market value
C. satisfy a client's needs
D. justify zoning requirements

40. The most recommended legal description of a property is
A. mailing address
B. topographical survey
C. metes and bounds
D. government survey

41. The number of square feet in an acre is
A. 34,650
B. 43,560
C. 34,560
D. 43,450

42. Vacant land can be valued by
A. Land Residual Approach
B. Ground Rent Capitalization
C. Sales Comparison
D. all of the above

43. Future value, used in the income approach to value, is used by investors based on the principle of
A. conformity
B. substitution
C. anticipation
D. contribution

44. Highest and best use always tries to estimate
A. the largest resale price
B. the greater density of land use
C. the reasonableness of zoning
D. the interim proper use

45. "Net return" is always used in the definition of
A. market value
B. highest and best use
C. economic usefulness
D. principle of anticipation

46. The life cycle of a neighborhood is an example of
    A. principle of balance
    B. principle of contribution
    C. principle of conformity
    D. principle of change

47. Economic obsolescence is also known as
    A. external obsolescence
    B. physical deterioration
    C. functional inability
    D. loss of amenities

48. Reproduction cost is an effort to
    A. duplicate insurable value
    B. duplicate an identical building
    C. duplicate a similar building
    D. duplicate cost of replacement

49. The Cost Approach is generally a reflection of
    A. value in exchange
    B. cost of construction
    C. cost of assemblage
    D. value in use

50. An important measurement in the valuation of a home is
    A. its height
    B. its square footage
    C. its length
    D. its width

51. Physical depreciation is a result of
    A. residual values
    B. deferred maintenance
    C. external forces
    D. functional obsolescence

52. A roof has an economic life of 20 years. It has a present effective age of 5 years. The amount of present depreciation is
    A. 20%
    B. 33%
    C. 25%
    D. 50%

53. "Quantity Survey" is used in
    A. estimating depreciation
    B. legal descriptions
    C. Cost Approach to Value
    D. Sales Comparison Approach

54. What two interests are created by a lease?
    A. Leased fee and land trust
    B. Fee determinate and leased fee
    C. Fee simple and leased fee
    D. Leased fee and leasehold

55. In the Sales Comparison Approach to Value, sales are adjusted
    A. to each other
    B. to the subject property
    C. to an ideal property
    D. to the highest priced sale

56. Highest and best use is that use which would result in
    A. largest building size
    B. highest density to the site
    C. highest value to the property
    D. present zoned use

57. It would be best to appraise a school building by the
    A. Sales Comparison Approach to Value
    B. Development Approach to Value
    C. Income Approach to Value
    D. Cost Approach to Value

58. The highest estate under which title to property is held is
    A. leased fee estate   C. fee simple estate
    B. leasehold estate   D. life estate

59. Another word for economic life is
    A. functional life   C. useful life
    B. physical life   D. effective age

60. What does GIM mean?
    A. Graduated Income Multiplier
    B. Graduated Investment Manager
    C. Gross Income Multiplier
    D. Greater Investment Model

61. The basic capitalization formula is
    A. rate times income equals value
    B. rate divided by income equals value
    C. rate plus income equals value
    D. rate less income equals value

62. A property with a gross income of $20,000 which sold for $100,000 has a gross income multiplier of
    A. 20   C. 5
    B. 10   D. 4

63. Site values for single-family homes are best valued by
    A. front feet   C. allocation
    B. abstraction   D. comparable sales

64. A recent sale of a two-family residence took place at $150,000. Monthly rents were at $600 for the lower half, and $400 for the upper half. The indicated gross rent multiplier would be
    A. 15   C. 8
    B. 12.5   D. 10

65. The cost of constructing an exact duplicate building, in the Cost Approach, is known as
    A. replacement cost   C. present cost
    B. original cost   D. reproduction cost

66. A 2,000-square-foot house costs $40 per square foot to build, and when completed will have an economic life expectancy of 50 years. It has an effective age of 10 years. Its estimated accrued depreciation is
    A. $8,000   C. $20,000
    B. $16,000   D. $40,000

67. A property recently sold for $185,000. Its site value is $37,000. The present estimated replacement cost is $180,000 and its effective age is 10 years. What is the yearly average depreciation rate?
    A. 2.3%   C. .05%
    B. 5%   D. 1.8%

68. In the valuation of single-family homes, the most general unit of comparison is
    A. square feet   C. cubic feet
    B. per room   D. per front foot

69. Cost manuals are used to
    A. compute expenses   C. estimate cost new
    B. determine square footage   D. estimate past depreciation

70. After estimating cost to replace or reproduce, the appraiser's next estimates are
A. unit cost
B. appreciation
C. entrepreneurial profit
D. depreciation

71. Functional utility best refers to
A. economic life
B. effective age
C. usefulness
D. marketability

72. The primary source of cost data is
A. supplies
B. builders
C. brokers
D. the local zoning officer

73. Five years ago a builder could build a typical townhouse for $30,000. Shortly thereafter, prices increased 25% above original costs, but then prices decreased to 15% below the high point. Approximately what would this townhouse cost today?
A. $34,500
B. $31,875
C. $33,000
D. $33,333

74. Paired sales analysis is best described as
A. qualitative analysis
B. comparative analysis
C. graphic analysis
D. rank analysis

75. The first step in analyzing sales data is to compute the differences between the subject and comparable properties so as to
A. adjust for financing
B. create a unit of comparison
C. adjust for location
D. adjust for special conditions

76. The best verification of a sale is
A. the title company
B. the closing attorney
C. the buyer
D. the broker of record

77. Real estate sale prices in a specific community would be most affected by
A. national employment trends
B. gross national product
C. inflationary statistics
D. local interest rates

78. The proper sequence of adjustments in the Sales Comparison Approach begins with an adjustment for
A. financing
B. market conditions
C. location
D. property rights

79. An acre of land recently sold for $200,000. Its sale can be reported on a square-foot basis for analytical reasons. The indicated square-foot price would be
A. $10.00 per s.f.
B. $ 9.18 per s.f.
C. $ 4.59 per s.f.
D. $ 2.20 per s.f.

80. A small apartment building is said to have a useful life of 50 years. On a straight-line basis, its annual depreciation rate can be estimated at
A. 5%
B. 4%
C. 2.5%
D. 2%

81. Market data is best verified from
A. multiple listing services
B. newspapers
C. buyers/sellers
D. brokers

82. A new garage can be built for $22,000. A check of comparable sales indicates that buyers would not be willing to pay more than $15,000 for a garage in this neighborhood. The $7,000 difference between cost and probable sales price is known as
A. locational obsolescence
B. functional obsolescence
C. physical underimprovement
D. externalities

83. External obsolescence is generally measured by
A. cost of rent capitalized
B. breakdown method
C. cost to cure deducted
D. age-life method

84. The process used to convert future benefits into present value at a yield rate is known as
A. direct capitalization
B. discounting
C. reversion
D. equity conversion

85. Gross income multipliers are used primarily in
A. all three approaches to value
B. the Income Approach
C. the Cost Approach
D. The Sales Comparison Approach

86. In the valuation process, value is reconciled
A. throughout the report
B. after each approach to value
C. after all three approaches are completed
D. after the limiting conditions

87. Sales of three comparable properties reflect $6.00, $6.50, and $7.00 per square foot. All three comparables are superior in size to the subject property by 10%. The range of probable value of the subject property is
A. $6.60 to $7.00
B. $5.40 to $6.30
C. $6.60 to $7.70
D. $6.00 to $7.70

88. A sale is always adjusted first for _____, before all other adjustments.
A. condition of the sale
B. date of the sale
C. financing of the sale
D. property rights of the sale

89. An appraiser should choose his/her comparable sales based first on
A. size
B. location
C. time
D. client's preference

90. Subtracting the improvement's current market value from its replacement cost new reflects
A. the overall sales price
B. the principle of substitution
C. entrepreneurial profit
D. accrued depreciation

91. What method of cost estimating is most often used by appraisers?
A. quantity survey
B. contractor's estimates
C. comparative unit
D. unit-in-place

92. In the Cost Approach, the site is valued as if it were
A. totally improved
B. vacant and at its highest and best use
C. to be improved
D. residual to the improvements

93. A frame single-family rancher costs $65.35 per square foot to build. It measures 28' by 42'. Entrepreneurial profit is estimated at 20%. Its cost new should be reported at
A. $91,728
B. $76,852
C. $92,222
D. $64,032

94. A new building has a future economic life of 80 years. Because of some shoddy construction, it is estimated to have an effective age of 10 years. The percentage of depreciation is

A. 10%

B. 13%

C. 14%

D. 8%

95. The subject property has direct costs of $125,000. Indirect costs are $20,000 and land value is $30,000. If entrepreneurial profit is measured at 15% of direct costs, what would it be for the subject property?

A. $21,750

B. $18,750

C. $26,250

D. $23,250

96. A building component with an estimated remaining life shorter than the remaining economic life of the entire building as a whole is called a(n)

A. short-lived item

B. long-lived item

C. incurable item

D. curable item

97. After estimating cost to replace or reproduce a structure, the appraiser next estimates and deducts

A. cost to cure

B. entrepreneurial profit

C. depreciation

D. land value

98. Divided or undivided rights in real property that are less than the whole are termed

A. determinable interests

B. partial interests

C. easement rights

D. leased for rights

99. Who benefits most when market rent exceeds contract rent?

A. The Tax Assessor

B. The leasehold interest

C. The leased fee interest

D. The property owner

100. A home recently sold for $250,000. When sold, the property rented for $1,200 per month. A similar home on the same street is rented at $800 per month. What is the indicated gross rent multiplier of the recently sold property?

A. 12.50

B. 17.36

C. 26.04

D. 20.83

TYPICAL APPRAISAL LICENSE EXAMINATION ANSWER KEY

1. C	21. C	41. B	61. B	81. C
2. A	22. A	42. D	*62. C	82. B
3. C	23. B	43. C	63. D	83. A
4. B	*24. B	44. A	*64. B	84. B
5. D	*25. D	45. B	65. D	85. D
6. C	*26. C	46. D	*66. B	86. C
7. A	27. C	47. A	*67. D	*87. B
8. B	28. D	48. B	68. A	88. D
9. A	29. B	49. D	69. C	89. B
10. C	30. B	50. B	70. D	90. D
11. A	31. D	51. B	71. C	91. C
12. D	32. B	*52. C	72. B	92. B
13. C	*33. A	53. C	*73. B	*93. C
14. D	34. A	54. D	74. B	*94. B
15. B	35. D	55. B	75. B	*95. B
16. D	36. C	56. C	76. C	96. A
17. B	37. D	57. D	77. D	97. C
18. A	38. D	58. C	78. D	98. B
19. D	39. B	59. C	*79. C	99. B
20. C	40. C	60. C	*80. D	*100. B

* Solutions provided

SOLUTIONS TO PROBLEMS REQUIRING MATHEMATICAL CALCULATIONS

24. **(B)** $120,000 ÷ $30,000 = 4.0
    Operating expenses do not enter into calculation of *gross* income.

25. **(D)** $\dfrac{\text{Effective Age}}{\text{Total Economic Life}} \times \text{Cost New} = \text{Accrued Depreciation}$

    $\dfrac{20 \text{ years}}{80 \text{ years}} \times \$192,500 = .25 \times \$192,500 = \$48,125$

26. **(C)** No calculation is needed. A one-week lapse of time is irrelevant. The current values of the identical houses are identical.

33. **(A)** $160,000 − $150,000 = $10,000 appreciation in one year.
    $10,000 ÷ $150,000 = .6666 = 6.7% appreciation per year.

52. **(C)** 5 years ÷ 20 years = .25 = 25%. One-fourth or 25% of the roof's economic life has passed.

62. **(C)** $100,000 ÷ $20,000 = 5

64. **(B)** Total monthly rents = $600 + $400 = $1,000.
Annual rents = $1,000 × 12 = $12,000.
$150,000 ÷ $12,000 = 12.5

66. **(B)** Total cost = 2,000 sq. ft. × $40 = $80,000

$$\frac{\text{Effective Age}}{\text{Total Economic Life}} = \frac{10 \text{ yrs.}}{50 \text{ yrs.}} = .2 \times \$80,000 \text{ cost} = \$16,000$$
accrued depreciation

67. **(D)**   Sale price = $185,000
  − Site value = − 37,000
    $148,000 present worth of building

    Cost new = $180,000
  Present worth − 148,000
    $ 32,000 depreciation
$32,000 ÷ $180,000 = .18 = 18% depreciation in 10 years
18% ÷ 10 = 1.8% average annual depreciation rate

73. **(B)** $30,000 × 125% = $37,500 cost to rebuild after prices went up 25%.
$37,500 × 85% = $31,875 cost to rebuild after prices dropped 15% from
their high point.

79. **(C)** $200,000 ÷ 43,560 sq. ft. = $4.59 per sq. ft.

80. **(D)** 100% depreciation ÷ 50 years = 2% per year.

87. **(B)** The range of comparables is $6.00 to $7.00 per sq. ft.
On the basis of size, subject property is worth 10% less.
$6.00 × 90% = $5.40; $7.00 × 90% = $6.30

93. **(C)** 28' × 42' = 1.176 sq. ft. × $65.35 per sq. ft. =
$76,851.60 to build × 120% to allow profit = $92,222 reported cost.

94. **(B)** 10 ÷ 80 = .125 = 12½%, which is closest to 13%.

95. **(B)** $125,000 × 15% = $18,750. Read carefully; indirect costs and land
value, though given to you, are irrelevant to the question as stated.

100. **(B)** $1,200 per month × 12 months = $14,400 annual rental.
$250,000 ÷ $14,400 = 17.36 gross multiplier. Ignore extraneous information.